About Island Press

Since 1984, the nonprofit organization Island Press has been stimulating, shaping, and communicating ideas that are essential for solving environmental problems worldwide. With more than 1,000 titles in print and some 30 new releases each year, we are the nation's leading publisher on environmental issues. We identify innovative thinkers and emerging trends in the environmental field. We work with world-renowned experts and authors to develop cross-disciplinary solutions to environmental challenges.

Island Press designs and executes educational campaigns, in conjunction with our authors, to communicate their critical messages in print, in person, and online using the latest technologies, innovative programs, and the media. Our goal is to reach targeted audiences—scientists, policy makers, environmental advocates, urban planners, the media, and concerned citizens—with information that can be used to create the framework for long-term ecological health and human well-being.

Island Press gratefully acknowledges major support from The Bobolink Foundation, Caldera Foundation, The Curtis and Edith Munson Foundation, The Forrest C. and Frances H. Lattner Foundation, The JPB Foundation, The Kresge Foundation, The Summit Charitable Foundation, Inc., and many other generous organizations and individuals.

PARKS AND RECREATION SYSTEM PLANNING

PARKS AND RECREATION SYSTEM PLANNING

A New Approach for Creating Sustainable, Resilient Communities

DAVID L. BARTH, PHD

ISLANDPRESS | Washington | Covelo

Library of Congress Control Number: 2019955368

All Island Press books are printed on environmentally responsible materials.

Manufactured in the United States of America

10 9 8 7 6 5 4 3 2 1

Keywords: Bicycle and pedestrian access, Collaborative planning, Commission for Accreditation of Parks and Recreation Agencies (CAPRA), Comprehensive plans, Economic development, Green infrastructure, Health and wellness, High-Performance Public Space, Land development regulations, Level-of-service guidelines, Livable community, Long-range vision, National Recreation and Park Association, Park classification, Plexus, Preliminary implementation framework, Public realm, Resilience, Signature parks, Social equity, Strategic planning, Sustainability, Trails and greenways, Urbanization

CONTENTS

ACKNOWLEDGMENTS

I would like to thank the many people who made this book possible. First, former University of Florida Landscape Architecture Chair Herrick Smith inspired me to seek the patterns, puzzle-making, and systems that define urban design. Bill Kercher at Glatting Jackson set me on the path to parks and recreation system planning and encouraged me to seek opportunities to generate multiple benefits from single actions. And my colleague Carlos Perez has been a creative and inspirational collaborator.

University of Florida Landscape Architecture Department Chair Tina Gurucharri encouraged me to return to school and pursue a doctoral degree, and my dissertation committee—Dr. Marilyn (Mickie) Switzer, Margaret (Peggy) Carr, Dr. Ruth Steiner, and Dr. David Hedge—guided and fostered my research.

My sister F. Diane Barth, an accomplished author, provided almost daily assistance and inspiration. My brother Dr. Richard Barth—and friends Dr. Jay Exum, Terry Clark, Lynn Hays, and Dr. Cathy DiBenedetto—provided continuous support and encouragement.

The very patient planner and graphic designer Sarah Ciccone did a terrific job of formatting all of the exhibits and images for the book. And Island Press editors Elizabeth Farry and Courtney Lix were spot-on with their edits and comments, making the book immeasurably more thoughtful and succinct.

Finally, thanks to my parents, Joy and George Barth, for their unconditional love; to my incredible children, Abigail and Elliot, for being such great boosters; and to my anchor and wife, Denise, for her unwavering patience, love, and support.

INTRODUCTION

A Framework for Community Sustainability and Resilience

Parks and recreation system planning has long been overlooked as an effective tool for community sustainability, resiliency, and livability. It has been over thirty years since the World Commission on Environment and Development published *Our Common Future* (also known as the Brundtland Report), proposing a multilateral, interdependent path for creating economically, socially, and environmentally sustainable communities. More recently, the concept of resilient communities—those capable of rebounding from both acute shocks and chronic stresses—seems to have superseded sustainability, perhaps because it is more accessible and quantifiable. And the concept of a livable community—one that is safe and secure, has a variety of affordable housing options, is connected by multiple modes of transportation networks, has clean air and water, protects its natural areas and wildlife habitat, and provides high-quality community facilities and services—has become part of the standard community planning lexicon.

Regardless of the preferred term, local communities in the United States and throughout the world have sought new approaches, tools, and techniques to become more balanced, healthy, and prosperous over the past several decades. They have created sustainability plans, climate action plans, stormwater plans, affordable housing plans, transportation plans, vulnerability analyses, sea-level mitigation plans, and other plans and initiatives. Yet one resource that is often overlooked as a tool for sustainability, resiliency, and livability—and is already owned and controlled by local communities—is their parks and recreation system.

Parks and recreation systems include parks, civic spaces, conservation areas, trails and greenways, historic and cultural sites, stormwater ponds, and other lands owned and managed by public agencies. Not only can they account for up to 50 percent of a community's landmass; they also can generate significant sustainability and resiliency benefits for a community. Such benefits can range from creating a framework for growth to combating climate change. Dr. John Crompton, University Distinguished Professor at Texas A&M University, identified nineteen community-wide benefits in particular, listed in box 0-1.

These benefits don't automatically accrue to a community, however; they require careful and thoughtful planning, design, maintenance, and operation of the parks and recreation system. Generating significant benefits also requires leadership, collaboration, and transcendence of organizational silos. None of this is easy, and there isn't much guidance available about how to change approaches steeped in the simpler aims of the 1950s. This book aims to change that.

Generating greater sustainability and resiliency benefits at a system-wide level requires embracing two big ideas. The first is that parks and recreation systems can generate multiple sustainability and resiliency benefits if they are thoughtfully planned, designed, and managed as part of a broader public realm that includes transportation, stormwater, and utility systems. The second idea is that we need a more comprehensive and collaborative parks and recreation system planning process to realize these benefits.

Generation of Significant Benefits

First, planners have long been aware of the potential benefits of parks and recreation systems. Frederick Law Olmsted, considered the father of landscape architecture and the American parks movement in the late nineteenth century, noted that "a park exercises a very different and much greater influence upon the progress of a city in its general structure than any other ordinary public work."[1] However, these ideas need public support, and Americans' appreciation of the value of parks and open spaces had waned by the second half of the twentieth century. This growing ambivalence may be due to

Box 0-1
Community-wide Benefits Generated by Parks and Recreation Systems

Economic Prosperity

- Attracting tourists
- Attracting businesses
- Attracting retirees
- Enhancing real estate values
- Reducing taxes
- Stimulation of equipment sales

Environmental Sustainability

- Protecting drinking water
- Controlling flooding
- Cleaning air
- Reducing traffic congestion
- Reducing energy costs
- Preserving biological diversity

Alleviating Social Problems

- Reducing environmental stress
- Community regeneration
- Cultural and historic preservation
- Facilitating healthy lifestyles
- Alleviating deviant youth behavior
- Raising levels of education attainment
- Alleviating unemployment distress

Source: John L. Crompton, *Community Benefits and Repositioning: The Keys to Park and Recreation's Future Viability* (Ashburn, VA: National Recreation and Park Association, 2007), 61.

a variety of factors, such as the growth and expansion of cities into suburbs, middle-class flight from urban areas, the diminished role of local governments in physical city planning, the degradation of urban parks and open spaces, and the privatization of public spaces.

As a result, many communities lost sight of the integral relationship between parks and a community's quality of life, as observed by the noted American urban planner, educator, and author Alexander Garvin in 2002.

> It has been many years since parks were thought of as central to the planning of cities. Their very existence has eliminated pressure for additional park development and made it possible for other issues to dominate the urban planning agenda. Nor is there the same certainty that existed during the 19th century that exposure to nature or active recreation can alleviate the effects of slums and poverty. Nevertheless, public open space remains an effective tool for shaping the American city.[2]

Perhaps as a reaction to loss of benefits provided by undermaintained parks and to urban growth with little regard for open space, a renewed appreciation of the role of parks and the public realm as a framework for livable communities has clearly emerged over the past two decades, evidenced by increased investment in urban signature parks, green infrastructure, and complete streets. Complete streets, for example, are intended to meet the needs of pedestrians, bicyclists, and transit riders—in addition to cars—to accommodate the needs of all users. "This is an exciting and remarkable time to be designing parks for American cities," wrote the noted landscape architect Joe Brown in 2000. "Urban parks are being recognized, at long last, as a critical part of any revitalization strategy, an impressive stimulus to development. . . . We are seeing a greater commitment to America's urban parks than we have seen for decades."[3] Greater awareness and commitment have brought higher expectations for a return on investment (ROI). In addition to providing traditional recreation benefits, parks and other elements of the public realm are expected to generate higher property values, improved water quality, reduced crime, and other societal benefits.

Many communities in the United States are already capitalizing on their parks and recreation systems to generate greater benefits, including Atlanta, New York, Philadelphia, Chicago, Minneapolis, Seattle, Denver, and Portland, Oregon. The New York City Department of Parks and Recreation, for example, leads a citywide

Public Realm Team that works collaboratively across divisions, departments, and agencies to generate a comprehensive set of community-wide benefits from every park project in the city; parks and recreation staff note that traditional government silos are "a luxury we can no longer afford." Benefits have included improved water quality, increased social equity, better mental and physical health, mitigation of climate change impacts, economic development, and better youth education and development. The department's commissioner, Mitch Silver, says that New York is a "deal-making city" that collaborates with other agencies to respond to residents' needs and emerging trends on every parks project.

A More Comprehensive Planning Process

The second idea that this book develops—that we need a more robust and collaborative parks and recreation system planning process to generate sustainability and resiliency benefits—is gaining traction. The scope of parks and recreation system planning has changed dramatically over the past two decades in response to numerous societal and lifestyle shifts. Parks and recreation system planners are having to constantly refine and update their planning approach in response to changing trends, lifestyles, demographics, land development patterns, and other influences. However, the typical parks and recreation planning process hasn't changed significantly over the past century and a half since architect Horace Cleveland presented his *Suggestions for a System of Parks and Parkways for the City of Minneapolis* in 1883!

The typical system planning process generally follows a strategic planning model (see chapter 4), including evaluation of existing conditions; identification of needs; development of a long-range vision; and creation of a funding, phasing, and implementation strategy. In 1995 the National Recreation and Park Association (NRPA) recommended more specific, quantitative procedures to "provide a framework for park, recreation and open space planning in a rational, internally consistent and justifiable process for defining and addressing all components of the system."[4] The procedures included physical components, such as parks, trails, and amenities, and planning components, such as level-of-service guidelines, parks classifications, and facility design guidelines. The 2006 planning and urban design standards published by the American Planning Association (APA) proposed that the parks and open space planning process also include a review of mission, mandates, and plan elements; public participation; supply and demand analysis; and alternative scenarios, leading to the adoption and implementation of a final plan.[5]

While these planning models are still basically sound, a new approach is needed to respond to the cultural, environmental, and economic changes of the past few decades. Parks and recreation systems have become more complex in response to public needs; while parks and recreation agencies used to focus primarily on recreation facilities and programs such as playgrounds, ball fields, boat ramps, and youth athletics, now they're also involved in socioeconomic and environmental issues such as social services, child care, habitat restoration, and homelessness. Peter Harnik, retired executive director of the Trust for Public Land's Center for City Park Excellence, noted that

> parks *seem* relatively simple and straightforward. In fact, they are immensely complicated. People frequently say, "It's not rocket science, it's just a park." Or, "If you think parks are tough, you should see how difficult highways are." No! For rockets and highways, you need to be good at math. Parks require math plus horticulture, hydrology, psychology, sociology, and communication.[6]

In recognition of these increased complexities, there are no longer any nationally accepted standards for parks and recreation planning. Each community must determine its own standards, level-of-service metrics, and long-range vision for its parks and recreation system based on community issues, values, needs, priorities, and available resources. The most recent publication on parks and recreation planning standards—the NRPA's 1996 *Park, Recreation, Open Space, and Greenway Guidelines*—stated that "a standard for parks and recreation cannot be universal, nor can one city be compared with another even though they are similar in many respects."[7] Similarly, the APA's 2008 publication *From Recreation to Re-creation* noted that "specific guidance on planning for parks and open space systems in a manner similar to other community resources is simply not available."[8]

Another complicating factor is urbanization across the United States and the accompanying demographic diversity. Most parks and recreation planning standards in the United States were developed for mid-twentieth-century suburban communities, focused on what architectural historian Galen Cranz called the "recreation facility."[9] The primary goal was to provide suburban families with access to basic active recreation activities and facilities such as playgrounds, basketball and tennis courts, athletics fields, and swimming pools. While many of those facilities are still in demand, today's urban and urbanizing residents are also demanding indoor recreation centers, pickleball courts, food trucks, yoga classes, outdoor movies, dog parks, special events, festivals, and other types of recreation experiences. Urban lifestyles are very different from suburban lifestyles; for example, the parks and recreation needs assignment we conducted for downtown San Diego several years ago revealed that "going out for a glass of wine" was a top recreation priority for many downtown residents. Also, the needs of different urban neighborhoods may vary significantly on the basis of demographic factors such as ethnicity, age, and income. Aging and active baby boomers may lobby for more indoor pickleball courts, while youth athletic leagues and travel teams demand more high-quality sports fields and tournament complexes. An added complication of urbanization is the rapidly diminishing supply of large tracts of land available to accommodate these needs.

Residents' expectations for high-quality parks and recreation facilities have also changed dramatically. In Cranz's suburban "recreation facility" era, each community was provided with the same standard equipment: concrete or asphalt sports courts, grass ball fields with backstops, slides and swings for the young kids, and basic swimming pools. Today's residents are requesting Har-Tru clay tennis courts to reduce impact on their knees; multigenerational playgrounds with rubberized surfaces to simultaneously accommodate adults and kids; laser-leveled or artificial turf fields with batting cages, covered bleachers, and concessions; competitive sports leagues; and aquatics centers with indoor/outdoor Olympic-size pools, diving wells, spray pads, lap pools, and lazy rivers. Americans are traveling more than ever before and expect their hometown community to provide the same or higher level of quality as the newest facility they visited on their latest travels. Such increased expectations not only have strained budgets for capital improvements but also have had a tremendous impact on most parks and recreation agencies' operations and maintenance workloads and budgets.

Related to these increased expectations, public involvement in parks and recreation system planning has also changed dramatically over the past several decades. One of my longtime clients, a parks and recreation director for a midsize city, quipped, "The only thing I used to ask residents was what color playground do you want—red or blue?" In contrast, today's elected officials are highly sensitive to the need to provide residents with every opportunity to participate in the parks and recreation planning process, employing an entire tool kit of public involvement techniques, including surveys, focus groups, online engagement, and open houses.

Rapidly changing trends and technologies are also affecting the parks and recreation planning process. For example, the increasing national popularity of pickleball has taken many agencies by surprise, and recreational trends such as e-gaming, Pokémon Go, and footgolf were unheard of a few years ago. While it may be desirable to forecast the future trends for a ten-year parks and recreation system master plan, or PRSMP, it is not very realistic. Instead, the parks system planning process could focus on building the flexibility and adaptability needed to respond more quickly to new trends as they arise without causing major disruption. New technologies are also affecting communications and data collection in the parks and recreation planning process; for example, the rapid decline in residential telephone landlines has forced a shift from telephone surveys to mail and online surveys. Similarly, social media and interactive websites have become de facto tools for parks and recreation needs assessments.

Finally, today's fiscal climate has had a tremendous impact on the practice of parks and recreation system planning. In spite of the renewed interest in parks and open spaces, particularly in urban communities, in many communities parks are still not considered an essential service akin to police, fire, sewer, and water services. Parks and recreation agencies are consistently underfunded and asked to do more with less. The situation has been exacerbated by a decrease in trust in government, an increase in demands for lower ad valorem taxes, and the concurrent increase in demand for parks and recreation services, as noted earlier. This emotionally charged climate has heightened the importance of thoughtful planning for implementation throughout the entire parks and recreation planning process.

A few communities in the United States have responded to these complexities through more robust, comprehensive, and collaborative parks and recreation planning processes. City departments in Bellevue, Washington, for example, concurrently planned their public realm, including parks, streets, and other community facilities. The city's comprehensive plan notes that "these facilities address multiple objectives, such as creating new open space and enhancing neighborhood character even as they meet basic functional requirements."[10] The City of Portland, Oregon, combines all of its subsystem plans (e.g., parks, streets, utilities) into a citywide systems plan. The cities of Lenexa, Kansas, and Philadelphia, Pennsylvania, have collaboratively planned their parks and stormwater systems to generate greater community-wide benefits from each. And in chapter 4, I discuss our parks and recreation system planning work with the City of Port St. Lucie, Florida, which annually engages in a collaborative interdepartmental process to update its strategic plan, translate its strategic goals into citywide initiatives, and form multidisciplinary teams to plan and implement each of the top-priority projects for the year.

These communities represent the exception, however; most still follow the traditional parks and recreation system planning model. Every phase of the traditional planning process, from the existing conditions analysis to the implementation strategy, must be reexamined—and possibly redefined—in response to the increasing complexities and profound societal shifts outlined here.

How This Book Is Organized

Parks and Recreation System Planning responds to these shifts from two different but overlapping perspectives. The first part of the book advocates for a broader scope and context of parks and recreation system planning in order to respond to societal shifts and expectations in a meaningful way. Parks and recreation facilities should no longer be regarded as isolated facilities but rather as elements of a larger, interconnected public realm that also includes streets, museums, libraries, stormwater facilities, utility corridors, and other civic infrastructure. Each element of the system should be designed to generate as many benefits as possible for the community. Therefore, parks and recreation agencies must transcend their silos—and leverage their resources—to plan and collaborate with other public and private agencies to meet as many of the community's needs as possible.

Part I offers three concepts related to the big idea of generating multiple community benefits through the parks and recreation system planning process. Chapter 1 discusses the idea of planning parks and recreation systems as part of the larger public realm, creating a plexus, or integrated system. Chapter 2 reviews the breadth and depth of alternative dimensions or perspectives of parks and recreation systems that could be addressed through the planning process. And chapter 3 introduces the concept of High-Performance Public Spaces (HPPSs) that generate multiple economic, social, and environmental benefits as an aspirational goal of the parks and recreation system planning process. Together, these three concepts—the public realm, multiple dimensions, and the HPPS—form the philosophical foundation of this book. They also help reframe and reposition parks and recreation systems as essential frameworks for achieving community sustainability, resiliency, and livability—and not just places for fun and games.

Part II outlines the proposed new process for parks and recreation planning based on the concepts presented in part I. It proposes that the parks and recreation planning process should be more comprehensive, collaborative, and focused on community-wide issues. Chapter 4 provides an overview of the traditional parks and recreation planning process and how it can be changed to generate greater community-wide benefits for sustainability and resiliency. Chapter 5 discusses how to initiate and plan the new approach, including the development of a project charter and project plan. Chapter 6 emphasizes the importance of developing a preliminary implementation framework as part of the planning process for the new approach and outlines the types of questions that should be asked.

Part III reviews each of the major phases of creating the PRSMP, including key differences between the new and traditional approaches. Chapter 7 discusses the evaluation of the existing parks and recreation system, based on the concepts in part I, and chapter 8 outlines a mixed-methods, triangulated approach to the needs assessment process. Chapter 9 deals with the thorny and often troublesome task of establishing parks and recreation level-of-service standards. Chapter 10 discusses how to create a long-range vision for a parks and recreation system that generates community-wide sustainability and resiliency benefits, including the elements of a decision-making framework. Chapter 11 tackles how to implement the vision by developing a realistic, actionable funding and implementation plan and offers recommendations for periodically updating the plan to keep it current.

Throughout the book, I present examples from parks and recreation master plans I led as principal-in-charge for the planning and design firms of Glatting Jackson Kercher Anglin, AECOM, and Barth Associates, using the pronoun "we" to refer to the project planning team for each project. I also use the phrase "our practice" to refer specifically to my firm, Barth Associates.

Finally, the conclusion summarizes the proposed new approach to developing a PRSMP to generate greater community-wide resiliency and sustainability benefits. The appendixes offer commonly used forms, questionnaires, worksheets, and other planning templates and tools that parks and recreation system planners may find useful.

Aspirations

I have had the honor of working with hundreds of communities throughout the United States during this time of great transition over the past forty years and have personally witnessed the increasing complexities of parks and recreation system planning—which has made my career all the more interesting and challenging! Upon reflection, I have three major aspirations for this book.

First, it is my hope that those involved in the planning and design of parks and recreation systems—including parks and recreation professionals, planners, design professionals, elected officials, parks commissioners, and others—will gain a greater appreciation of the importance of their work and of the incredible opportunities they have to significantly influence the quality of life in their communities. For far too long, many have accepted the tired old axiom that parks and recreation systems are nonessential facilities for fun and games rather than essential frameworks for community livability, sustainability, and resiliency.

A second, related aspiration is that those same professionals will use parks and recreation system planning as a platform for community leadership. I've witnessed the ascension of numerous professionals and departments that, like New York City's public realm team, have assumed community leadership positions, increased their funding, and helped transform their communities by advocating for an integrated public realm. Miami-Dade County's Parks, Recreation, and Open Spaces Department, for instance, has steadily increased its community-wide influence in the decade since we developed its "50 Year, Unifying Vision for a Livable, Sustainable Miami-Dade County" (see figure 0-1). We engaged more than three thousand residents to create a shared vision for an integrated public realm including great parks, public spaces, and natural and cultural areas connected by greenways, trails, waterways, and complete streets. The plan was adopted by the county commission, the school board, thirty-four municipalities, three state parks, and two national parks and was codified in the county's comprehensive development master plan. To date, the plan has resulted in the development of 140 miles of greenways to improve access to parks, schools, and businesses; the design of the Underline, an internationally recognized ten-mile bike and pedestrian corridor running beneath the Metrorail through Miami's densely populated urban core; more than one hundred acres of new neighborhood parks; and the evidence-based Fit2Play out-of-school program, which is improving the health of thousands of children. Health outcomes have been published in five public health and medical journals, extolling the benefits of a properly designed and programmed urban public realm.

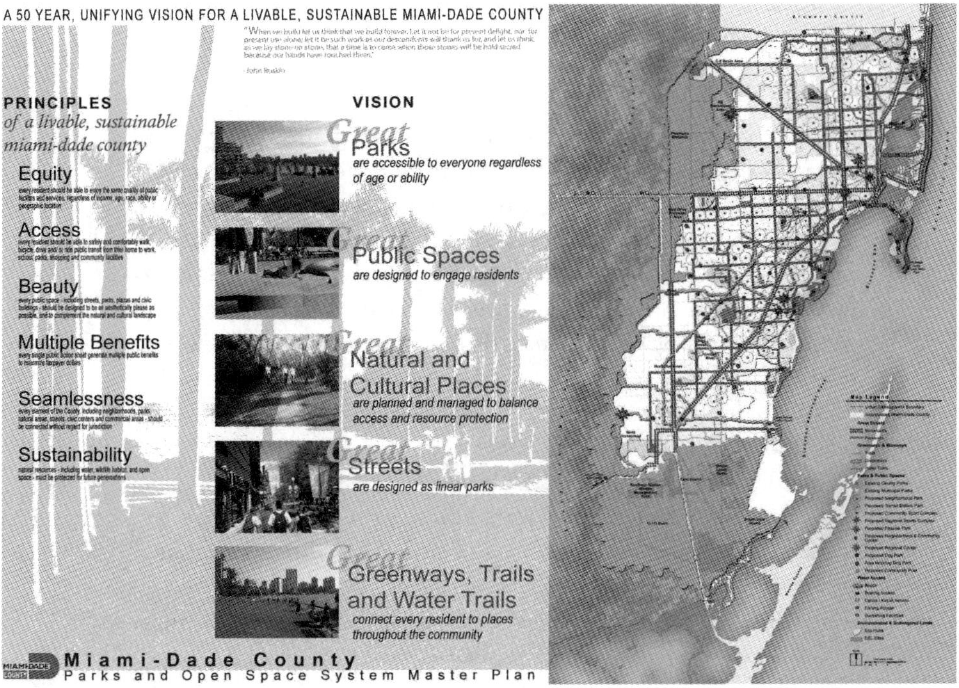

Figure 0-1: Summary poster for the 2007 Miami-Dade County Parks and Open Space System Master Plan (Glatting Jackson Kercher Anglin, Inc.)

Third, and more specific to the point of this book, I hope that readers will recognize the need for a far more rigorous, robust, and collaborative process for planning parks and recreation systems to both increase their influence and generate greater community-wide benefits. The proposed new approach to parks and recreation system planning requires a greater commitment of time and resources than did the traditional model, as well as significant skills in leadership, team building and collaboration, public engagement, social science research, facilitation, financial analysis, and political strategy. However, the ROI can be significant; many of those who have embarked on such processes have been rewarded with heightened community respect and influence, increased funding, boosted morale, more collaborative relationships, and leadership positions in transformative projects that have significantly improved the livability, sustainability, and resiliency of their communities.

Box 0-2
Terminology

For ease of reading, I've simplified some terms in this book that are unwieldy or vague. First, the term "planner" refers to any agency or individual leading a parks and recreation system planning process. Typically, this may include parks and recreation departments and professionals, city and county planners, parks commissions and commissioners, landscape architects, and urban designers.

Second, as detailed elsewhere in the introduction, the pronoun "we" refers to project teams I led for Glatting Jackson Kercher Anglin, AECOM, and Barth Associates, and "our practice" refers to my current firm, Barth Associates.

Third, the acronym PRSMP (plural PRSMPs) is used for a parks and recreation system master plan, also known as a parks and recreation master plan, a parks master plan, and a parks and recreation strategic plan.

Finally, "the planning process" refers to the process of preparing a PRSMP, regardless of the specific scope of work.

PART I

GENERATING MULTIPLE BENEFITS

01 PARKS AND THE PUBLIC REALM

Parks and recreation system master plans (PRSMPs) are typically developed in departmental silos in cities and counties throughout the United States, totally independently of comprehensive transportation plans, stormwater master plans, bikeway and trail plans, and other public infrastructure planning processes. However, in order for parks and recreation systems to generate greater economic, social, and environmental benefits for their communities; contribute to community livability, sustainability, and resiliency; and be regarded as more essential, they should be planned and designed as part of an integrated public realm.

While there is no commonly accepted definition for the term "public realm," it generally refers to a community's system of streets and sidewalks, parks and civic spaces, historic and cultural areas, and natural areas and trails. It also includes public infrastructure such as drainage swales, stormwater treatment ponds, utility corridors, and other lands owned and managed by city, county, regional, state, and federal agencies. Alexander Garvin may have given the best definition: the public realm is "our common property. It is the fundamental element in any community—the framework around which everything grows."[1]

A Brief History of the Public Realm in the United States

The modern public realm in the United States, including streets and parks, evolved from the sanitary reform movement in the mid-nineteenth century, which arose in response to the health needs of urbanizing communities: "wide straight streets, open prospects, and the generous distribution of green reinforced the preachings of the increasingly vocal sanitation movement."[2] For example, an 1850 report on a sanitary survey of Massachusetts recommended that "in laying out new towns and villages, and in extending those already laid out, ample provisions must be made for a supply, in purity and abundance, of light, air and water; for drainage and sewerage, for paving and cleanliness."[3] Sanitarians also agreed that cities should be designed as airy, verdant places free from excessive crowding and congestion; there should be abundant parks and trees to refresh the air and to provide opportunities for outdoor exercise; there should be a pure water supply and a fully developed sewage system; and building sites should be well drained. "Freedom from organic wastes, stagnant water, ground moisture, and human congestion, and the presence of abundant clean water, fresh air, and sunlight formed the basis of townsite consciousness."[4]

As a result of the sanitation movement, the second half of the nineteenth century was a boom time for public parks in the United States. While no municipal parks existed in the United States in 1852, over one hundred cities had parks by 1892, and ten years later almost eight hundred cities and towns were working on park projects; over the same period of time, park committees and commissions grew from none in 1852 to about 200 in 1877 and to 2,300 in 1902.[5] By the end of the late nineteenth century there was a growing sense of responsibility for the public welfare in the United States, "nurtured for three or four decades by interrelated movements for developing pure water supplies, controlling contagious diseases, creating effective sewerage systems, and providing parks, particularly large, romantic pleasure grounds, such as Central Park and Franklin Park."[6] Today it is estimated that over one hundred thousand parks have been constructed in the United States, managed by over twelve thousand agencies.[7] Streets, sidewalks, trails, greenways, and stormwater facilities are being designed as multipurpose "green infrastructure," and the public realm "remains an effective tool for shaping the American city."[8]

Figure 1-1 illustrates a typical community public realm system. It is estimated that the public realm comprises as much as 25–50 percent of a community's landmass; public rights-of-way alone account for up to 35 percent of the developed lands in US cities.[9] Figure 1-2 shows the public realm of the City of Norfolk, Virginia, as an

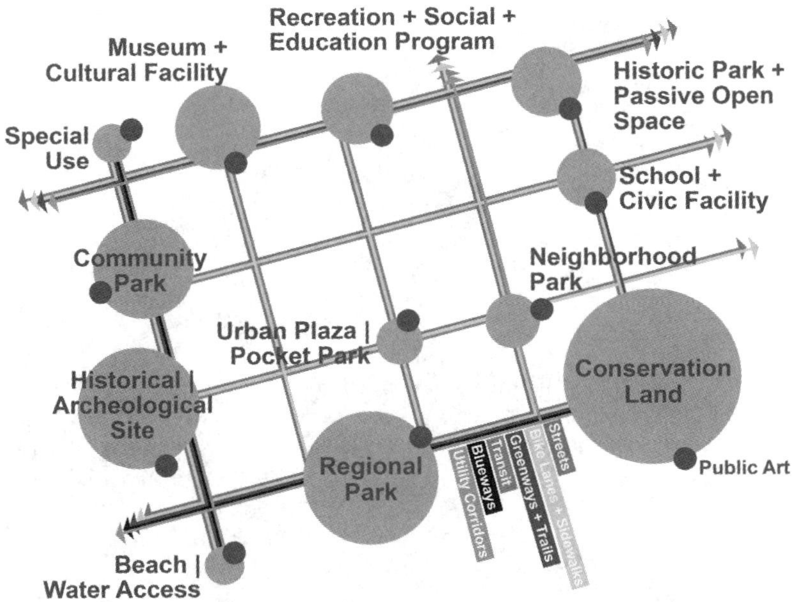

Figure 1-1: The public realm system (David Barth and Carlos F. Perez)

example. Such a landmass could generate numerous societal benefits if collaboratively planned as a single, integrated system.

The Public Realm as a Tool for Sustainability and Resiliency

Despite the advantages of a well-crafted public realm, many cities and counties have overlooked this important asset over the past thirty years as they've strived to make their communities more sustainable. They've prepared ambitious and hopeful strategic plans, climate action plans, health assessments, economic development plans, sea-level mitigation plans, public transportation plans, affordable housing plans, redevelopment plans, vulnerability assessments, and other plans to help solve economic, social, and environmental issues. For example, the extensive flooding damage caused by superstorm Hurricane Sandy in 2012 prompted renewed calls for climate change planning and adaptation, including improved energy systems, transportation systems, coastal communities, and landscaping.[10]

Figure 1-2: Public realm of the City of Norfolk, Virginia; areas in black include parks, rights-of-way, and other public lands owned by the city, estimated to account for 40–50 percent of the city's landmass (Glatting Jackson Kercher Anglin, Inc.)

However, a growing number of communities are now recognizing the potential of their public realm—including their parks and recreation systems—as a means of addressing many of these issues.

The concepts of sustainability and resiliency are closely related (see box 1-1). Sustainability was defined by the World Commission

Box 1-1

An Integrated Framework for Realizing the "Future We Want for All" in the Post-2015 UN Development Agenda

Inclusive Social Development

- Adequate nutrition for all
- Quality education for all
- Reduced mortality and morbidity
- Gender equality
- Universal access to clean water and sanitation

Environmental Sustainability

- Protecting biodiversity
- Stable climate
- Resilience to natural hazards

Inclusive Economic Development

- Eradicating income poverty and hunger
- Reducing inequalities
- Ensuring decent work and productive employment

Peace and Security

- Freedom from violence, conflict, and abuse
- Conflict-free access to natural resources

Source: United Nations, "UN System Task Team on the Post-2015 UN Development Agenda: Realizing the Future We Want for All, Report to the Secretary-General," June 2012, 24, https://www.un.org/millenniumgoals/pdf/Post_2015_UNTTreport.pdf.

on Environment and Development in 1987 as "meeting the needs of the present without compromising those of future generations." A good definition of resiliency is "the capacity of individuals, communities, institutions, businesses, and systems within a city to survive, adapt, and grow no matter what kinds of chronic stresses and acute shocks they experience."[11]

Many communities have struggled to develop meaningful metrics, strategies, and actions to address these broad goals and objectives, and the more esoteric concept of sustainability remains difficult to grasp and operationalize. However, some communities are trying to mobilize more quickly to address the more immediate and urgent concept of resiliency, including responses to the shocks and stresses that are making headlines daily. Shocks are acute natural and human-caused disasters such as coastal storms and flooding, wildfires, civil disturbances, and severe economic recessions; stresses are chronic challenges to natural and human systems such as drought, the urban heat island effect, nuisance flooding, poverty and inequality, and climate change. The Rockefeller Foundation's City Resilience Index suggests that the resilience of a community

> relates to four key dimensions: health and well-being, ensuring the health and well-being of everyone living and working in the city; economy and society, the social and financial systems that enable urban populations to live peacefully, and act collectively; infrastructure and environment, man-made and natural systems that provide critical services [and] protect and connect urban citizens; and leadership and strategy, the need for informed, inclusive, integrated, and iterative decision making in our cities.[12]

As mentioned in the introduction, the public realm can be an important tool in both mitigating the shocks and stresses associated with resiliency and accomplishing the long-range aspirations inherent in sustainability. A case in point is the seventeen-acre Historic Fourth Ward Park in Atlanta, Georgia, a "glistening oasis" where there once stood little more than cracked asphalt, trash-strewn fields, and an empty promise of something more.[13] The park was designed as a stormwater detention basin to increase storm sewer capacity, reduce the burden on the city's aging infrastructure, and minimize downstream flooding and property damage. It was also designed as a central gathering space to help stabilize the surrounding neighborhoods. Amenities include open lawns, two playgrounds, a splash pad, an outdoor amphitheater, a "world-class" skate park, and a large multiuse athletics field.

As in many transformative projects that increase local sustainability and resiliency, the Historic Fourth Ward Park also serves as a model of collaboration. Public and private partners included the

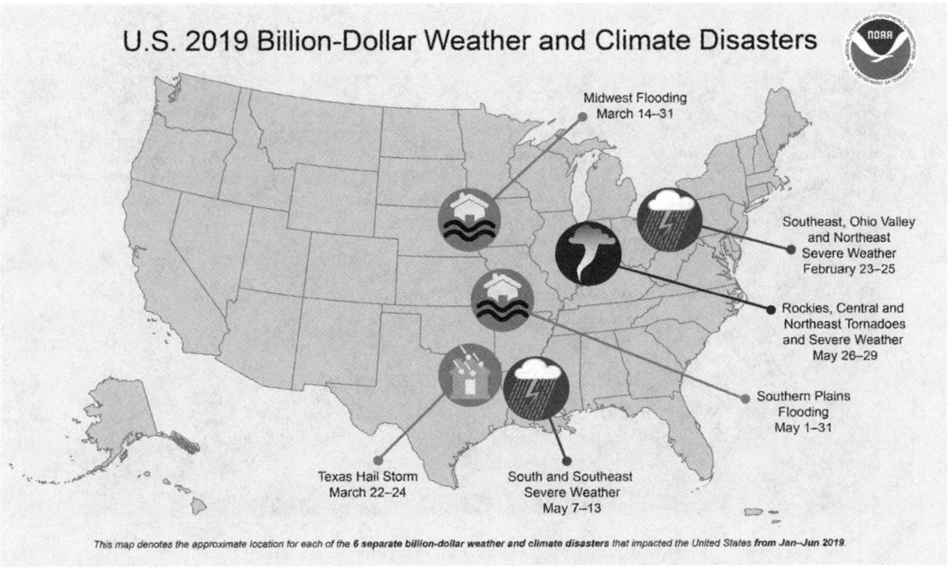

Figure 1-3: Resiliency shocks (National Oceanic and Atmospheric Administration, National Centers for Environmental Information, "U.S. 2019 Billion-Dollar Weather and Climate Disasters," https://www.ncdc.noaa.gov/billions/)

Atlanta BeltLine Partnership, the Atlanta Department of Watershed Management, the Georgia Power utility, and the BB&T bank. In addition to addressing flooding and stormwater issues, the project has significantly increased surrounding property values; stabilized surrounding neighborhoods; attracted thousands of residents and visitors for fitness, recreation, socialization, and special events; and saved the city more than $15 million over the original plans to build a traditional stand-alone stormwater facility. Additionally, ongoing irrigation and maintenance costs have been reduced through the use of native plants, dynamic soils (soils that change in response to natural and man-made disturbances and stressors), and solar panels.

Another well-known example is New York City's High Line, an old elevated rail line that was retrofitted into an incredibly popular park. Constructed at a cost of approximately $153 million, the High Line has brought in an estimated $2 billion in new development. A 2011 post on Smartplanet.com describes the incredible return on the city's investment.

Figure 1-4: Historic Fourth Ward Park, Atlanta, Georgia (Photo courtesy of Carlos F. Perez)

> In the five years since construction started on the High Line, 29 new projects have been built or are under way in the neighborhood, according to the New York City Department of City Planning. More than 2,500 new residential units, 1,000 hotel rooms and over 500,000 square feet of office and art gallery space have gone up.
>
> "Cities recognize parks are good for their economies. They're no longer a nice thing to have, but a must," said Will Rogers, president and chief executive of the Trust for Public Land, a national conservation group. . . .
>
> The area around the park, sprinkled with small offices under 200,000 square feet, has become a draw for start-ups and creative companies.[14]

In addition to serving as a catalyst for new development, the High Line has become one of the city's most visited tourist destinations, attracting millions of visitors per year. It also serves as a central gathering space for city residents, providing opportunities for strolling, socializing, viewing the skyline, exercising, and enjoying quiet contemplation. Recreation and cultural programs include stargazing, teen nights, music and dance performances, and family activities. The High Line also reduces stormwater runoff, mediates

Figure 1-5: New York City's High Line (Photo courtesy of David Barth)

the heat island effect created by hard and reflective city surfaces, and provides shade, oxygen, and habitat for insects and birds.

Planning the Public Realm as a Plexus

The ability of the public realm to generate broad community benefits cannot be realized without coordinated planning. However, as mentioned previously, very few communities plan, design, and manage their public realm as a plexus: an interwoven combination of parts or elements in a structure or system.[15]

Unlike a plexus, the public realm is typically segregated into subsystems planned and managed by different departments or agencies, such as parks and recreation, planning, public works, engineering, transportation, and water management. Each agency separately plans and manages its subsystem according to its own planning principles, goals and objectives, methodologies, metrics, constituents, stakeholders, mandates, and funding requirements. Examples include parks and recreation master plans, comprehensive transportation plans, bikeways and trails master plans, stormwater master plans, school and library master plans, public art master plans, and environmental lands acquisition and management plans. While some departments collaborate with others during the planning process, much of the work is done in departmental or agency silos. For instance, as mentioned earlier, the original plan to address stormwater and flooding problems in Atlanta's Historic Fourth Ward was to build a traditional stand-alone stormwater facility.

The planning processes for all of these subsystems are very similar, usually following the same basic strategic planning steps discussed in the introduction.

1. Evaluate existing conditions.
2. Determine needs and gaps between existing and desired future conditions.
3. Develop alternative scenarios and solutions to meet needs and gaps, including capital improvements, programs, policies, codes, and other initiatives.
4. Estimate costs and funding projections.
5. Develop a phased implementation plan, including short-term, mid-term, and long-term actions.

The three subsystems that would generate the most benefits with collaborative planning are parks and recreation, stormwater, and transportation. Together, they often account for well over 75 percent of the public realm, including both sites and corridors. Sites include parks and recreation facilities such as parks, sports complexes, community centers, civic spaces, cultural and historical facilities, and preserves; transportation facilities such as public parking lots, structures, and trailheads; and stormwater treatment facilities such as retention and detention ponds. Corridors for all three subsystems include streets, sidewalks, bike lanes and cycle tracks, off-road trails, greenways, stormwater swales, and drainage canals. Utility corridors (a fourth subsystem) also include water, gas, sewer, and electric utility corridors and easements.

The desired outcomes for these subsystem planning processes are very similar. Parks and recreation agencies, for example, prepare PRSMPs to identify parks and recreation needs; to identify projects, programs, and policies to meet those needs; and to reconcile desired projects with available funds through capital improvement programs (CIPs), grants, and other funding sources. Municipal, county, and regional transportation departments typically prepare comprehensive transportation plans (CTPs) to identify transportation needs; to identify projects, programs, and policies to meet those needs; and to reconcile desired projects with available funds through transportation improvement programs, state and federal grants, and other funding sources. And stormwater system plans are prepared by local and regional agencies to identify existing and anticipated problems with water quality or quantity; to define projects, programs, procedures, and practices that address those problems; and to reconcile desired projects with available funds through CIPs, state and federal grants, and other funding sources.

Dissimilarities among the subsystem planning processes include the different levels of quantitative analysis and modeling used to determine needs and evaluate alternatives; the availability of standards; and the primary sources and mandates for funding. For instance, parks and recreation planning relies more heavily on qualitative techniques to determine needs and demand, such as stakeholder interviews, focus groups, and public workshops. Quantitative techniques used in PRSMPs are typically limited to surveys, benchmarking, and various models for determining local levels of service. Funding for parks and recreation improvements is mostly local, with the exception of state and federal grants. And, as mentioned previously, there are no standards for parks and recreation levels of service; the authors of the latest edition of the National Recreation and Park Association's *Park, Recreation, Open Space, and Greenway Guidelines* "provide guidance to communities so that each community can create its own custom standards rather than applying an absolute national standard."[16]

In contrast, stormwater and transportation subsystem planning rely much more heavily on sophisticated computer modeling to calculate levels of service and determine travel demand for various modes of transportation, calculate stormwater runoff rates and the required areas needed for water quality treatment and storage, and develop alternative future scenarios in response to the demand. Far more federal and state funds are available for stormwater and transportation improvements, along with the accompanying mandates.

And quantitative standards are used to inform modeling of both stormwater and transportation systems.

Interestingly, all three processes have evolved over the past several decades from being prescriptive to more contextual, perhaps in response to the growing complexity of urbanizing communities—and the public's desire for more sustainable and resilient solutions that balance functionality and livability. For example, the current approach to transportation planning is starting to focus on moving people rather than just cars, incorporating a wide variety of transportation modes (e.g., bicycle, pedestrian, transit, automobile) and alternative design solutions based on urban, suburban, and rural contexts. Similarly, an increasing number of stormwater projects are being designed as green infrastructure, using natural systems and landscapes—rather than pipes and concrete structures—to reduce and treat stormwater at its source. And, as discussed throughout this book, parks and recreation systems are being planned and designed within the context of an interconnected, multidimensional public realm. Since the planning processes for the various elements of the public realm are more similar than dissimilar—and since concurrent and collaborative planning could help leverage resources and generate multiple benefits—it seems logical that more communities would prepare their subsystem planning processes concurrently.

The 2035 comprehensive plan for the City of Portland, Oregon, updated in 2018, offers perhaps one of the best examples of an integrated public realm system plan. The plan integrates parks, open spaces, greenways, and trails with land use and transportation, transit, development centers and corridors, and neighborhoods. It is based on a compelling vision for Portland as "a prosperous, healthy, equitable and resilient city where everyone has access to opportunity and is engaged in shaping decisions that affect their lives."[17] An equity framework comprising three integrated strategies—thriving educated youth, economic prosperity and affordability, and healthy connected city—is being used as the basis for implementation. The five guiding principles that influence the city's decision making are economic prosperity, human health, environmental health, equity, and resilience. Figure 1-6 graphically illustrates how the various elements of the comprehensive plan form an integrated public realm

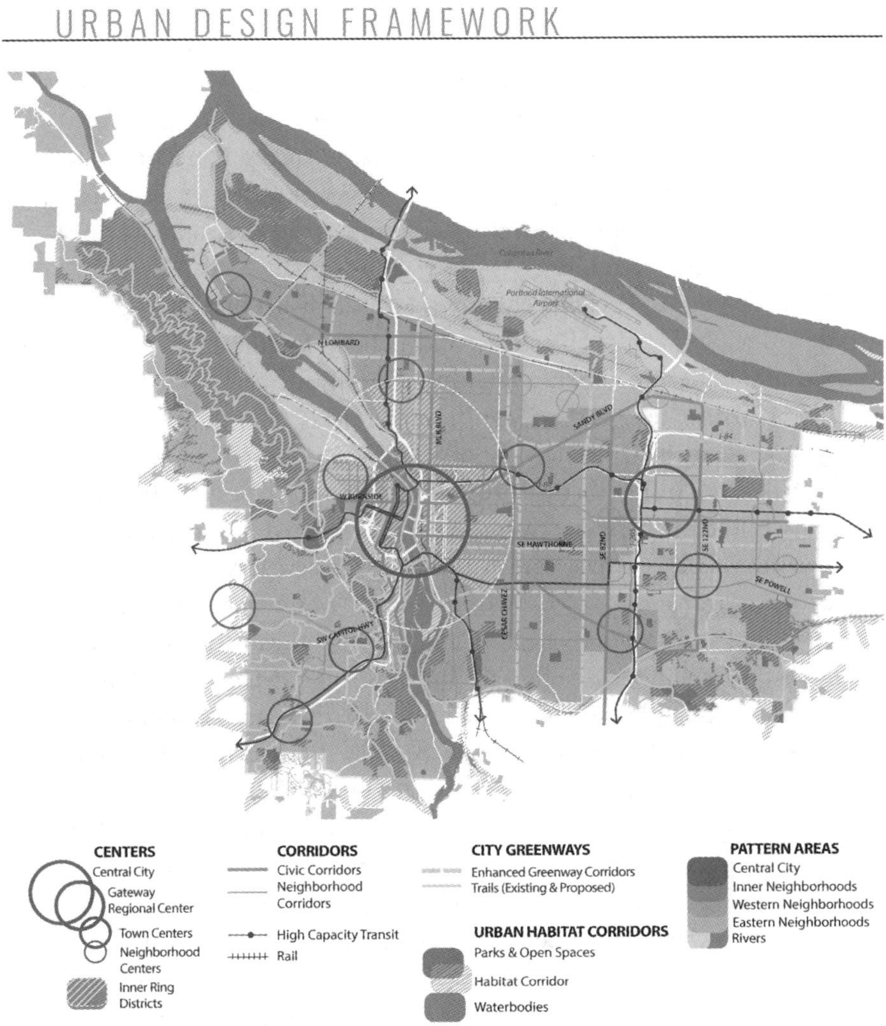

Figure 1-6: Portland, Oregon, urban design framework (City of Portland, Oregon, "2035 Comprehensive Plan," December 2018, I-9, https://beta.portland.gov/sites/default/files/2019-08/comp_plan_intro.pdf)

that defines the physical form of the city and creates numerous environmental, social, and economic benefits.

Most important, the city treats parks, streets, and trails; water pipes and reservoirs; and stormwater swales and sewers as basic systems needed to protect the health, safety, and well-being of Portland households and businesses. The city also acknowledges the importance of these systems for its long-term sustainability and resiliency. "High quality basic services are essential to Portland's future success. Infrastructure, like sidewalks, developed streets, stormwater management systems, and parks and open space, ensure that Portlanders can move around the city, recreate, drink clean water and have reliable sewer service. They also help protect the environment and support the city's economy."[18]

While Portland's comprehensive plan establishes the vision, guiding principles, goals, objectives, and policies for the public realm, two additional documents relate specifically to parks and public infrastructure: the "List of Significant Projects" and the "Citywide Systems Plan" (CSP). The "List of Significant Projects" includes the city's planned infrastructure projects, based on each of the subsystem plans, while the CSP is a twenty-year coordinated municipal infrastructure plan for areas within Portland's urban service boundary, including transportation networks; water storage and distribution; sewer and stormwater collection and treatment facilities; parks and recreation facilities; and other facilities such as city hall, office buildings, and fire and police. City bureaus (departments) collaborate on projects that will generate multiple benefits. For example, Portland Parks & Recreation recently collaborated with the city's Bureau of Environmental Services to acquire a one-hundred-acre parcel that will provide recreation, habitat, and stormwater treatment. While the individual subsystems were not all planned concurrently, the CSP acknowledges the need for collaboration.

> The Citywide Systems Plan . . . serves as a long-range, coordinated plan to guide future public infrastructure investments. . . .
>
> The CSP goes beyond the State planning requirements and includes a more coordinated and comprehensive look at the City's infrastructure based on community values and best practices. . . . The CSP recognizes the critical roles these systems play in meeting the needs of Portlanders and supporting the overall mission of the City of Portland. . . .
>
> The CSP . . . improves coordination between infrastructure planning efforts, and considers the community's infrastructure priorities in a consistent manner.[19]

Figure 1-7: Seattle's Pavement to Parks program (Photo courtesy of the Seattle Department of Transportation)

Other examples of coordinated subsystem planning include the Rain to Recreation program of the City of Lenexa, Kansas, which integrates water quality and flood control planning with parks and natural resource planning. In Washington, the Seattle Department of Transportation's Pavement to Parks program has converted over thirteen street ends and other roadway areas to basketball courts and miniparks (figure 1-7). And the City of New York is receiving great accolades for its conversion of street lanes to more bicycle- and pedestrian-friendly bike lanes, urban plazas, and miniparks.

Barriers to Collaborative Planning

So, what keeps public realm planners from working more collaboratively? First, funding mandates often prescribe specific planning practices. A case in point is the Federal Highway Administration's requirement that a CTP include a proactive public participation process conducted by the area's metropolitan planning organization, the state department of transportation, and transit operators in order to receive federal transportation funds. Therefore, transportation planners may focus on "checking the boxes" of federal transportation requirements rather than on collaborative public realm planning, according to one of the project planners I interviewed. There are no similar federal or state mandates regarding the development of parks and recreation master plans; planners are free to define the scope and products of local parks and recreation planning processes.

Second, budget constraints may limit the level of collaboration among departments or agencies. PRSMP budgets range from approximately $100,000 to $300,000, while stormwater and CTP budgets may exceed $1 million. While stormwater and transportation planners may focus on meeting state and federal requirements, parks and recreation planners focus on addressing local issues such as defining levels of service, determining residents' needs, securing funding for both capital improvements and ongoing operations, and maintaining the existing system. Little time, money, or energy may be available for addressing other elements of the public realm.

A third, related reason may be control. While transportation planners, stormwater planners, and parks planners may make broad recommendations in their subsystem plans regarding other elements of the public realm, few may be comfortable suggesting specific capital improvements under another agency's jurisdiction. A project planner I interviewed stated, "You don't want to make bold recommendations for properties you don't control."

Finally, collaboration among agencies is difficult, time-consuming, and often counterintuitive. Public employees are typically evaluated using fairly narrow, mission-related metrics, and few agencies have adopted a truly collaborative culture. According to Karyl Ramsey's doctoral research at Saybrook University, collaborative planning "does not lend itself to mechanistic or predictable implementation. Instead, it is an emergent process that reflects the interconnected, complex nature of social systems. This requires a shift in how public agencies are perceived, from independent entities with separate functions, to interdependent entities within a cultural context—that is, a culture of collaboration."[20]

Shifting Perspectives and Promoting Collaboration

Creating a culture of collaboration within the parks and recreation system planning process begins with the project leader, be it an elected official, department or agency head, city manager, parks commissioner, project manager, or other individual. To generate the most benefits for the community, he or she must first commit to conducting a multidimensional planning process, as discussed in the next chapter. Inherent in this approach is the need to collaborate with other agencies and departments to leverage available resources. Once the decision has been made to adopt a multidimensional, interdependent approach, there are numerous opportunities for collaborative planning, including integrated needs assessment processes, coordinated CIPs, mandatory planning cycles, and coordinated small area plans.

First, an integrated needs assessment process can provide opportunities to identify projects and initiatives that can generate multiple benefits. We often collaborate with other departments and agencies to develop questions about broader community issues in our public workshops, interviews, and surveys. Topics have included traffic congestion, community safety, homelessness, climate change, crime, poverty, and sea-level rise. For instance, a recent needs assessment process identified the need for twenty-five to thirty integrated stormwater parks to accomplish two objectives: increase walking access to neighborhood parks and improve the quality of stormwater runoff. This integrated approach will allow the parks and recreation agency to leverage parks and stormwater funding while also generating multiple benefits from land acquisition.

Another opportunity to promote collaborative planning—and to plan the public realm as a plexus—is the coordination of CIPs. Quite simply, this entails the sharing of proposed projects and initiatives among various agencies and departments to identify opportunities to generate multiple benefits. Similar to the example of stormwater parks, coordination of CIPs could identify opportunities for joint street and trail projects, such as complete streets; joint park and transit projects, such as transit-oriented urban parks; and joint school parks for both indoor and outdoor recreation. One of our clients, for example, recently identified the opportunity to design bus stops and trailheads as public art projects within parks.

Mandatory planning cycles may also foster more collaborative planning. For example, many states require local comprehensive plans to be evaluated on a regular basis, such as every seven years.

Perhaps local transportation, stormwater, and parks agencies—along with other public realm partners such as public works departments, school boards, and libraries—could be required to update their long-range plans at the same time. Concurrent planning cycles, including the needs assessment and capital improvement phases discussed earlier, may lead to more collaborative public realm planning.

Finally, small area planning provides a tool for planning the public realm as a plexus at the more meaningful local level. The City of Denver, Colorado, notes that small area plans "can cover three different geographic scales—neighborhood, corridor, and district regardless of the size of the area. Small area plans cover a specific geography that often has a cohesive set of characteristics." These plans allow local government to address disinvestment and deteriorating housing; public facilities and physical improvements that need to be addressed; opportunities for substantial infill or redevelopment; opportunities to influence site selection, development, or major expansion of a single large activity generator; and transit station development opportunities.[21] Small area plans transcend the different elements of the public realm and focus on the overall quality of the neighborhood, corridor, or district, which requires the participation and collaboration of all of the public realm managers. A Washington, DC, planner stated that small area plans provide an opportunity to "test scenarios and develop alternatives" at a local level on the basis of the system-wide plans.

In summary, planning the public realm as a plexus requires a commitment to transcend agency silos, spend extra time, and engage other public realm partners in a transdisciplinary planning process focused on community goals and values. It can be messy, time-consuming, and more expensive than single-disciplinary planning processes. But the payoffs can be big. In addition to increasing community sustainability and resiliency, integrated and collaborative planning can yield significant cost savings and increased efficiencies, improve teamwork and morale, and earn greater recognition and support for public projects from elected officials and the general public.

02 MULTIPLE DIMENSIONS OF PARKS AND RECREATION SYSTEMS

—

Planning a parks and recreation system within the context of an integrated public realm requires broader thinking. Parks and recreation systems are often generalized as being one-dimensional, focused mostly on recreation. However—in order to contribute to community sustainability and resiliency—we must first recognize the true multidimensional potential of these systems.

Multidimensionality is another broad concept related to the generation of multiple community benefits through the parks and recreation system planning process. For example, *Parks & Recreation*, the monthly publication of the National Recreation and Park Association (NRPA), lists numerous potential sustainability and resiliency dimensions that could be addressed, including health determinants, income inequality, educational opportunities, environmental conditions, gentrification, neighborhood stabilization, homelessness, sea-level rise, and social cohesion. Additional dimensions characterized as upcoming trends—for better or worse—in parks and recreation include opioid abuse in parks; the use of technology such as drones, beacon counters, and geofencing; e-sports; commercial recreation opportunities; and consolidation of health services, social services, cemeteries, and after-school care in parks.[1]

This is not to say that every parks and recreation system master plan (PRSMP) needs to address every possible dimension. The sheer breadth and depth of alternative dimensions—particularly if conducted within the context of the entire public realm—can present a dilemma for the parks and recreation planner: Should we just focus on traditional parks and recreation issues such as parks, recreation facilities, and trails, which will typically require less time and money? Or should we consider broader community-wide dimensions such as climate change, economic development, and homelessness, as discussed in chapter 1, which will undoubtedly require more of both time and money? Every community must determine the most appropriate scope for its PRSMP process. For this reason, we always conduct a scoping meeting before starting a new PRSMP to discuss the alternative dimensions with key stakeholders. We also discuss their expectations for the project and the desired outcomes. The defined dimensions, expectations, and desired outcomes can help define the specific scope of work for the project, as discussed in chapter 5.

A case in point is the 2007 Parks and Open Spaces Master Plan of Miami-Dade County, Florida. Dimensions of the plan included population growth, traffic congestion, inadequate housing, diminishing supply of developable land and potable water, affordable housing, loss of agricultural lands, income disparity, crime, educational attainment, history, design standards, neighborhood stabilization, redevelopment, walkability, and others. Box 2-1 is a short list of more than fifty potential dimensions of parks and recreation systems that could be addressed during the planning process; many communities may have others, based on local values, issues, and opportunities. For example, some PRSMPs are program driven; others focus on placemaking; some emphasize capital improvements; and some are driven by regulations. It can depend on the catalyst for development of the plan, the specific agenda of the person or agency leading the process, or both.

In my experience, the top ten dimensions most commonly addressed through the PRSMP process are (1) accreditation; (2) bicycle and pedestrian access; (3) priority needs and social equity; (4) updates to the comprehensive plan and land development codes, including level-of-service (LOS) standards; (5) funding and implementation; (6) green infrastructure and stormwater treatment; (7) health and wellness; (8) organizational mission, role, and structure; (9) park classifications and service delivery models; and (10) recreation, social, and educational programs. And while economic development is not often a top-priority dimension for parks and recreation planners, it should be, and it is included here as the eleventh dimension. John Crompton, University Distinguished Professor at Texas A&M University and the author of several books documenting the economic value of parks, noted that "the key to sustaining or

Box 2-1

Potential Dimensions of Parks and Recreation Systems

- Accreditation by the Commission for Accreditation of Parks and Recreation Agencies (CAPRA)
- Before- and after-school care
- Bicycle and pedestrian access
- Branding
- Capital improvement program
- Commercial recreation
- Compliance with Americans with Disabilities Act (ADA)
- Comprehensive plan goals
- Construction delivery methods
- Cost recovery
- Crime prevention through environmental design (CPTED)
- Design standards and details
- Economic development
- Educational opportunities
- Environment
- E-sports
- Flood control
- Funding
- Gentrification
- Green infrastructure
- Health and wellness
- Homelessness
- Impact fees
- Income inequality
- Land development codes
- Land use
- Level-of-service standards
- Marketing
- Mental health
- Needs and priorities
- Neighborhood stabilization
- Operations and maintenance
- Opioid abuse
- Organizational mission and role
- Organizational structure
- Park classifications
- Partnerships
- Permitting
- Political priorities
- Programs—recreation, social, educational
- Quality of life
- Redevelopment
- Resource protection
- Safety
- Sea-level rise
- Service delivery models
- Social equity
- Staffing
- Stormwater treatment
- Technology
- Tourism
- Transportation
- Wildlife habitat
- Youth development

Source: Barth Associates, LLC.

increasing investments in park and recreation services is for them to be repositioned so they are perceived to contribute to alleviating problems that constitute the prevailing political concerns of policy makers who are responsible for allocating tax funds."[2] Economic development, he continued, "is widely viewed as being central to a community's economic prosperity because it is viewed as a means of enhancing the tax base."[3]

Following is a discussion of each of these eleven dimensions as examples of the broader thinking required in the new PRSMP process. Consideration of each dimension has the potential not only to improve the parks and recreation system but also to generate broader community-wide resiliency and sustainability benefits.

1. Accreditation

Many parks and recreation agencies wish to become accredited by the Commission for Accreditation of Parks and Recreation Agencies (CAPRA) as a primary or secondary goal of a parks and recreation system planning process. CAPRA is administratively sponsored by the NRPA but acts independently to determine accreditation standards and to confer accreditation to applicant agencies. The NRPA cites many benefits of accreditation, both for the public and for agencies.

Benefits for the Public

- Assurance and validation of well-administered services in accord with approved professional practices
- Potential for external financial support and savings to the public
- External recognition of a quality governmental service
- Holds an agency accountable to the public and ensures responsiveness to meet their needs
- Improves customer and quality services

Benefits for the Agency

- Public and political recognition
- Increased efficiency and evidence of accountability

- Answers the question, "How are we doing?" through extensive self-evaluation
- Identifies areas for improvement by comparing an agency against national standards of best practice
- Enhances staff teamwork and pride by engaging all staff in the process
- Creates an environment for regular review of operations, policies and procedures, and promotes continual improvement
- Forces written documentation of policies and procedures[4]

The accreditation process also provides agencies with the opportunity to revisit their mission and vision, to collaborate with other departments and agencies, and to redefine their role in making their community more livable, sustainable, and resilient.

Agencies wishing to use the planning process for accreditation should become familiar with the CAPRA certification standards to make sure that the proposed scope of work includes as many of the standards as possible. Alternatively, they may want to "flip" the process, using the standards and accreditation process as a means of producing a parks and recreation system plan. The standards are available online (https://www.nrpa.org/certification/accreditation/CAPRA/capra-standards/) and include 151 standards for national accreditation. Many of the 37 fundamental standards could be addressed through a typical parks and recreation system planning process, including agency mission, goals, and objectives; vision; role of the agency and relationships with other providers; involvement with local planning initiatives; a parks and recreation system master plan; a strategic plan; community involvement; organizational structure; a recreation programming plan; and maintenance and operations management standards.

2. *Bicycle and Pedestrian Access*

Parks and recreation needs assessments in communities throughout the United States consistently reveal that one of residents' top priorities is improved bicycle and pedestrian access through sidewalks, bikeways, and trails. This is not surprising, given that the post–World War II focus on suburban land development patterns, which replaced the traditional grid with winding roads and dead-end cul-de-sacs, has led to disconnected, automobile-dependent subdivisions. Communities across the country are slowly and gradually retrofitting their streets, utility corridors, and abandoned rail lines with bike lanes, wide sidewalks, and multipurpose trails. Bikeways and trails can generate numerous community-wide benefits, including reduced traffic congestion, increased fitness, reduced obesity, opportunities for festivals and special events, and multigenerational social interactions.

Bicycle and pedestrian access is typically addressed through long-range comprehensive transportation plans (CTPs) led by regional transportation agencies, as discussed in chapter 1. While parks and recreation master plans typically address most of the sites within the public realm—including parks, community centers, trails, civic spaces, cultural and historical facilities, public art, environmental preserves, and greenways and blueways—CTPs typically address most of the linkages or connectors within the public realm, including streets, sidewalks, bikeways, and transit.

Parks and recreation agencies that wish to address bicycle and pedestrian access as part of the parks and recreation system planning process should collaborate with their local transportation planning agency to conduct concurrent planning processes. Both parks and recreation planning and bicycle and pedestrian planning require some type of need-demand analysis including quantitative and qualitative assessment techniques. Both processes also include a capital improvement program (CIP); a collaborative process could lead to the identification of multiuse projects that meet both recreation and transportation needs. The findings and recommendations from such collaborative processes could also be integrated into other community-wide plans, such as comprehensive plans and neighborhood plans.

Parks and recreation planners should also engage with other nongovernmental organizations (NGOs) that advocate, plan for, and implement bicycle and pedestrian facilities—such as the Washington Area Bicyclist Association and Charleston Moves—to get direct feedback from citizens who bike and walk. One of the most successful municipal-NGO relationships is between the City of Atlanta, Georgia, and Atlanta's nonprofit PATH Foundation, which initiates,

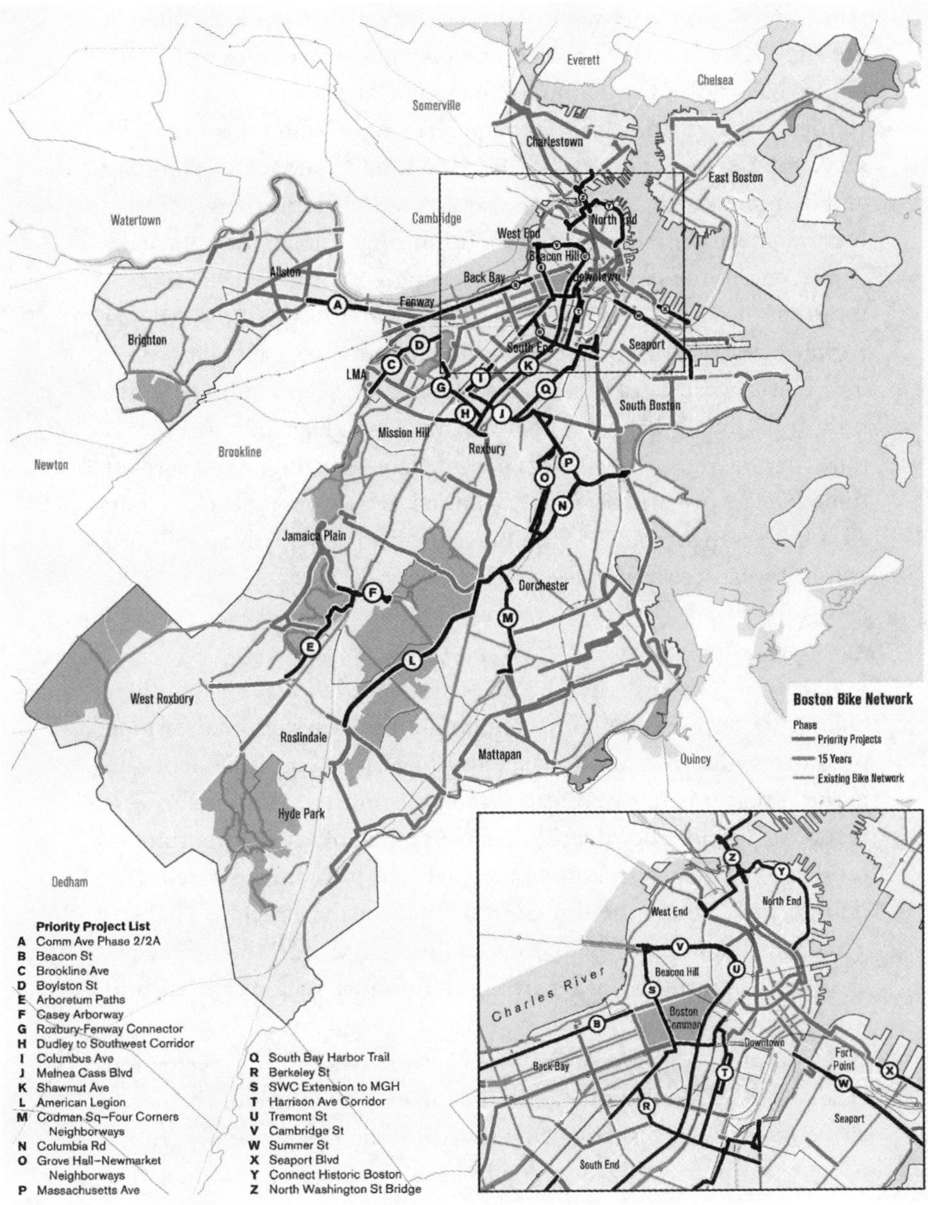

Figure 2-1: Boston Bike Network (Toole Design)

plans, and implements many of the bicycle and pedestrian facilities in the city's CTP. The PATH Foundation works to develop a network of off-road trails in and around the Metro Atlanta area for walkers, runners, skaters, and cyclists; to connect neighborhoods; and to preserve the regional character.[5] The foundation's success in planning and designing over 250 miles of trails since 1991 is partly responsible for the enormous support for the multidimensional Atlanta BeltLine, "one of the largest, most wide-ranging urban redevelopment programs in the United States [and] the catalyst for making Atlanta a global beacon for equitable, inclusive, and sustainable city life."[6] The BeltLine isn't just a trails project: in addition to 33 miles of multiuse trails and 1,300 acres of parks, proposed elements include 22 miles of rail transit; 2,600 units of affordable housing; 1,100 acres of remediated brownfields; $10–$20 billion in economic development; 30,000 permanent jobs; 48,000 one-year construction jobs; public art; and historic preservation (see figure 2-2).

3. *Priority Needs and Social Equity*

One of the top reasons for developing a parks system master plan is to determine residents' needs and to ensure equitable access to parks, programs, and recreational opportunities. A needs assessment can also identify the broader issues that are most important to residents, such as community safety, jobs, traffic congestion, climate change, and any of the dimensions listed in the previous chapter. This information can help park planners redefine their agency's mission, vision, and roles regarding community-wide resiliency and sustainability.

Most parks and recreation agencies are aware of the recreation needs of their regular users, but they may not be sure of the needs of the majority of residents who don't use their parks or programs. Also, some marginalized residents of a community may not feel empowered or motivated to participate in traditional government processes, and their needs may not be well represented. For example, according to the survey database of ETC Institute, a leading parks and recreation market research firm, only approximately 34 percent of US households have participated in recreation programs. A needs

Figure 2-2: Atlanta BeltLine (Photo courtesy of Carlos F. Perez)

assessment could help determine why residents are not using the programs and what programs they would like to see offered.

Also, a public agency's perception of needs may be distorted by the most vocal members of the community. For example, organized groups such as youth athletics associations frequently contact agency staff and elected officials to express their need for additional athletics fields. However, community surveys consistently find that residents' top priorities include walking and biking trails, adult fitness programs, aquatics centers, and other nonathletic facilities and programs.

A thoughtful and comprehensive needs assessment process can provide a sound, scientific basis for good decision making. As discussed in chapter 7, it should include multiple quantitative and qualitative techniques and should engage as many residents as possible. Planners need to reach out to the community through multiple venues, potentially including public workshops and open houses, neighborhood and church meetings, special events booths, online forums, mail and online surveys, and interviews and focus groups. When planning the scope of work for a needs assessment, planners need to make sure that the methodology and process will hold up to the scrutiny of elected officials, residents, and other stakeholders. A needs assessment is often the foundation of a parks and recreation master plan; any doubts regarding the validity and credibility of the needs assessment can sabotage the entire planning process.

An interesting question regarding the scope of a needs assessment process is "Should an agency's mission define the scope of the needs assessment; or should the findings from the needs assessment help shape the agency's mission?" For example, if an agency's mission doesn't include connectivity, should the needs assessment ask whether there's a need for bikeways, trails, or greenways? Conversely, if a needs assessment reveals that bikeways and trails are a top priority for residents (as they have been in almost every needs assessment we've conducted over the past ten years), maybe an agency should include connectivity in its mission. This is a good question to ponder when planning a needs assessment process. I believe the needs assessment should be as broad as possible, and I remind my clients that they are not obligated to meet residents' priority needs unilaterally, particularly if the need is contrary to an agency's mission. With bikeways and trails as an example, an agency could respond to a community's need for more bicycle and pedestrian facilities by designating certain parks as trailheads (with amenities such as parking, restrooms, water fountains, information kiosks, and air stations) and collaborating with another agency (e.g., transportation, public works, or engineering) to design and construct trails within and between parks. The appropriate response to community needs is addressed in more detail in the discussion of long-range vision in chapter 8.

4. Updates to the Comprehensive Plan, Land Development Codes, and LOS Standards

Public planning departments often initiate a PRSMP to update their comprehensive plan, LOS metrics, land development regulations, impact fees, and other regulatory documents. A regulation-driven planning process can be very different from other planning processes because the emphasis is often on the external implementation of a parks system through private property owners and developers rather than on internal implementation through public agencies. For example, a needs assessment may be less relevant to the process

Figure 2-3: Public needs assessment workshop (Photo courtesy of David Barth)

if the focus is on regulating new development rather than on meeting the needs and priorities of existing residents.

Addressing the regulatory dimension requires close coordination among multiple agencies to align goals, objectives, policies, and metrics. For instance, the recreation and open space element of a comprehensive plan should include the community's guiding principles and long-range vision for its public realm, including its parks and recreation system. It should also include the proposed implementation strategy, including specific roles of the public agency, private developers, and other public or private partners. The specific details of the parks and recreation master plan should also be adopted into the comprehensive plan by reference.

Land development regulations and impact fees require the development of regulatory LOS metrics, presumably ensuring that new development is providing the same level of service as the existing system. The process of determining LOS metrics is often slow and laborious; therefore, many communities simply adopt existing metrics, which are often based on obsolete or long-forgotten rationales. Before initiating a regulatory-based process, planners must identify all of the stakeholders who should be involved, the specific techniques that will be used to refine or develop preliminary LOS metrics, and the specific LOS review and approval process. This is discussed in more detail in chapter 9, along with a description of typical levels of service.

Recently, our practice has focused on revising land development regulations to mandate the construction of new local (neighborhood) parks as required infrastructure (along with roadways, sewer, water, etc.); and to require that they be designed and constructed in accordance with prescriptive prototypes (see figure 2-4). These prototypes define the size and configuration of the park, the relationship to adjacent streets and land uses, and the facilities and amenities that must be included according to guiding principles and current trends. They also require the integration of bikeways, bus stops, and stormwater treatment facilities wherever appropriate. The codes are also being refined to clarify the role of developers in meeting residents' needs for larger facilities—such as recreation centers and athletics fields—outside the boundaries of proposed new developments.

5. Funding and Implementation (including Capital and Operations)

Many PRSMPs are driven by funding issues. Public agencies are challenged to fund the parks and facilities needed to accommodate new growth while also maintaining and repairing existing facilities. Many agencies fell behind during the recent recession and are struggling to find funding for deferred maintenance, new construction, and increased operations and maintenance costs.

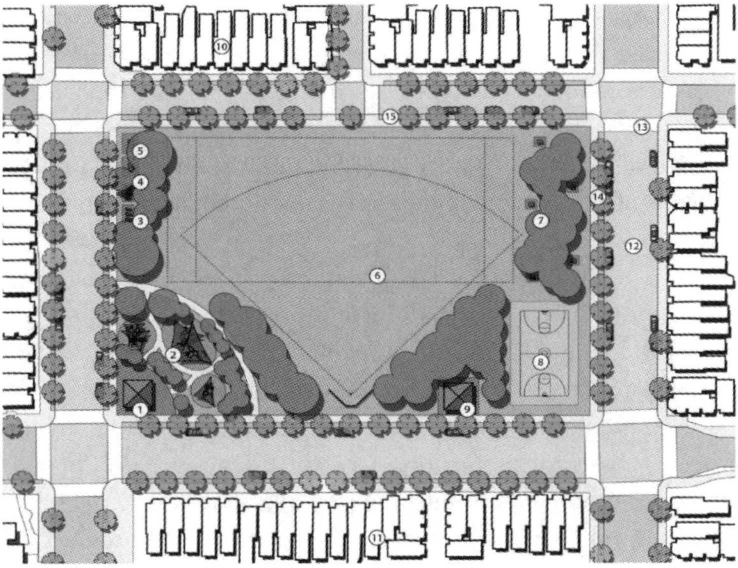

Example Park Amenities

1. Pavilion + concession + restrooms
2. Playground + shade structure
3. Chess + checker table games
4. Outdoor fooseball table
5. Outdoor ping-pong table
6. Multi-purpose open space
7. Picnic table(s)
8. Basketball/Tennis/Pickleball/Multi-purpose court
9. Pavilion

Park Context

10. Park-oriented residential development
11. Park-oriented mixed use (residential/commercial development)
12. Park zone traffic calming
13. Crosswalk
14. On-street parking
15. Sidewalk + tree zone/buffer

Figure 2-4: Local park prototype (Perez Planning + Design)

A funding-based plan should focus on implementation from the beginning of the planning process, asking questions such as the following:

- What is our agency's role in meeting needs and providing parks and recreation services?
- What other public or private organizations can we partner with to reduce costs?

- What sources of funding are available to us over the next one, five, and ten years, including both pay-as-you-go sources, such as grants and ad valorem taxes, and borrowing sources such as bonds?
- Do we have cost recovery goals for both the direct and indirect costs of providing facilities, programs, and management?

Most of these questions are policy based, requiring meetings and workshops with agency administrators and elected officials to discuss and determine policy. To facilitate these meetings, we typically develop and distribute a preliminary implementation framework (PIF) memorandum at the beginning of the planning process to provide a basis for discussion. A recent PIF for a South Florida city included estimated capital and operating costs based on a hypothetical long-range vision; deferred maintenance costs provided by the parks and recreation department; approved funding for parks and recreation improvements in the city's five-year CIP; estimates of available and potential funding from viable sources such as future CIPs, grants, municipal service taxing units (MSTUs), bonds, local option sales tax, and other potential funding sources provided by the city's finance department; potential spending priorities based on preliminary findings from the needs assessment; and a proposed funding and phasing plan based on all of the above. Because it was completed early in the process, the PIF provided the basis for open, honest dialogue about parks and recreation needs and issues, politically feasible funding options, and realistic funding and phasing strategies long before the planning process was completed. These discussions then helped inform the visioning and implementation phases of the project.

A multidimensional PRSMP provides more funding opportunities than a one-dimensional plan. Local, state, and federal funds for transportation, stormwater treatment, flood control, utilities, and other public realm improvements can be leveraged to generate multiple benefits, including parks and recreation improvements. Involvement of other departments and agencies—as discussed in the previous chapter—can result in the development of a more robust, integrated CIP.

The PIF should be revisited and refined once the long-range vision is developed. It is important to note that the cost estimates developed from most parks and recreation master plans are based on vague descriptions or conceptual plans rather than on detailed design and construction documents. Rarely is the project budget large enough for detailed designs. Therefore, planners should add a 25–50 percent contingency to cost estimates for budgeting purposes.

6. Green Infrastructure and Stormwater Treatment

Many communities wish to focus on the protection and enhancement of wildlife habitat, water quality, tree canopy, and other natural resources. Others have the ambitious goal to create a biophilic city, which is "a place that learns from nature and emulates natural systems, incorporates natural forms and images into its buildings and cityscapes, and designs and plans with nature," wrote Timothy Beatley in *Biophilic Cities*. "Biophilic cities cherish what already exists . . . but also work hard to restore and repair what has been lost or degraded."[7] An ecologically driven plan focuses on integrating natural and built systems to create a community environment within which both can function and thrive. The planning process generally follows the same steps as a typical parks planning process—including existing system mapping and analysis, needs assessment, vision, and implementation strategy—but the emphasis is on the much broader ecological framework, requiring a comprehensive analysis of urban, suburban, rural, and natural ecosystems. For example, the City of Atlanta is initiating its first urban ecology study

> in an effort to evaluate and inventory the City's natural environs, including rivers and creeks, forest and tree canopy, ridges and watersheds, public and private green spaces, and other features that encompass and define the City's existing landscape. The Urban Ecology Framework identifies what natural features are unique to the City of Atlanta, how ecosystems or habitats can be restored, and which policies promote development aligned with those features and systems. This inventory will be used to define a better future condition for the natural environment, including high-level

recommendations about future green spaces, green connections, and green policies.[8]

It is anticipated that the project will require the participation of dozens of local, state, federal, and nonprofit agencies as well as thousands of local residents.

Another green infrastructure and stormwater initiative is the City of Philadelphia's Green City, Clean Waters plan to reduce stormwater pollution currently entering the city's combined sewer system. The program's website states that the plan "represents a major shift in the way we think about and deal with stormwater in Philadelphia."[9] The city is adding green space to its parks, streets, schools, and other elements of the public realm to create "living landscapes" that slow, filter, and consume rainfall in order to reduce the stormwater pollution of its waterways by as much as 85 percent.

As discussed in chapter 1, planners interested in addressing green infrastructure, habitat, stormwater, and flooding issues in the parks and recreation system planning process must engage engineers, ecologists, planners, and other experts in the planning process. Ideally, long-range stormwater, habitat, and sewer master plans would be developed concurrently with the parks and recreation master plan in order to maximize opportunities to generate multiple benefits of resiliency and sustainability from each element of the public realm.

7. Health and Wellness

Some parks and recreation system planning processes are driven by the desire to create healthier communities. The PRSMP of the Town of Pittsboro, North Carolina, for example, was partially funded through a grant from the county health department and prominently featured health goals.

There is broad consensus—and compelling research and scientific evidence—that a well-planned and maintained public realm contributes to healthier communities. Various organizations have established specific principles and policies for designing communities to generate health benefits. For example, the American Planning Association's "Healthy Communities Policy Guide" states that

Figure 2-5: Philadelphia's Green City, Clean Waters initiative (City of Philadelphia Water Department)

how a community is planned and designed has a direct effect on the health of its residents. Land development patterns, zoning ordinances, and land-use classifications impact walkability, access to key services like healthy food, and access to transportation options. An understanding of how the built environment affects public health is a vital component in the creation of vibrant, active spaces, and places that have a strong positive impact on an individual's health. It is also critical for planners to use this understanding . . . as the standard for creation of good public policy.[10]

Similarly, the Robert Wood Johnson Foundation and the University of Wisconsin Population Health Institute compiled a ranking of health-related policies based on the degree to which they're scientifically supported. Policies are assessed in terms of their effect on factors that drive health outcomes (see box 2-2).[11]

Box 2-2
Scientifically Supported Policies Directly Related to Parks, Recreation, and the Public Realm

- **Activity programs for older adults:** Offer group educational, social, or physical activities that promote social interactions, regular attendance, and community involvement among older adults
- **Community fitness programs:** Offer exercise classes (e.g., yoga, Tai Chi, cycling, etc.) and fitness program support in community centers, senior centers, fitness, and community wellness centers
- **Community-based social support for physical activity:** Build, strengthen, and maintain social networks that provide supportive relationships for behavior change through walking groups or other community-based interventions
- **Complete streets and streetscape design initiatives:** Enhance streetscapes with greater sidewalk coverage and walkway connectivity, street crossing safety features, traffic calming measures, and other design elements
- **Exercise prescriptions:** Provide patients with prescriptions for exercise plans, often accompanied by progress checks at office visits, counseling, activity logs, and exercise testing
- **Extracurricular activities for social engagement:** Support organized social, art, or physical activities for school-aged youth outside of the school day
- **Mixed-use development:** Support a combination of land uses (e.g., residential, commercial, recreational) in development initiatives, often through zoning regulations or Smart Growth initiatives
- **Outdoor experiential education and wilderness therapy:** Support outdoor pursuits that emphasize inter- and intra-personal growth through overcoming obstacles (e.g., challenge courses, wilderness excursions, etc.)

(*continued*)

(Box 2-2 *continued*)

- **Places for physical activity:** Modify local environments (e.g., parks) to support physical activity, increase access to new or existing facilities for physical activity, or build new facilities
- **Public transportation systems:** Introduce or expand transportation options that are available to the public and run on a scheduled timetable (e.g., buses, trains, ferries, rapid transit, etc.)
- **Rain gardens and other bioretention systems:** Establish bioretention systems (e.g., rain gardens, bioretention cells, green roofs, planter boxes, bioswales, etc.) to make city landscapes more permeable
- **Safe routes to schools:** Promote walking and biking to school through education, incentives, and environmental changes; often called SRTS
- **Traffic calming:** Modify the built environment to affect traffic speed and patterns via speed bumps, pedestrian center crossing islands, roundabouts, etc.

Source: Robert Wood Johnson Foundation and University of Wisconsin Population Health Institute, County Health Rankings & Roadmaps, "Policies & Programs: Policies and Programs That Can Improve Health," 2018, filtered by "Scientifically Supported," http://www.countyhealthrankings.org/take-action-to-improve-health/what-works-for-health/policies?f%5B0%5D=field_program_evidence_rating%3A1.

The broad scope of these policies emphasizes the need to assemble a holistic, multidisciplinary team to develop a parks and recreation system plan focused on health and wellness dimensions. Collaborators may include public health agencies, transportation planners, school district staff, urban designers, stormwater engineers, developers, health-care providers, fitness specialists, geriatricians, and others involved in health, wellness, and the built environment.

8. Organizational Mission, Role, and Structure

The focus of some PRSMPs is to establish or realign their agency's mission, vision, role, and organizational structure in response to some type of change. For example, a new administrator, council, or commission may establish new priorities; a parks and recreation department may emerge from a public works department; or an existing planning agency may assume responsibility for additional public services such as libraries or conservation lands management. Typically, the agency or department wishes to define or refine its mission and vision; define and distinguish its specific role versus the roles of other agencies or providers; and organize or reorganize its staff in alignment with the new mission and role. This is a perfect time to determine which dimensions the agency wishes to address and to incorporate them into the PRSMP process.

One of our clients is a newly formed parks and recreation department that was previously part of the public works department. Because it was a new department, its staff had significant latitude regarding where to focus their resources. Through the planning process, we found that residents, city commissioners, and department staff all valued youth development, safety, equity, economic opportunity, and environmental sustainability. The city also valued the integration of the parks and recreation system with other elements of the public realm, including streets and sidewalks, trails, and stormwater facilities. Therefore, the parks and recreation department's new mission is "to help young people realize their potential; to provide recreational opportunities for residents and visitors; and to contribute to the city's sustainability." A new organizational chart was developed to reflect the new mission, identifying key staff positions to be filled within the coming years.

Existing agencies can use the process to refine or redefine their mission and role, particularly if they have experienced recent changes such as budget cuts, increased responsibilities, changes in leadership, new mandates such as cost recovery goals, or reorganization. For example, another one of our client agencies has become incredibly skilled at "doing more with less" and consistently tries to maintain an unsustainable level of service even as its budgets are reduced by an economic downturn. This can often result in demotivated or burned-out staff, deferred maintenance, and park safety issues. Therefore, we used the parks and recreation system planning process—including the multiple opportunities it provides to meet with elected officials—to more narrowly define the mission and role of the department in order to align with its actual funding.

Planners should recognize the significant amount of time required for organizational planning. The scope of organizational planning can include organizational structure, partnerships,

Figure 2-6: Organizational alignment (Barth Associates, LLC)

programs, physical resources, maintenance and operations, information technology, public relations, human resources, finances, budgeting, risk assessment, law enforcement and security, and evaluations and metrics. Figure 2-6 illustrates the concept of aligning each of these elements with the agency's guiding values and mission as well as its day-to-day operations. Organizational alignment and consensus building can be a slow, laborious, and time-consuming process; planners should carefully determine which of these elements should be addressed during the master planning process.

9. Park Classifications and Service Delivery Models

Some parks and recreation agencies desire to reassess how they deliver services to the community. They may be delivering facilities and services because "that's how we've always done it" without taking time to reassess current service delivery models for efficiency, effectiveness, and customer satisfaction.

A service delivery approach focuses on the identification and assessment of service delivery models for parks and recreation subsystems, facilities, programs, and maintenance. Typical examples include an equity-based, decentralized model for neighborhood playgrounds; a centralized venue model for a central aquatics complex and swimming lessons; and a roving crew model for parks maintenance. A service delivery approach may begin with the assessment of current models, and possibly the development of new models, as the framework or context for the planning process (see chapter 10 for a more in-depth discussion of service delivery models). For example, Washington, DC, chose to deliver indoor recreation services via a decentralized equity-based model. A goal was set to provide access to a recreation center within one mile of every resident's home. Centers were classified as neighborhood, community, district, and specialty centers; specific criteria for service areas and facilities were developed for each type of center. Once the model was created, the city used the planning process to determine needs, priorities, costs, and implementation strategies.

The service delivery approach may also extend to the delivery of services beyond traditional parks and recreation services, such as stormwater treatment, social services, and wildlife habitat. Such an approach may also lead to new classifications that reflect the full scope of services and benefits being delivered.

10. Recreation, Social, and Educational Programs

Similar to the question of which comes first—mission or needs—is the question of facilities versus programs. A facilities perspective focuses on physical infrastructure, that is, what types of parks and recreation facilities need to be constructed to meet residents' needs. A programming perspective focuses on the desired recreation, social, and educational programs to be offered by an agency and asks what types of facilities are needed to support those programs.

Planners wishing to focus on the programming dimension of a PRSMP must first understand the needs of the community, as discussed in chapter 8. If they wish to explore social and educational programs—in addition to the traditional recreation programs—they'll need to collaborate with appropriate social and educational partners to help design the needs assessment process. Once they understand the community's needs, they can discuss the appropriate service delivery models, as discussed in chapter 10, which will lead to the types of facilities needed to provide the services. And, of course, the appropriate response to programming needs will also relate to the missions and roles of the departments and agencies involved.

A parks and recreation planning process that is focused on social issues requires extensive outreach efforts to engage residents and stakeholders who may not otherwise participate in the process. For example, the Atlanta Regional Commission notes that "the concept of social equity (or environmental justice) requires that minority and low-income communities get special attention from public agencies during public decision-making processes" and has incorporated social equity methodologies in its planning processes. These include a social equity advisory committee; Hispanic and Asian American advisory councils; focus groups and listening sessions in affected neighborhoods; and community conversations on diversity.[12]

Communities focused specifically on addressing health issues through the parks and recreation planning process may wish to include potential partners such as hospitals, health-care providers, insurance companies, public health agencies, drugstores, and others. Miami-Dade County's Parks, Recreation, and Open Spaces Department, for example, developed a partnership with Walgreens to provide Healthy Choices Clinics at fourteen recreation centers throughout the county. Each clinic offered free blood pressure, glucose, and cholesterol screenings, along with flu, pneumonia, and shingles immunizations for adults aged fifty-five and older. A registered pharmacist was also present to answer questions regarding medications.

Another example of social programming is the City of Los Angeles's Summer Night Lights program, a public-private partnership undertaken by the Mayor's Office of Gang Reduction and Youth Development (GRYD) and the GRYD Foundation to address gang violence. The program operates at thirty-two locations across the city, keeping recreation centers and parks open and adding extended programming between 7:00 p.m. and 11:00 p.m. during the summer. Such an effort requires extensive collaboration with law enforcement and judicial agencies, neighborhood associations, elected officials, social service agencies, and others.

Similarly, we're currently working with the Valdosta-Lowndes County Parks and Recreation Authority (VLPRA), which provides youth sports programs for an estimated ten thousand participants every year. One of the county's challenges is to improve high school graduation rates, which have a direct effect on unemployment rates and the availability of an educated workforce to attract new businesses. During our stakeholder interviews, one of the local school principals mentioned the University of Minnesota's app-based Check & Connect program, which trains mentors to help keep students on track toward graduation. The program's website states, "C&C is the only dropout prevention intervention listed on the IES What Works Clearinghouse found to have positive effects on staying in school."[13] The VLPRA board may consider using the program to train its coaches to help mentor the students participating in the youth sports programs, using sports as a tool to improve graduation rates and an educated workforce.

11. Economic Dimension: Property Values, Jobs, Tourism

Cities have become increasingly aware of the economic role of parks and open spaces over the past two decades. Signature projects such as Chicago's Millennium Park, New York City's High Line, Houston's Discovery Green, and Atlanta's Historic Fourth Ward Park have generated extensive economic benefits including increases in downtown visitors, new residents, increased property values, and additional jobs. The $270 million Millennium Park, for example, is credited with generating nearly $2.45 billion in new condominium, office, and hotel construction near the park over the past ten years.[14]

There has also been a boom in sports tourism, although the economic benefits are hotly debated. Many communities question whether economic benefits of sports tourism—typically measured in increased sales taxes through increased hotel, restaurant, and equipment sales—are adequate to offset the costs of building and maintaining state-of-the-art sports facilities.

A parks and recreation planning process focused on economic development must be strategically planned to generate the desired results. Rather than assuming a "build it and they will come" approach, parks planners must first identify specific assets and opportunities with the greatest potential to generate economic benefits. They must also coordinate with public and private sector partners such as community redevelopment agencies, sports commissions, tourist development councils, convention and visitor bureaus, chambers of commerce, private developers, and others knowledgeable about economic development. For example, when we prepared the PRSMP for the City of Raleigh, North Carolina, we worked with the planning director to identify targeted areas for redevelopment, where new urban parks could serve as catalysts for the redevelopment of surrounding properties. Similarly, the Buckhead (Atlanta) PRSMP identified several transit-oriented sites to be acquired as urban green spaces to catalyze redevelopment of blighted areas.

Summary

These eleven dimensions—while all very important—are just examples of the type of broad multidisciplinary thinking needed to generate broad community-wide sustainability and resiliency benefits from the PRSMP process. Chapter 5 discusses the importance of considering these and other potential dimensions of parks and recreation system planning from the very beginning of the PRSMP process, when developing the project plan and scope of work.

Alternative dimensions may also be identified after the planning process has begun, particularly during the needs assessment process (discussed in chapter 8). Stakeholder interviews, focus group meetings, public workshops, interactive websites, and surveys can all be used to identify dimensions that are important to elected officials and residents. For instance, we are working with a parks and recreation department that traditionally has focused almost exclusively on youth sports. During the needs assessment process, however, we found that many of the elected officials and residents—although very supportive of the sports programs—are also eager to address alternative dimensions of their parks and recreation system, including homelessness, gangs, drug use, economic development, environmental protection, education and graduation rates, water access, safety, tourism and community branding, health and wellness, infrastructure, retention of residents and businesses, transportation, and downtown redevelopment. Ultimately, each community must determine the specific issues and dimensions it wishes to address through the PRSMP process—and then design its process accordingly to identify opportunities to generate the desired future outcomes and benefits.

03 HIGH-PERFORMANCE PUBLIC SPACES

The broad ideas of understanding the interconnected public realm and considering the multiple dimensions of parks and recreation projects provide important background for this chapter's focus on High-Performance Public Spaces (HPPSs). The genesis of this concept was my experience with the Kissimmee Lakefront Park in Kissimmee, Florida, a seventy-thousand-person community south of Orlando known mostly for its proximity to Walt Disney World.

In 2007, the City of Kissimmee began evaluating strategies to revitalize its downtown. During the previous century, the waterfront town had served as the railroad and shipping hub for citrus and cattle, and the quaint, historic downtown area would have been bustling with activity. With the opening of Walt Disney World in the early 1970s, the decline of shipping on the waterfront, and new suburban development sprawling throughout the metropolitan Orlando area, downtown Kissimmee had gradually faded into obscurity.

One strategy to revitalize the downtown was to redevelop the waterfront parkland along Lake Tohopekaliga, just a few blocks away. The city solicited proposals from developers who—much to the chagrin of residents—proposed to develop much of the waterfront for new multifamily housing. At that point, we were asked to develop a new plan for the park, maintaining its role as a public space while also helping to revitalize downtown.

The city staff and the design team understood the potential of the park to generate multiple economic, social, and environmental benefits for the community. Our concept was for the park to serve as the city's common front yard on the lake. The surrounding roadway network was reconfigured to provide easy bicycle and pedestrian connections to the adjacent historic downtown, including wide sidewalks, shade trees, brick streets, and on-street parking.

Figure 3-1: Kissimmee, Florida, waterfront, 2008 (Photo courtesy of Kimley-Horn)

Park elements included a new waterfront promenade (replacing the roadway that separated the park from the lake), elegant Old Florida–themed picnic pavilions with ceiling fans and movable chairs and tables, concessions, numerous event lawns, memorials, a small marina and bait shop, lawn chairs, an interactive animal-themed water playground, and other features that now attract residents and visitors to the park until late at night.

Both the park and downtown are now bustling again. The estimated benefits generated by the park revitalization include over five hundred thousand visitors to downtown; improved stormwater treatment, lake water quality, and lakefront habitat; increased property values; new jobs; additional revenues from fee-based park venues, booked six months in advance; greater social equity and a sense of community; and over $75 million worth of new, planned residential and retail development, a new transit station, and a public parking garage adjacent to the park.

After my experience on the Kissimmee project—as well as on hundreds of other park planning and design projects—I wondered why the Kissimmee design team, including both city staff and

Figure 3-2: Kissimmee waterfront, 2017 (Photo *A* courtesy of Mike Brown, AECOM; photo *B* courtesy of Mike Steigerwald, City of Kissimmee)

consultants, had been so willing to adopt sustainable design innovations during the planning design process, whereas many other teams I had been involved in had not. This led to my research into the factors that lead to the adoption of innovation in the planning and design process.

The research involved identifying and analyzing case studies of projects similar to the Kissimmee Lakefront Park that generated multiple sustainability benefits for their communities. Since no name for such parks existed, I referred to them as High-Performance Public Spaces (HPPSs), defined as publicly accessible spaces that generate economic, environmental, *and* social sustainability benefits for their local community. An HPPS can be a park, trail, square, green, natural area, plaza, or any other element of the public realm that generates all three types of benefits. Although the actual implementation of HPPSs is accomplished through the design and construction of individual sites, it is important for planners to incorporate the principles and criteria for HPPSs into the entire system planning process in order to identify as many opportunities as possible to generate multiple benefits.

HPPSs can be found throughout the United States, especially in urban and urbanizing areas that have embraced the role of public open spaces in addressing resiliency- or sustainability-related issues such as social inequity, decaying infrastructure, flooding, or economic depression. New York City's High Line and Bryant Park, Boston's Lawn on D, Atlanta's BeltLine and Historic Fourth Ward Park, Houston's Discovery Green, and Chicago's Millennium Park have all been credited with community benefits such as increased property values, new jobs, cleaner water, enhanced wildlife habitat, additional tourism, flood mitigation, neighborhood stability, and others.

Box 3-1 lists the twenty-five criteria that were developed to identify an HPPS, based on the principles of good public spaces and performance indicators used to measure sustainable development. The criteria were refined through a Delphi process involving twenty-two sustainability experts. Any public space that meets 80 percent or more of the criteria could be considered an HPPS that contributes to community sustainability and resiliency.

The HPPS criteria were used to identify and select three public spaces in Florida for further study: the City of Lakeland's historic downtown Lake Mirror Park, named by the American Planning Association as one of the top ten public spaces in America in 2014; the City of Clearwater's Beach Walk, a beachfront roadway realignment and pedestrian promenade that revitalized the city's tourism district; and the City of Tallahassee's Gaines Street, a vibrant commercial street once planned as a six-lane arterial road. All of these public spaces were noteworthy not only for the benefits they generated for

Box 3-1

Criteria for a High-Performance Public Space (HPPS)

Economic Criteria

- The space creates and facilitates revenue-generating opportunities for the public sector, the private sector, or both.
- The space creates meaningful and desirable employment.
- The space indirectly creates or sustains good, living-wage jobs.
- The space sustains or increases property values.
- The space catalyzes infill development, the reuse of obsolete or underused buildings or spaces, or both.
- The space attracts new residents.
- The space attracts new businesses.
- The space generates increased business and tax revenues.
- The space optimizes operations and maintenance costs (compared with other similar spaces).

Environmental Criteria

- The space uses energy, water, and material resources efficiently.
- The space improves the quality of both surface water and groundwater.
- The space serves as a net carbon sink.
- The space enhances, preserves, promotes, or contributes to biological diversity.
- Hardscape materials were selected for longevity of service; social, cultural, and historical sustainability; regional availability; low carbon footprint; and other related criteria.
- The space provides opportunities to enhance environmental awareness and knowledge.
- The space serves as an interconnected node within larger-scale ecological corridors and natural habitat.

Social Criteria

- The space improves the neighborhood.
- The space improves social and physical mobility through multi-modal connectivity—automobile, transit, bike, and pedestrian.
- The space encourages the health and fitness of residents and visitors.
- The space provides relief from urban congestion and stressors such as social confrontation, noise pollution, and air pollution.

(continued)

(Box 3-1 *continued*)

- The space provides places for formal and informal social gatherings, art, performances, and community and civic events.
- The space provides opportunities for individual, group, passive, and active recreation.
- The space facilitates shared experiences among different groups of people.
- The space attracts diverse populations.
- The space promotes creative and constructive social interaction.

Source: David L. Barth, "The Adoption of Innovation in the Planning and Design Process: Creating High-Performance Public Spaces That Contribute to Community Sustainability" (PhD diss., University of Florida, 2015).

each community but also for their role as catalysts for revitalization and renewal. HPPSs are often transformative, generating benefits far beyond the boundaries of the site or district.

For example, Lakeland's downtown had declined in the 1970s and 1980s as residents and businesses relocated to the suburbs, and the once-celebrated Lake Mirror Park and promenade became neglected and began deteriorating. Planners proposed to restore the park and promenade as the centerpiece of the 1990 downtown redevelopment plan. The community's positive response to the restoration and reactivation of the park and promenade led to additional improvements around the lake over the next decade, as well as public and private investments in downtown Lakeland.

Similarly, in the 1990s the City of Clearwater Beach became concerned about the declining physical conditions on the island, the lack of reinvestment in business properties in the area, declining tourism, poor traffic and pedestrian circulation, and poor aesthetic conditions. The city's proposed redevelopment plan included recommendations for transportation and parking; redevelopment of hotel, retail, entertainment, and multifamily districts; and upgrading of the beach. At the heart of the city's development vision was the proposed Beach Walk public space project, a proposal to realign the beachfront road to create a scenic drive and beachfront promenade, to replace existing ugly beachfront parking lots with new parking structures integrated into the proposed redevelopment of off-beach properties, and to create new redevelopment parcels for high-quality resort development. Six years after completion of the project, an article in the *Tampa Bay Times* touted its success.

> "The Beach Walk . . . has changed the whole complexion of Clearwater Beach," [the county's top tourism official] said. "The city leaders had the vision to push Beach Walk, and it has been extremely successful."
>
> Remember how asphalt parking lots and hundreds of parked cars used to separate S Gulfview Boulevard from the beach's sugary white sand? The Beach Walk project, finally completed in 2008 after years of discussion and planning, replaced those lots with a wide, meandering pedestrian walkway right on the edge of the sand. It provides an unobstructed view of the gulf. It's a great public space where people can walk, jog, watch sunsets. It was beautifully designed. And it draws people like a magnet.
>
> Developers and merchants couldn't resist its appeal. That section of S Gulfview is bustling now, and projects to build more hotels, more condos, more restaurants and stores, are spreading east, north and south from Beach Walk.
>
> And most of the development is high-end. That is perhaps the most surprising part of the change on Clearwater Beach. A place that for decades drew mostly middle-income families and retirees who stayed in mom-and-pop motels and spent little on their frugal vacations has in the space of 10 years been so transformed that it now legitimately markets itself as a west coast resort for the well-to-do.[1]

Recently, for the second year in a row, TripAdvisor named Clearwater Beach the number one beach in America.

The third HPPS case study, Tallahassee's Gaines Street, generated similar benefits for the community. Initially envisioned by the Florida Department of Transportation as a six-lane arterial road, the street was reconceptualized in the city's 2000 Gaines Street Revitalization Plan as a two-lane complete street and an eighteen-hour-per-day, six-day-per-week urban activity center. Today the street is featured on the website of Visit Florida, the state's tourism agency.

> The G Street area is recently renovated, surprisingly sophisticated, and a destination venue for anyone in search of a low-cost, high-impact experience. The Street itself forms the spine of the campuses of Florida State University to the north and Florida A&M University to the south. It's also the heart and soul of the local arts, music, food and fashion communities.
>
> Gaines Street is a three-mile stretch that begins at Cascades Park and works its way west to Doak Campbell Stadium, home of FSU's defending national championship football team. Whether you're looking to fill a solitary hour or savoring a weekend in Tallahassee with family and friends, there's something for every age and interest.[2]

On the surface, these three HPPSs—a historic park, a beachfront promenade, and a downtown street—could not be more different. Yet each of these transformational public realm projects met 80 percent or more of the HPPS criteria, as illustrated in figure 3-3, and generated resiliency and sustainability benefits for their respective communities well beyond their physical boundaries.

While it is not realistic to think that every public park or public space could meet 80 percent or more of the HPPS criteria, every public space has the potential to generate some type of sustainability or resiliency benefits, or both, either directly or indirectly. Parks planners can use the HPPS criteria as a guide or checklist during the parks and recreation system planning process to prompt discussions regarding the types of benefits they wish to generate. A community that strives to plan and design its parks system and its public realm as a plexus of HPPSs could contribute significantly to its aspirations and goals for sustainability and resiliency.

My research also identified six common factors that appear to influence innovation in the planning and design of HPPSs. The three strongest factors appear to be a strong leader, collaborative relationships, and external characteristics including system openness and stakeholder involvement. Three secondary factors included the perception of the innovation, perceived economic benefits and return on investment, and the presence of a long-range vision. The study also theorized that planning and design innovations are adopted in two stages: early conceptual planning and design innovations, and

	Tallahassee Gaines Street	Lakeland Lake Mirror Park	Clearwater Beachwalk
ECONOMIC			
Creates and facilitates revenue-generating opportunities for the public and/or the private sectors	●	●	●
Creates meaningful and desirable employment	●	●	●
Indirectly creates or sustains good, living wage jobs	●	●	●
Sustains or increases property values	●	●	●
Catalyzes infill development and/or the re-use of obsolete or under-used buildings or spaces	●	●	●
Attracts new residents	●	●	●
Attracts new businesses	●	●	●
Generates increased business and tax revenues	●	●	●
Optimizes operations and maintenance costs (compared to other similar spaces)		●	●
ENVIRONMENTAL			
Uses energy, water, and material resources efficiently	●	●	●
Improves water quality of both surface and ground water	●	●	●
Serves as a net carbon sink			
Enhances, preserves, promotes, or contributes to biological diversity			
Hardscape materials were selected based on longevity of service, social/cultural/historical sustainability, regional availability, low carbon footprint and/or other related criteria	●	●	●
Provides opportunities to enhance environmental awareness and knowledge	●	●	●
Serves as an interconnected node within larger scale ecological corridors and natural habitat		●	

Figure 3-3: High-Performance Public Space (HPPS) case study evaluations (David L. Barth, "The Adoption of Innovation in the Planning and Design Process: Creating High-Performance Public Spaces That Contribute to Community Sustainability" (PhD diss., University of Florida, 2015)

(Figure 3-3 *continued next page*)

(Figure 3-3 *continued*)

	Tallahassee Gaines Street	Lakeland Lake Mirror Park	Clearwater Beachwalk
SOCIAL			
Improves the neighborhood	●	●	●
Improves social and physical mobility through multi-modal connectivity – auto, transit, bike, pedestrian	●	●	●
Encourages the health and fitness of residents and visitors	●	●	●
Provides relief from urban congestion and stressors such as social confrontation, noise pollution, and air pollution	●	●	●
Provides places for formal and informal social gathering, art, performances, and community or civic events	●	●	●
Provides opportunities for individual, group, passive and active recreation	●	●	●
Facilitates shared experiences among different groups of people	●	●	●
Attracts diverse populations	●	●	●
Promotes creative and constructive social interaction	●	●	●
TOTAL (out of 25 possible criteria)	21	23	22

Figure 3-4: Lake Mirror Park, Lakeland, Florida (Photo courtesy of Rut Patel)

Figure 3-5: Beach Walk, Clearwater, Florida (Photos courtesy of VisitStPeteClearwater.com)

Figure 3-6: Gaines Street, Tallahassee, Florida (Photo courtesy of David Barth)

detailed design and implementation innovations. These factors have significant implications for the parks and recreation system planning process and are discussed in more detail in part II.

Putting It All Together: The Public Realm as Plexus, Multiple Dimensions, and HPPSs

The first three chapters of this book—focusing on the concepts of the public realm, multiple dimensions, and HPPSs—form the ideological framework for the new approach to parks and recreation system planning to create more sustainable, resilient communities.

The scope, context, and aspirations of parks and recreation system planning must be broadened in order to respond to societal shifts, issues, and expectations in a meaningful way.

First, parks and recreation system master plans (PRSMPs) should be developed concurrently—or at least collaboratively—with the other subsystems of the public realm, including stormwater, transportation, and utilities systems. Potential benefits of integrated public realm planning include increased opportunities to address community sustainability and resiliency; leveraging of available resources; increased efficiencies and cost savings; improved communication,

Figure 3-7: Creating more sustainable and resilient communities through parks and the public realm (Barth Associates, LLC)

teamwork, and morale; and greater recognition of and support for public projects.

Second, PRSMPs should be more multidimensional. In addition to considering the other elements of the public realm, they should explore opportunities to tackle sustainability and resiliency issues such as health, economic development, climate change, traffic congestion, homelessness, social equity, and any of the other dimensions discussed in chapter 2.

Finally, PRSMPs should emphasize that every public realm improvement—including parks, streets, stormwater facilities, civic spaces, and natural areas—should be planned and designed as an HPPS to generate as many economic, social, and environmental benefits as possible. If each public space within the public realm is thoughtfully planned, designed, and managed as an HPPS—and if the entire public realm is planned and designed as an integrated system to address broader community-wide issues—then the true power of the public realm can be harnessed to make a community more resilient and sustainable.

Figure 3-7 illustrates the relationships between these foundational concepts. Part II of this book, "Planning a Comprehensive Approach," discusses a new approach to plan and execute each step of parks and recreation system planning process to realize the benefits promised in part I.

PART II

PLANNING A COMPREHENSIVE APPROACH

04 A NEW APPROACH TO PARKS AND RECREATION SYSTEM PLANNING

Many communities are already realizing sustainability and resiliency benefits on a project-by-project basis, such as those mentioned in the previous chapters. The Landscape Architecture Foundation's Landscape Performance Series has documented over one hundred exemplary built projects with quantified environmental, economic, and social benefits, including the following:

- Canal Park in Washington, DC, captures and treats 95 percent of average annual runoff from the site and neighboring streets—approximately 3 million gallons per year—helping to prevent combined sewer overflows into the Anacostia River. The park draws almost 28,000 annual visitors through year-round programming and special events and provides forty-three jobs, with a minimum of six reserved for low-income persons residing in public housing and members of the local community.
- SoundScape Park in Miami Beach sequesters approximately 9.5 tons of atmospheric carbon in 355 newly planted trees; prevents approximately 1.2 million gallons of stormwater from entering Miami Beach's stormwater system annually; and contributed to a 60 percent increase in the total assessed value of properties within a block of the park from 2010 to 2015, leading to a $1.2 million increase in yearly property tax revenues.
- Railroad Park in Birmingham, Alabama, increased the number of bird species observed on the site by 250 percent; attracts over six hundred thousand visitors annually and improved the perception of downtown Birmingham for 98 percent of

ninety-five survey respondents; and catalyzed $324.5 million in public and private investment in the area since the park's opening, with over $200 million more in private investment pending.

- Klyde Warren Park in Dallas (figure 4-1) hosted over 1 million park visitors in its first year; is projected to generate $312.7 million in economic development and $12.7 million in tax revenue; and sequesters 18,500 pounds of carbon dioxide annually through newly planted trees, equivalent to the carbon dioxide emitted by driving approximately 22,636 miles in a single-passenger vehicle.
- Vista Hermosa Park in Los Angeles provides habitat within the Pacific Flyway corridor for sixty bird species observed on-site; educated an average of 1,485 visitors per year through an average of sixty-seven programs in English and Spanish between 2008 and 2012; and generates a projected $87,000 in annual revenue for park operating expenses from fees associated with professional filming activities.[1]

While these projects are laudable, imagine how many more benefits could be generated if communities took a more comprehensive, systematic approach to improving sustainability, resiliency, and quality of life through the planning and design of their parks and recreation systems and the broader public realm. Such an approach would require that parks and recreation system master plans (PRSMPs) be developed concurrently—or at least collaboratively—with the other subsystems of the public realm, including stormwater, transportation, and utilities systems. It would require PRSMPs to be more multidimensional, as discussed in chapter 2. And it would require that every public realm improvement—including parks, streets, stormwater facilities, civic spaces, and natural areas—be planned and designed as High-Performance Public Spaces to generate as many economic, social, and environmental benefits as possible.

However, most of today's parks and recreation system planning processes are based on a fairly linear and narrowly defined process that includes an evaluation of existing conditions (primarily parks and recreation facilities); a needs and priorities assessment; a long-range vision; and an implementation strategy that includes

Figure 4-1: Klyde Warren Park, Dallas, Texas (Photo by Joe Mabel, CC BY-SA 3.0, https://commons.wikimedia.org/w/index.php?curid=24515285)

funding, staffing, programs, policies, and partnerships (see figure 4-2).

While there is nothing inherently wrong with this traditional approach—and it is often effective in identifying and addressing common parks and recreation needs—it is not intended to generate the types of community-wide sustainability and resiliency benefits discussed in part I, such as job creation, improved water quality, economic development, reduced crime, and climate change mitigation. As discussed in previous chapters, this may be due in part to organizational silos, narrowly defined missions, one-dimensional mind-sets, or lack of collaboration. It also may be due to the very linear, check-the-box nature of the traditional PRSMP process itself. Regardless of the reason, an expanded approach to parks and recreation system planning is clearly needed to comprehensively address broader community issues and generate greater benefits.

Chapter 1 outlined several ideas for improving the PRSMP process, including an integrated needs assessment process, coordinated capital improvement plans (CIPs), mandatory planning cycles, and coordinated small area plans. Additionally, best practices and principles from the disciplines of project management, strategic planning,

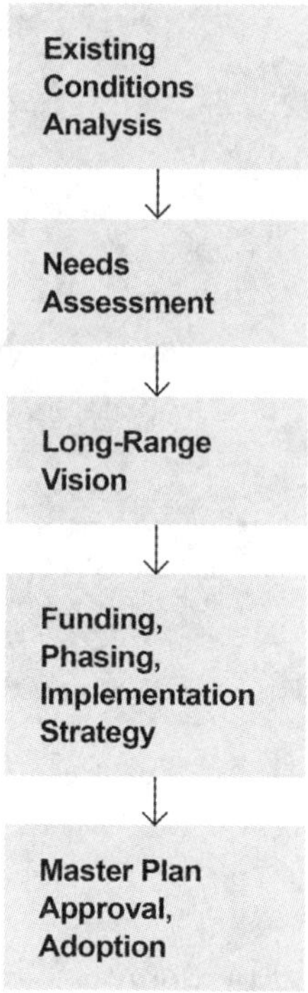

Figure 4-2: Traditional linear process for parks and recreation system planning (Barth Associates, LLC)

and applied social science research provide insights into how the PRSMP process can be improved to generate greater benefits to improve community resiliency and sustainability.

Project Management

First, good project management practices ensure that adequate time is spent to initiate and plan the project, as discussed in chapter 5. Such preplanning is necessary to thoughtfully and purposefully select the dimensions of the PRSMP; to determine whether the agency is prepared to initiate and implement the plan; to develop a detailed project charter, project plan, and schedule; to identify expectations and desired outcomes; and to form the collaborative team and leadership necessary to be successful. Good project management also requires that interim submittals and reviews—particularly by elected officials and other decision makers—are scheduled throughout the

PRSMP process to build gradual support for the ultimate findings and recommendations.

Strategic Planning

Second, insights from the strategic planning discipline can help the PRSMP process generate greater benefits to improve community resiliency and sustainability. The United Nations Educational, Scientific and Cultural Organization (UNESCO) defines a strategic plan as "a management tool to help an organization to improve its performance by ensuring that its members are working to the same goals and by continuously adjusting the direction of the organization to the changing environment on the basis of results obtained."[2] The primary benefit of a strategic planning approach—and the reason it is useful in parks and recreation system master planning—is its emphasis on change and implementation. Box 4-1 summarizes the distinctions, which are definitely applicable to parks and recreation system plans, between traditional and strategic planning processes.

Box 4-1
Blueprint Contrasts between Traditional and Strategic Planning

Traditional Planning	**Strategic Planning**
Input-oriented	Result-oriented
Technocratic	Participatory
Neutral	Mobilization instrument
Linear planning	Iterative planning
Rigid implementation	Flexible implementation
Routine-based	Change-oriented
Compliance monitoring	Performance monitoring
Emphasis on the plan document	Emphasis on plan implementation

Source: United Nations Educational, Scientific and Cultural Organization (UNESCO), International Institute for Educational Planning (IIEP), "Strategic Planning: Concept and Rationale," Working Paper 1, 2010, 13, http://unesdoc.unesco.org/images/0018/001897/189757e.pdf.

A strategic planning approach also requires a PRSMP to be developed through a thoughtful, step-by-step process to carefully build a foundation for implementation. The ten steps of the strategic planning process, as outlined in *Strategic Planning for Public and Nonprofit Organizations*, are as follows:

1. Initiate and agree on a strategic planning process.
2. Identify organizational mandates.
3. Clarify organizational mission and values.
4. Assess the organization's external and internal environments to identify strengths, weaknesses, opportunities, and threats.
5. Identify the strategic issues facing the organization.
6. Formulate strategies to manage these issues.
7. Review and adopt the strategic plan or plans.
8. Establish an effective organizational vision.
9. Develop an effective implementation process.
10. Reassess strategies and the strategic planning process.[3]

The key difference between a traditional PRSMP process, which generates only parks and recreation benefits, and a strategic planning process, which generates the broader benefits associated with more resilient and sustainable communities, is the breadth and depth of time and thought given to each step in the process, providing enough "space" to explore various dimensions and issues. This type of robust, thoughtful, and comprehensive PRSMP approach could not be undertaken in a traditional linear, check-the-box type of process. The strategic plan for Seattle's recreation centers, for example, began with a business-focused approach including marketing, sales, and revenues. During the process, however, we began exploring the role of the recreation centers in addressing some of the city's most pressing social problems, such as homelessness, drug use, transportation access, racial equity, and integration of education, medical, and social services.

Applied Social Science Research

Finally, the discipline and structure of applied social science research can significantly strengthen the PRSMP process—particularly during the existing conditions analysis and needs assessment phases—leading to more credible and defensible findings and conclusions, as discussed in more detail in chapters 7 and 8. "To say [needs assessment] is a type of *social research*," wrote Susan Berkowitz, coeditor of *Needs Assessment: A Creative and Practical Guide for Social Scientists*, "means that needs assessment entails a systematic process of conceptualizing a research design, and gathering and analyzing data according to commonly accepted standards of social science. To say it is *applied social research* means that the results of needs assessments are used to inform policy and program development."[4] The PRSMP process can gain greater credibility—and increase the chances for adoption of innovative ideas for greater resiliency and sustainability—if it adopts the practices of the more scientifically based applied social research approach. A social research approach can also provide the basis for exploring the specific needs and priorities related to the desired dimensions of the PRSMP, as discussed in chapter 2.

Historically, many PRSMP needs assessments were based solely on public meetings and perhaps a basic level-of-service (LOS) analysis for park acreage and facilities. While both techniques are valid components of a needs assessment, they often offer a distorted view of needs and priorities when used alone. Public meetings, for example, are often dominated by special interest groups lobbying for specific facilities, such as athletics fields. And levels of service are often arbitrary, meaningful only when they're based on agreed-upon metrics, community surveys, common values, or other agreed-upon criteria.

In contrast, the adoption of a more rigorous applied social research approach can generate findings that are much more credible and defensible. In order to meet the level of applied social research, planners need to follow commonly accepted standards of social science regarding identification of the targeted population, sampling size, data reporting, questionnaire design, and appropriate use of secondary data. Compliance with these standards requires more time and thought but yields far greater reliability and validity.

Numerous textbooks are available to guide the design and execution of both quantitative and qualitative social research techniques. Parks planners may also wish to consult with qualified statisticians or researchers to assist with these tasks. A more rigorous PRSMP needs assessment process, based on the more scientific practices of applied social research, can result in greater acceptance of the findings by the community (e.g., elected officials, residents, and key stakeholders)—and can eventually lead to broader support and adoption of proposed resiliency and sustainability initiatives.

The other benefit of adopting an applied social research approach to a PRSMP needs assessment is that the methodology provides the foundation for exploring alternative dimensions. The first step, for example, is to conceptualize the research design for the process. This is the ideal time to discuss the desired dimensions of the PRSMP, such as opportunities to increase social equity or improve water quality through the parks and recreation system, and to design the needs assessment process to generate the desired data. In our practice, for example, we typically use a mixed-methods, triangulated approach to a PRSMP needs assessment. Mixed-methods research combines both quantitative and qualitative research techniques and data. Quantitative techniques include statistically representative surveys, online surveys, and LOS analysis. Qualitative techniques include public workshops, interactive websites, focus groups, and interviews. Mixed-methods research may also include secondary data that has been gathered by others, such as census information or previous reports. "Triangulation" means that we compare the data from the various techniques to identify common themes and priorities.

If we wish to explore alternative dimensions, such as economic development or community health, we may expand or modify the research design to collect additional data related to those dimensions. For example, the needs assessment for a PRSMP designed to explore opportunities to improve community health and wellness may include health-related questions in surveys; interviews with public and private health-care providers; and review of secondary data such as local health department reports and studies. Similarly, a PRSMP designed to investigate opportunities to promote economic development may include interviews with local economists, real estate developers, or other experts in economic development in the needs assessment process; and review of market trends, redevelopment studies, land-use analyses, jobs reports, and other related studies. Careful design of the needs assessment process, based on the desired dimensions to be studied, establishes the basis for development of a long-range parks and recreation vision and recommendations that can generate multiple community benefits.

A Proposed New Approach

The proposed new approach to the PRSMP process expands and enhances the traditional process through incorporating these practices and principles from project management, strategic planning, and applied social science research. The proposed approach, illustrated in figure 4-3, is no longer linear but is cyclical to suggest (1) a constant feedback loop and (2) a continuous process that regularly repeats every one to five years. Box 4-2 outlines the specific tasks in the process, followed by a more detailed description. Chapters 5–11 discuss each phase of the process in more detail.

Initiation and Planning

The new approach to parks and recreation system planning begins with a more thoughtful initiation and planning phase to ensure a more multidimensional, collaborative, and implementable PRSMP, as discussed in chapter 5. It includes a review of the broad community-wide vision, mission, mandates, and goals contained in the community's comprehensive plan or strategic plan to help guide the plan, and a review of the organizational mission to determine whether it adequately acknowledges the role of the parks and recreation system and agency to address broader sustainability and resiliency issues.

The initiation and planning phase also includes a project charter to clearly define the scope, purpose, and expectations for the process, including the proposed dimensions to be addressed, and to gain the necessary approvals and resources (money, staff time, etc.) to proceed. A readiness audit should be conducted to determine the agency's readiness to conduct the PRSMP process and—more important—its willingness and ability to implement the recommendations.

This phase also includes a project plan, complete with a detailed scope of work, project deliverables, project schedule, and milestones. This may be the most important step in initiating and planning the PRSMP process; opportunities to realize sustainability and resiliency

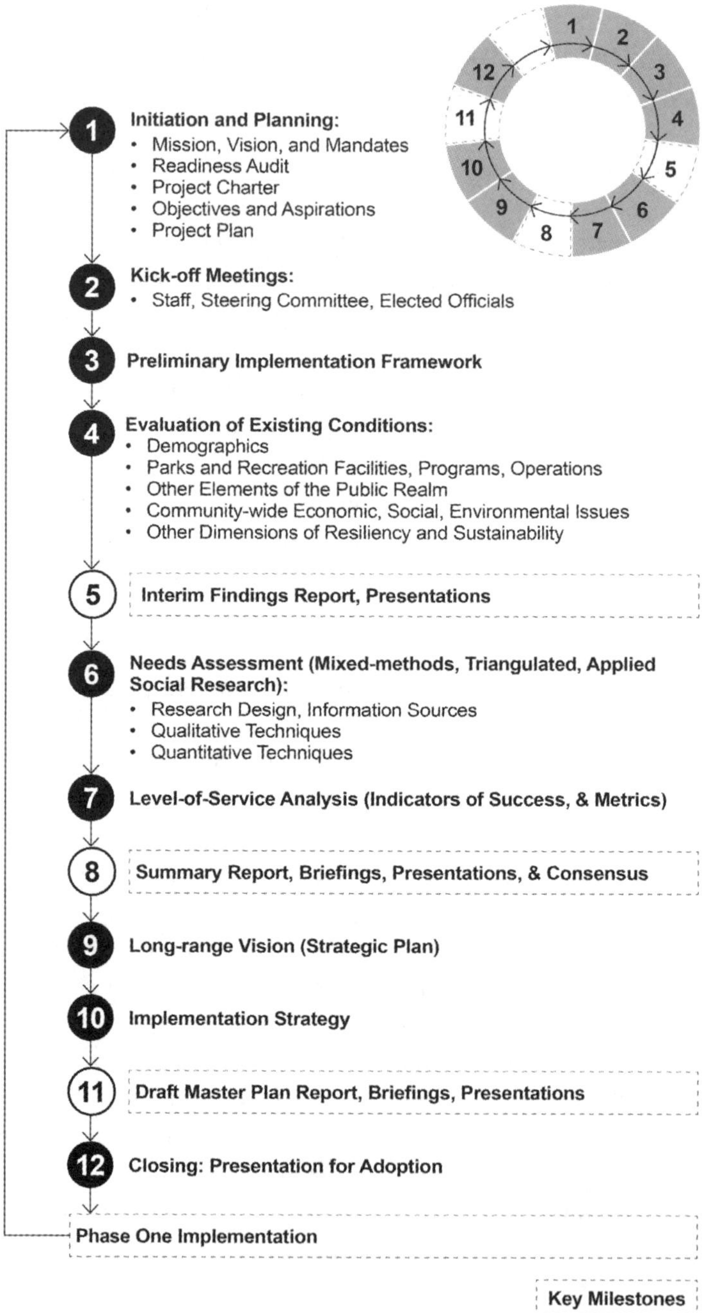

Figure 4-3: Proposed new approach to parks and recreation system planning (Barth Associates, LLC)

Box 4-2

Outline of Tasks in the Proposed New Approach

1. Initiation and planning
    - Readiness audit
    - Project charter (project manager, team, description, scope, costs, roles)
    - Objectives and aspirations
        - Traditional parks and recreation system
        - Alternative dimensions
        - Integrated public realm
        - Community resiliency and sustainability
        - High-performance public spaces
    - Project plan
        - Project team, consultants, participants, stakeholders
        - Opportunities for integrated, collaborative public realm planning
        - Scope and schedule
        - Methodologies
        - Steering or advisory committee
        - Deliverables
        - Review and approval process
2. Kickoff meeting(s): staff, steering committee, elected officials
3. Evaluation of existing conditions
    - Demographics
    - Parks and recreation facilities, programs, operations
    - Other elements of the public realm
    - Community-wide economic, social, and environmental issues
    - Other dimensions of resiliency and sustainability
4. Preliminary implementation framework (building the runway)
    - Hypothetical vision: parks and recreation system, dimensions, resiliency and sustainability initiatives
    - Estimated costs
    - Potential funding sources and amounts
    - Regulatory implementation
    - Staffing, operations, and maintenance
5. Interim findings report, presentations

(*continued*)

(Box 4-2 *continued*)

6. Needs assessment (mixed-methods, triangulated, applied social research)
   - Research design, identification of information sources
   - Qualitative techniques
     - Site evaluations
     - Interviews and focus groups
     - Public meetings (open houses)
     - Interactive website
     - Other community outreach
   - Quantitative techniques
     - Mail survey
     - Online survey
   - Secondary data (comprehensive plan, census, other reports)

7. Level-of-service analysis (indicators of success, metrics)
   - Community values, desired future conditions
   - Parks and recreation system
   - Other dimensions
   - Service delivery models
   - Classifications
   - Metrics
   - Benchmarking

8. Summary report, briefings, presentations, and consensus

9. Long-range vision (strategic plan)
   - Foundational values
   - Mission and role
   - Guiding principles
   - Priorities
   - Visioning workshop
   - Alternative and preferred strategies to address needs
   - Service delivery models and classifications
   - Capital improvements, programs, and other initiatives
   - Operations
   - Maintenance
   - Organizational structure and staffing
   - Illustrations, graphics
   - Executive summary

(*continued*)

(Box 4-2 *continued*)

10. Implementation strategy
    - Estimate of costs
    - Alternative funding projections
    - Partnership opportunities
    - Implementation workshop
    - Prioritization criteria
    - Prioritization
    - Funding, phasing strategy including milestones, metrics
    - Construction delivery methods
    - Codification: comprehensive plan, land development codes, capital improvement plans, department work plans, project charters
11. Draft master plan report, briefings, presentations
12. Closing: presentation for adoption

Phase one implementation

(Repeat!)

Source: Barth Associates, LLC.

benefits will not materialize if they are not carefully and thoughtfully integrated into the planning process. The project plan must reflect all of the aspirations expressed in the project charter, including alternative dimensions to be addressed; opportunities and mechanisms for concurrent and collaborative public realm planning; desired benefits; the relationships between subsystems; the needs assessment methodologies and public engagement processes; and the review and approval process leading up to approval and adoption. It is important to note that our most successful processes have provided numerous opportunities to meet with elected officials—both individually and in workshops—to discuss these aspirations and to review and discuss interim findings from the PRSMP as they develop. At a minimum, elected officials should be briefed on the project's scope of work and methodology; preliminary implementation framework; existing conditions and needs assessment findings; long-range vision; and final funding, phasing, and implementation strategy.

Kickoff Meetings

Project kickoff meetings provide opportunities to educate and inform key stakeholders about the importance of the PRSMP process and the opportunities to generate community-wide benefits. Separate kickoff meetings are often scheduled with agency staff and department heads, the project steering or advisory committee, and elected officials. Hosting the meetings in a prominent building outside of the sponsoring agency's offices, such as the mayor's office, a civic center, or a conference center, can help signal the significance of the project.

A typical agenda for a kickoff meeting includes a review of elements within the project plan, with particular emphasis on the desired outcomes and expectations for the project. Discussions should be recorded and transcribed, summarized in meeting minutes, and distributed to all participants as a reminder of what the team hopes to accomplish. Perhaps surprisingly, some of the most thoughtful and innovative ideas for a PRSMP are often discussed at the kickoff meeting, and they should be memorialized in the minutes.

Preliminary Implementation Framework

The new approach to parks and recreation system planning recommends the development of a preliminary implementation framework (PIF) early in the planning process, as discussed in chapter 6. The PIF provides a vehicle to initiate discussions regarding alternative strategies, potential funding sources, and preliminary implementation strategies from the very beginning of the project, beginning with the kickoff meeting. Our PIFs begin as draft memoranda or white papers that reflect our understanding of implementation options—based on preliminary discussions and review of existing documents—and then distributed to team members for review and comment. The PIF is refined as the project proceeds to reflect the latest information regarding needs, priorities, proposed initiatives, estimated costs, and funding projections. Ultimately it serves as the basis for the final PRSMP implementation strategy.

Existing Conditions Analysis

The existing conditions analysis phase of the new approach includes an assessment of community-wide issues in addition to the traditional evaluation of the parks and recreation system. The exact scope of this phase, as discussed in chapter 7, will vary depending on the dimensions selected for the project; for example, the existing conditions analysis for the Town of Pittsboro, North Carolina, included an overview of community-wide health issues, since improved health and wellness was a focus of the plan. The community-wide analysis also focuses on understanding the context of the parks and recreation system within the community's history, values, demographics, land-use patterns, and standards. This phase typically includes a review of previously prepared guiding documents such as the comprehensive plan, strategic plans, related studies, redevelopment plans, previous parks and recreation master plans, and other documents related to the issues being addressed in the process.

Evaluation of the parks and recreation system is more site specific, including site visits to evaluate individual parks, trails, and open spaces on the basis of agreed-upon criteria, and evaluation of the existing parks and recreation levels of service using metrics adopted by the community. Members of the project team, the steering committee, and the public could be invited to participate in the analysis to share their unique perceptions.

The key to a successful existing conditions analysis is curiosity, as exemplified in the deep dive analogy discussed in chapter 7. Planners must set aside their preconceived perspectives and opinions (known in social sciences as researcher bias) and work to gain firsthand understanding of the real conditions of the parks and recreation system, public realm, or community. A recent *Washington Post* article noted that researchers use the term "science curiosity" to describe the character trait that suppresses biased judgment. "Science curiosity is different from science knowledge. Science-curious folk always chose to look at new evidence, whether it aligned with their beliefs or not. . . . A reasonable conclusion is that curiosity—and a broad range of knowledge—might be a kind of superpower."[5]

Needs Assessment

The concept of science curiosity is even more important during the needs assessment process; the new approach adopts the principles and practices of applied social science research to the process to generate more credible and valid findings, as discussed in chapter 8. Planners must form a hypothesis regarding potential needs and then develop a research design—a mixed-methods, triangulated needs assessment process—to determine actual community priorities. The process must be designed to withstand the scrutiny of elected officials, staff, residents, and other stakeholders, and the findings must be perceived as credible and valid.

LOS Analysis

The LOS analysis, discussed in chapter 9, is typically conducted as part of the existing conditions analysis or the needs assessment. However, if the scope of work includes the development of new LOS metrics—particularly those related to sustainability and resiliency goals—additional time may be needed. The process to develop LOS metrics should include the determination of long-range desired future conditions, identification of indicators of success, and the development of metrics to measure such success. It is not unusual to allow three to six months to build consensus and approval for new LOS metrics.

Long-Range Vision

The traditional approach to long-range visions often relied heavily on outdated LOS standards. The new approach, discussed in chapter 10, proposes the collaborative development of a long-range vision based on the community's vision and goals, the agency's mission, the PIF, the findings from the existing conditions evaluation and needs assessment, best planning practices and principles, the unique desires and aspirations of the community, and political and fiscal realities. To be consistent with a strategic planning approach, planners should consider alternative strategies to address the community's issues and needs, with an emphasis on change and implementation. The visioning process should be as collaborative as possible, and participants should represent many different perspectives and backgrounds to reflect the various dimensions of the PRSMP. Participants in our visioning workshops have included parks and recreation professionals, planners, artists, social activists, historians, city managers, health officials, developers, residents, elected officials, bicycle advocates, business owners, environmental educators, climate scientists, ecologists, school principals, budget directors, landscape architects, extreme sports enthusiasts, economic development directors, tourism directors, hoteliers, business owners, music promoters, and others. They have also included representatives of faith-based groups, environmental advocacy groups, youth sports associations, universities, homeowners' associations, mothers' groups, seniors' and youth groups, millennials, LGBTQ+ communities, disability-rights groups, indigenous communities, and other special interest groups.

Implementation Strategy

The new approach to parks and recreation system planning comes full circle with the implementation strategy, which builds on the initial PIF throughout the process. This is arguably the most important phase of the PRSMP process, potentially including recommendations for funding, phasing, partnerships, capital improvements, programs, operations, maintenance, staffing, policies, regulations, and other means of accomplishing the long-range vision. The implementation phase also includes recommendations for updates to the community's comprehensive plan, impact fee ordinance, land development regulations, and other policy and regulatory documents to reflect the new vision or standards for parks and recreation. If the PRSMP is not memorialized in these documents, it will quickly become obsolete. David Rouse, former research director for the American Planning Association, notes that the comprehensive plan is the framework defining how all city plans, investments, and programs fit together to support a common direction. At a minimum, the key elements of the PRSMP that should be included in the comprehensive plan are the summary of findings from the existing conditions analysis and needs assessment; proposed guiding principles, projects, and initiatives from the long-range vision; and an overview of the proposed implementation strategy. Other details of the PRSMP could be adopted into the comprehensive plan by reference.

The PRSMP vision and recommendations should also be integrated into the community's land development regulations to ensure that new parks and recreation facilities and programs are provided concurrently with new residential construction. Too many communities have been hesitant to require developers to provide local parks as part of their infrastructure requirements—or charge impact fees to offset the costs of new athletics fields or other regional facilities—only to find themselves drastically deficient in their parks and recreation levels of service years later. For example, Nassau County, Florida—historically known as a laid-back rural coastal community within commuting distance of metropolitan Jacksonville—has been "discovered" in recent years and is struggling to keep up with increasing demands for parks and recreation facilities. Our firm is working with the county to update its land development regulations to require developers of new communities to build new local parks in accordance with county-mandated prototypes and standards and to require perpetual operations and maintenance to be assumed by new homeowners' associations. At the same time, we have worked with the county to reevaluate and increase its park impact fees, which will focus on the acquisition and development of regional parks and recreation facilities such as greenways and trails, recreation and aquatics centers, and athletics fields and complexes.

Insights from the City of Port St. Lucie

A recent example of a PRSMP process that incorporated practices from project management, strategic planning, and applied social science research was the PRSMP for the City of Port St. Lucie in South Florida. One of Florida's many preplatted communities, Port St. Lucie was designed for retirees in the 1960s, but it is now one of Florida's fastest-growing cities. The increasingly diverse population is expected to increase from approximately 200,000 residents to over 360,000 residents within the next twenty years. In addition to the need for additional parkland and facilities to keep up with demand—as well as improvements to activate existing parks—the city is facing numerous resiliency and sustainability issues, including the need for increased economic development, stormwater treatment, improved water quality, neighborhood branding and identity, multimodal connectivity, and other issues related to rapid growth and the transition from a suburban retirement community to a vibrant, diverse city. Key adopted recommendations from the PRSMP included several sustainability and resiliency initiatives that will generate recreation, economic, social, and environmental benefits for the city, including the following:

- Expand the city's signature waterfront project to attract new businesses, promote tourism, and meet many of residents' top-priority recreation needs, such as walking and biking trails, an amphitheater, and multipurpose open spaces.
- Acquire land to improve equitable access to local neighborhood parks and provide additional stormwater treatment to improve the quality of adjacent water bodies.
- Improve and activate existing parks to incorporate best practices regarding branding, placemaking, and green infrastructure.
- Develop a new water park as the centerpiece of a proposed development initiative in an older area of the city.
- Improve multimodal access within this historically suburban community through complete streets, bikeways, and trails.
- Improve community health and fitness through expansion of the city's indoor recreation facilities, and increase collaboration with the county school district.

Several key factors led to the success of the plan, incorporating methods from both applied social research and strategic planning. First, the PRSMP was developed concurrently with the city's annual update to its strategic plan, providing numerous opportunities for research into specific topics, feedback loops, and workshop discussions with the city council. The process also provided multiple opportunities to plan and discuss the initial scope of work—as well as interim findings—with council members, the city manager, department heads (e.g., of parks, public works, planning, finance, economic development), and other key staff and stakeholders. These frequent communications and feedback loops with community leaders, agencies, and departments throughout the process were critical to defining and addressing parks and recreation needs as well as community sustainability and resiliency issues.

Second, the city council had clearly defined and updated citywide goals, initiatives, and projects through its annual strategic plan update, which provided mandates and clarified values for the PRSMP. The seven broad strategic goals for the city were as follows:

1. High-quality infrastructure and facilities
2. Quality education
3. Vibrant neighborhoods
4. High-performing government organization
5. Diverse economy and employment opportunities
6. Safe, clean, and beautiful city
7. Culture, nature, and fun activities

It was important that each proposed parks and recreation initiative or project be reviewed in terms of its potential contribution to one or more of these goals.

Third, the parks and recreation department, along with other city departments, refined its strategic business plan during a series of half-day retreats to better align with the city council's strategic goals (figure 4-4). The retreats also helped the department identify the resources needed to implement the council's priorities.

Consistent with methods from applied social research, the combined needs assessment process for the PRSMP and strategic plan update included multiple qualitative and quantitative techniques to identify residents' needs regarding parks, recreation, sustainability, and resiliency. Quantitative techniques included two citywide statistically representative surveys conducted at two different times (one related specifically to parks and recreation, the other to citywide issues, needs, and levels of satisfaction); an online survey; an LOS analysis; and benchmarking against the city's list of comparable communities. Qualitative techniques included several open houses held in different areas of the city; a centralized citizens' summit featuring interactive exhibits and exercises with each of the city departments, food, music, and opportunities to talk with council members (figure 4-5); and interviews and focus groups with key leaders and stakeholders from throughout the region. Additionally, secondary data (such as previous parks and recreation plans, transportation studies, stormwater studies, redevelopment studies, CIPs, deferred maintenance estimates, and water supply studies) was reviewed and analyzed for its relevance regarding citywide issues and residents' needs and priorities. Each assessment technique yielded new information for decision makers, which was incorporated back into the process. In this regard, the PRSMP needs assessment process never really ends; it is a continuous process to collect data regarding residents' needs and issues, establish and implement top priorities, and repeat annually. Findings from the needs assessment were presented to city staff, a project steering committee, and the city council to get their buy-in before proceeding with the next step of the process; experience has shown that this step is critical to build support for the ultimate recommendations from the PRSMP.

Another key factor that led to the success of the plan was the extensive number of workshops conducted to discuss the appropriate response to residents' needs and priorities, since each community must determine its own priorities based on policies, budgets, values, and other factors. A series of workshops was conducted with the parks and recreation department, the PRSMP steering committee (including city department heads), and the city council to discuss alternative strategies to address issues and needs and to determine preferred solutions. The council specifically discussed residents' concerns, opinions, and needs; proposed additions, deletions, and revisions to the strategic plan; and identified priority projects for the coming year.

A final factor for the plan's success was the level of detail provided for the funding, phasing, and implementation plan. Parks and recreation staff and staff of other departments met for one-day retreats to develop project charters for each of the top priorities, defining the scope and expectations for each initiative or project; which department or departments would be managing or participating in the project; what resources would be needed; and who specifically would manage the project and be part of the project team. The assigned project manager then prepared a detailed project plan that included the scope of work, budget, schedule, public involvement plan, and project deliverables. Meanwhile, each city department also

Figure 4-4: Strategic planning retreat for council and department heads of the City of Port St. Lucie, Florida (Photo courtesy of David Barth)

Figure 4-5: Port St. Lucie, Florida, citizens' summit (Photo courtesy of the City of Port St. Lucie)

met for a one-day retreat to determine its response to city council priorities, including department priorities, workload, and needed resources. All of this information—the project charter, project plans, schedule, budgets, and so forth—was incorporated into the updated strategic plan for city council review and consideration. The updated plan was adopted (with revisions, as necessary) in time for the city's annual budgeting process, which ultimately drives the city's CIP.

Port St. Lucie's city manager, Russ Blackburn, concluded that "the convergence of traditional parks master planning with strategic planning provides communities with a powerful tool. Governments should address as many infrastructure needs as possible with scarce resources. Parks which also serve as stormwater basins, wellfield recharge areas, or urban buffers add richness to the park while potentially adding funding to the park construction budget."

05 INITIATING AND PLANNING THE PRSMP PROCESS

A noteworthy differentiator between the traditional parks and recreation system master plan (PRSMP) and the proposed new approach is the amount of time and thought given to the initiation and planning phase of the project. Careful and thoughtful planning is critical to identifying opportunities to generate greater resiliency and sustainability benefits for the community as well as building the credibility and support needed to implement key recommendations. The eventual success or failure of many plans can be traced to the amount of time spent initiating and planning the process. Once a PRSMP process has begun, it is very difficult to change its scope, budget, and deliverables midstream.

In *Project Management for Planners*, Terry Clark noted that all planning projects include five phases: initiating, planning, executing, controlling, and closing. He estimated that the first two phases of the planning process—initiating and planning—should account for as much as 40 percent of the project manager's time for the entire project, underlining the critical importance of taking the necessary time to plan the PRSMP process.[1] However, in reality many PRSMPs are initiated with little forethought or preplanning and are often based on previously prepared plans or scopes of work. Some agencies simply update their existing plans periodically to satisfy their comprehensive plan requirements, with little thought given to changing trends or practices. Not surprisingly, such an approach will not generate the types of benefits discussed in this book. Fortunately, there are three helpful tools to maximize opportunities to generate sustainability and resiliency benefits during the initiating and planning phases of the PRSMP process: a readiness audit, a project charter, and a project plan.

The Readiness Audit

In chapter 3, I discussed the concept of High-Performance Public Spaces and the factors that lead to the adoption of sustainability innovations in the planning and design of public spaces. The three strongest factors are a strong leader, collaborative relationships, and external characteristics such as system openness and stakeholder involvement. Three secondary factors include the perception of the innovation, perceived economic benefits and return on investment (ROI), and the presence of a long-range vision (see box 5-1).

Parks and recreation planners can use these findings to help determine their readiness to adopt and implement innovative PRSMPs at the very beginning of the planning process. First, a strong leader, or champion, is absolutely necessary for successful adoption and implementation of the PRSMP. The leader can be an elected official, a community activist, a business leader, or someone else who can "create and communicate a clear vision that inspires and unites, thereby changing the perceptions of values of others"; "cope with resistance and skepticism, thereby overcoming all kinds of hurdles"; "create a coalition of the willing"; and "create a context for change."[2] Everett Rogers, author of *Diffusion of Innovations*, characterizes such a champion as "a charismatic individual who throws his or her weight behind an innovation, thus overcoming indifference or resistance that the new idea may provoke in an organization."[3] Actually, two types of leaders are necessary for the adoption of innovative plans and designs: (1) the bold, visionary leader needed to persuade others of the benefits and make the decision to adopt planning-level innovations, and (2) the steady, persistent leader needed to implement detailed design-level innovations. The readiness audit asks whether both types of leaders are present and ready to implement the plan.

The second most important factor is a collaborative relationship among the members of the team assigned to implement the plan. Prior to my research, I thought that a "collaborative relationship" simply meant that the team members enjoyed working together. I was only partly correct. My research found that collaborative teams work well together, respect one another's opinions, solicit input from numerous public and private stakeholders, participate in decision making, and share a common purpose or passion for the project.

But good collaboration also often requires the strong leader to "hold people together" and "motivate team members for collaboration."[4] In other words, collaboration is not always voluntary; a strong leader mandates it, particularly during the implementation phase of the project. If a PRSMP team is not prepared to be collaborative, leaders may help prepare them for implementation through team-building classes, workshops, and training.

The third most influential factor identified by my research was external characteristics and system openness. Openness is the degree to which the members of a system are linked to other individuals who are external to the system; in other words, the adoption of innovation requires a willingness of the team to be transparent in every action and to reach out to the community in a meaningful and authentic way. A perfunctory series of public workshops is not sufficient; the team should be ready to use multiple techniques to engage and communicate with stakeholders, similar to the needs assessment process discussed in chapter 8. My research found that successful teams went to extraordinary lengths to engage residents and key stakeholders in the planning and design process, both before and after the proposed plans had been developed. Common public involvement tools and techniques included public meetings and presentations, workshops, videos, special events, press releases, fact sheets, posters, brochures, newspaper editorials and articles, and social media. Openness also extends well beyond the dissemination of information and attendance at public meetings; successful teams are willing to meet with stakeholders at their homes, businesses, churches, or institutions; listen carefully to their concerns and issues; and work hard to develop thoughtful, responsive solutions to meet their specific needs. For example, one of our clients conducted a yearlong series of meetings with homeowners' and condominium associations to vet the recommendations from our PRSMP and to refine the implementation strategy in response to their concerns or ideas. During the readiness audit, parks system planners should discuss the process for getting buy-in from stakeholders and residents, particularly if a tax increase or assessment is anticipated to implement the plan.

Secondary factors that should be considered during the readiness audit are the perception of costs, economic benefits, and perceived ROI and the presence of a long-range vision. Compelling ROI charts and vision documents (system-wide visions, conceptual site plans, illustrations, photographs, etc.) should be developed during the visioning phase of the PRSMP. Both tools can be instrumental in communicating proposed innovative ideas to elected officials, residents, and other stakeholders; helping them to recognize the value of the proposed improvements; and approving proposed funding initiatives.

The readiness audit can significantly increase the likelihood for successful implementation. For example, a self-audit of the three most important factors would ask the following questions:

- Is there a strong and influential champion—such as a mayor, commissioner, or community activist—willing to advocate for funding of the planning process, adoption of the plan, and implementation of the recommendations?
- Is there a collaborative planning team—potentially comprising parks and recreation professionals, landscape architects, civil engineers, transportation planners, ecologists, urban designers, health officials, and others—whose members are willing to work together, brainstorm, and share ideas throughout the planning process?
- Is there a comprehensive and robust public outreach plan to seek out and involve residents and other stakeholders in the master planning process?

A self-audit of the secondary factors might include the following questions:

- Do public officials, residents, and other stakeholders perceive the need for innovative parks and recreation improvements that contribute to community sustainability and resiliency?
- Do public officials, residents, and other stakeholders perceive the economic benefits and ROI that could be generated by the proposed parks and recreation improvements?
- Will the PRSMP process create a compelling long-range vision and implementation strategy that will help public officials, residents, and other stakeholders recognize the benefits of the proposed improvements?

A negative response to any of these questions may indicate that the team isn't really ready to initiate the master planning process and should delay the project until the key factors are in place. Suppose, for example, that there is not an apparent champion for the project who will be willing to advocate for adoption, funding, or implementation of the recommendations. Often this may be due to budget concerns, particularly in communities struggling to meet essential needs for public safety, transportation, and utilities. In response, members of the planning team may wish to meet one-on-one with elected officials to determine why they are not enthusiastic about the project and the conditions under which they would be willing to support it.

Similarly, if there is not a collaborative team in place—for example, if representatives from the city manager's office, public works department, or planning department are not interested in participating in the process—then it would be worth the time and effort to meet with them individually to discuss their resistance. Describe the value of participation and the eventual return on their investment of time.

It is not an exaggeration to suggest that a PRSMP process should not proceed unless these key factors are in place. For instance, I was recently asked to intercede in a yearlong PRSMP process that had little support from elected officials, city management, and other departments. Although the parks and recreation director and advisory committee were pleased with the plan, it appeared to have little chance of being implemented. The director could have saved significant time, money, and frustration by conducting a readiness audit before initiating the project.

The Project Charter

The next step in planning the PRSMP process is to prepare what some agencies call a project charter, which outlines the basic requirements and expectations for the project. For example, the Community Redevelopment Agency of the City of Gainesville, Florida, requires its project managers to prepare a charter before any project is approved and funded. The purpose of the charter is to make sure that decision makers understand the reasons for the project; to define

Box 5-1
Readiness Audit

Project Preplanning Checklist

Primary Factors

- Presence of a strong leader or advocate for the innovation
- Collaborative relationship of the planning and design team
- External characteristics, including system openness and stakeholder involvement

Secondary Factors

- Costs, economic benefits, and perceived return on investment
- Presence of a long-range vision

Other Possible Factors

- Perception of the innovation
- Internal characteristics of the organization
- Funding
- Passion

Source: David L. Barth, "The Adoption of Innovation in the Planning and Design Process: Creating High-Performance Public Spaces That Contribute to Community Sustainability" (PhD diss., University of Florida, 2015).

the required resources and expected deliverables; and to secure management support for the time, staff, and funding required. Similar to the readiness audit, the project charter helps ensure that elected officials and management are fully committed to the PRSMP process before it begins. The charter should answer the following questions:

1. *Project purpose, goals, and expectations:* Why are you doing this project? What are you trying to achieve? What are the expected outcomes? What are your elected officials expecting? How will you measure whether the project is successful when it is completed?
2. *Project scope:* What is the basic scope of work for the project? For example, will it include an assessment of existing conditions, a needs assessment, a long-range vision, and an

implementation strategy? Will it address key objectives? Will it address the entire public realm or just the parks and recreation system? Will it include ways in which parks and the public realm can address community-wide concerns such as economic development, climate change, and health?

3. *Project budget (hours of staff time and funding for consultants):* What is the budget for the project? Is it adequate for the proposed scope? How does it compare with budgets for projects of similar scale?
4. *Project team:* What skills and expertise will be required for this project? Which of these will be provided by in-house staff and which will be provided by outside consultants? What other departments, agencies, or stakeholders should be involved in the process?
5. *Project schedule:* Is anything driving the completion date for the project, such as a grant proposal, citywide budget, or other catalyst for completion? How many months will be allocated for the project? What key dates or milestones must be met, such as presentations to key decision makers? Does the schedule allow adequate time for surveys, public involvement, and the review and approval of interim and final documents?

According to *Project Management for Planners*, the basic components of a project charter may include, but not be limited to, the following:[5]

- Project title
- Sponsoring agency or department
- Project management oversight team—the managers responsible for oversight and review
- Project manager
- Project team, including staff and consultants
- Project description (including the dimensions to be addressed)
- Preliminary scope and methodology (and schedule)
- Estimated costs and resources
- Assumptions
- Constraints
- Roles and responsibilities

Taking the time to create a project charter also provides the opportunity to discuss three other topics critical to the success of the PRSMP: the issues and dimensions to be addressed in the process, the use of consultants, and a preliminary scope of work and schedule.

Chapter 2 lists over fifty potential dimensions of parks and recreation systems that could be addressed during the planning process, including the top ten dimensions most commonly addressed through the PRSMP process. It also discussed the need to conduct a scoping meeting with key stakeholders to discuss alternative dimensions and determine the most appropriate scope for the PRSMP process. The project charter provides the opportunity to have these discussions and to determine the breadth and depth of the scope of work. I would encourage planners to use the list in chapter 2 as a checklist for the discussions, providing a potential menu for the dimensions to be included in the project's scope of work.

Once the dimensions of the PRSMP have been decided, the project planners need to determine the composition of the project team, including both public agency staff and consulting planners. Two critical considerations are the available time and expertise of the sponsoring agency staff. A basic PRSMP (not including any additional dimensions) requires approximately one thousand to two thousand hours of work over a nine- to twelve-month period, which equates to twenty-five to fifty weeks of work for one individual working full-time. However, few individuals have all of the skills needed to execute and produce even the most basic conventional PRSMP; traditional PRSMP teams include parks planners, landscape architects, recreation planners, operations and management planners, market researchers, communications and public relations planners, geographic information systems (GIS) technicians, editors, and graphic designers.

The time and expertise required to implement the new approach may be much greater, depending on the selected dimensions of the project. Additional subject matter experts could include, among others, stormwater engineers, urban designers, transportation planners, public health professionals, sociologists, public education professionals, bicycle and pedestrian planners, climate scientists, comprehensive plan and code planners, financial planners, and grant writers.

The project scope, schedule, and budget should adequately reflect the required team members and their level of involvement.

Representatives of the sponsoring agency also need to discuss whether the agency has the general experience to conduct a PRSMP internally. I believe that one benefit of hiring a consulting team that specializes in parks and recreation system planning is the knowledge and expertise team members have gained in conducting hundreds of similar projects in different communities across the United States. In our practice, for example, we are constantly refining and improving our approach on the basis of what we've learned from previous projects. This allows us to offer our clients the latest proven and most effective processes, tools, and techniques to meet their goals.

Once the team has been selected, a project description and preliminary scope of work need to be developed. For the purposes of the charter, the description and scope need be only detailed enough to define the project's preliminary expectations, deliverables, budget, and schedule. These can also be used as the basis for a request for qualifications (RFQ), if the sponsoring agency has decided to hire a consulting team to lead or assist with the project.

The Project Plan

Once the project charter has been approved, the next step is to prepare a detailed project plan that includes a detailed, task-by-task scope of work that includes the products (deliverables) from each phase of work; a detailed project schedule that includes the time frame for each task, key milestones, and key meeting dates; and a project budget that includes the estimated hours for each task (for each person on the team) and anticipated project expenses such as printing and travel.

This is the most important step in initiating and planning the PRSMP process! As mentioned earlier, many agencies simply duplicate the scope from a previously prepared PRSMP or copy a scope from another similar process. However, it is vitally important to develop a scope, schedule, and budget that reflect the proposed dimensions and desired outcomes of the PRSMP process. For those not experienced in project management, it is well worth the time to get training or read one of the many available publications on the subject. For those planning to hire a consultant, the project plan should be developed as part of the contract between the consulting firm and the sponsoring agency.

Some advice for those planning to issue an RFQ: First, don't spend a lot of time preparing a detailed scope of work, particularly if you have not been through the PRSMP process before; a simple description will suffice. Instead, ask consultants to submit their proposed approach in their qualifications, based on their own knowledge and experience.

Second, it is preferable to issue an RFQ rather than a request for proposal (RFP). Better yet, the RFQ should include the agency's project budget, which allows the consulting team to tailor an appropriate approach. It should be clear by now that PRSMPs are not an exact science, and comparing fee proposals is not a reliable method for selecting a consultant. The scope and fees for a PRSMP can vary wildly depending on the project's dimensions, the role of agency staff, the number of meetings, the level of detail, the number of graphics, the review and approval process, and other variables.

Rather than comparing fee proposals, the sponsoring agency should commit to spend the necessary time with the selected consulting team to clearly and collaboratively define the project objectives, goals, expectations, and deliverables for the project and to develop a fee in accordance with the project budget and the level of effort required for the project. In our practice, once we've been selected for a project, we conduct a scoping meeting with the client to discuss the desired dimensions, expectations, outcomes, and budget for the project as a basis for developing the scope of work. Some of our clients wish to focus only on the traditional dimensions of a parks and recreation system, such as needs, capital improvements, and costs; others aspire to fully explore opportunities to address community-wide sustainability and resiliency issues. In addition to defining the specific planning tasks, discussion should include coordination with other departments or agencies, the review and approval process, and the formation of a project steering or advisory committee.

Coordination with Other Departments or Agencies

The project scope should also define when and how interagency coordination will take place throughout the process. Too often, parks and recreation plans are prepared within the silos of parks and recreation departments or planning departments. One advantage of considering the entire public realm and other dimensions of a parks and recreation system (as opposed to the traditional parks and recreation plan) is that it forces planners to invite other participants to collaborate in the planning process. Considering the entire system helps avoid the shortsighted, one-dimensional perspective common in traditional planning. A robust public realm planning process would include representatives from the departments of parks and recreation, public works, health, environmental lands, transportation, engineering, planning, administration, and finance. It would also include the school district, athletic associations, water management districts, land developers, business owners, and other key stakeholders. Bringing in these voices enriches the process, ensuring that multiple perspectives and dimensions of the parks and recreation system will be considered.

Review and Approval Process

The project scope and schedule should also clearly outline the proposed review and approval process at each milestone. For example, three typical milestones for interim review are (1) the findings from the needs and priorities assessment, (2) the proposed long-range vision, and (3) the proposed implementation strategy. Different communities have different protocols, processes, and sequences for approval. Typically, both interim and final plans and presentations are reviewed by the following:

- Project manager and department staff
- Department head
- Other staff
- Administration
- Steering or advisory committees, boards, and other citizen groups

- Elected officials
- General public

Most interim and final plans and documents can be discussed at public meetings and workshops. However, it is often useful to conduct one-on-one interviews and meetings with elected officials at the critical milestones in the process, as outlined earlier. In our practice, we've found that these one-on-one meetings have a direct impact on our rate of success in PRSMP adoption and implementation. One-on-one meetings provide the opportunity for open and honest discussions regarding issues or concerns with the plan—and the opportunity to make critical revisions before the plan is considered for approval and adoption. The Port St. Lucie PRSMP example discussed in the previous chapter reinforces the benefits of having these types of interim, in-depth discussions throughout the proposed new approach to PRSMP planning. Multiple discussions with members of the city council, the city manager, department heads, and staff helped us to continually refine and position the plan for adoption, funding, and implementation.

Steering or Advisory Committee

The scope of work should also define the role and composition of a fifteen- to twenty-five-member project steering or advisory committee, which can be a very useful tool for soliciting feedback from a cross-section of the community at the key milestones mentioned previously. These committees are usually more diverse than the typical planning board or parks and recreation advisory board, including representatives from the following:

- Municipal and county jurisdictions
- Public and private recreation providers, leagues, and associations
- Environmental groups
- Business groups
- Faith-based organizations
- Social service and health agencies
- School districts
- Developers

- Property owners
- Law enforcement agencies
- Homeowners' associations
- Youth groups
- Seniors' groups
- Other community-specific groups

There are several benefits to creating a more diverse committee for the new approach to PRSMP planning. First, many of these committee members can provide significant expertise regarding the alternative dimensions of a PRSMP, such as community health, wildlife habitat, and economic development. Second, a diverse committee helps challenge conventional thinking about parks and recreation systems. For instance, a committee dominated by youth sports representatives may focus primarily on traditional sports-related needs and issues, but a more rounded committee may have a broader perspective. Finally, consistent with the need for a strong leader or project champion, a diverse committee that includes influential community leaders will lend significant credibility to the PRSMP process and increase the odds of successful implementation.

The Importance of Initiating and Planning the New Approach

At the risk of being redundant, I reemphasize that there is absolutely no substitute for taking the time to initiate and plan the new approach to the PRSMP process, especially if the goal is to generate greater sustainability and resiliency benefits for the community. Opportunities to realize these benefits simply will not materialize if they are not carefully and thoughtfully integrated into the planning process. Conducting the readiness audit and preparing the project charter and project plan—including the formation of the PRSMP scope of work, interdepartmental and interagency coordination process, review and approval process, and influential steering or advisory committee—will help ensure that the planning team has thoroughly considered the desired future outcomes for their community and designed a PRSMP process that will help them achieve their goals.

06 THE PRELIMINARY IMPLEMENTATION FRAMEWORK

—

The next step in the new comprehensive approach to a parks and recreation system master plan (PRSMP) is to develop a preliminary implementation framework (PIF). One of my favorite quotes, attributed to Ted Levitt of Harvard Business School, is "Don't let the airplane take off until you've built the runway." Much too often, PRSMPs are initiated without adequate forethought regarding their implementation, which eventually leads to frustration with and disappointment in the entire process. Implementation shouldn't be a crapshoot with an unpredictable outcome; it should be planned from the very beginning of the project.

The purpose of the PIF is to initiate implementation discussions as early in the process as possible, in order to "build the runway" for ultimate implementation. This is particularly important for plans that address numerous dimensions outside of traditional parks and recreation issues, such as transportation, stormwater, and social services, that will be implemented by agencies other than a parks and recreation or planning department. Most elected officials, parks and recreation professionals, and parks planners agree that "implementability" is one of the most important characteristics of a good plan and that implementation is the ultimate goal of every PRSMP; otherwise, there is little to show for the significant investment of time and money. A typical PRSMP's life span is only about five to ten years before it needs to be updated to reflect changing trends and demographics, urbanization, leadership, political priorities, and other influences on the parks and recreation system.

Forms of Implementation

Before examining the specifics of the PIF, it is important to understand that implementation comes in many forms. It is not limited to funding of capital improvements, additional staffing, new programs, and increased maintenance—although these are major objectives of most PRSMPs. Other forms of implementation include updates to comprehensive plans or land development regulations; partnerships with other agencies, businesses, or nonprofit organizations; changes to staffing or organizational structure; refocused delivery of programs and services in response to the agency's mission or residents' priorities; and changes to maintenance and operations procedures. Accreditation by the Commission for Accreditation of Parks and Recreation Agencies (CAPRA) is another form of implementation.

Each of these forms of implementation should be discussed during the PIF phase of the project to determine those that are most applicable or feasible for the community. This allows planners to establish realistic expectations for the PRSMP before the process begins—as opposed to finding out that the planning recommendations are impractical at the conclusion of the project. Following is a discussion of the most common forms of implementation for consideration.

Funding

Parks and recreation funding generally falls into two categories: pay-as-you-go and borrowing. Pay-as-you-go funding is based on incoming revenues such as ad valorem (property) taxes, sales taxes, special assessments, grants, user fees, and other revenues regularly collected by a public agency. A budget is established each year on the basis of anticipated revenues, and the governing body (e.g., city council, county commission, parks commission) of the agency determines what will be included. Funding for parks and recreation facilities, renovation, repairs, programs, and staffing may vary from year to year according to projected revenues. It is very difficult to rely solely on pay-as-you-go funding for parks and recreation capital improvements, operations, and maintenance because of its unpredictability from year to year and the difficulty of amassing sufficient funds for significant projects.

When pay-as-you-go funding is not adequate to pay for major new projects, renovations, or deferred repairs, agencies often increase ad valorem or sales taxes. For example, an increase of one mil ($1 per $1,000 of assessed value) in ad valorem taxes generated approximately $10 million per year for a community of approximately 60,000 residents. A half-cent increase in local sales taxes is generating approximately $20 million per year for a county of approximately 270,000 residents. Residents are often asked to vote on the increase through a referendum, which underscores the need for a political champion or strong community advocate to lead the effort, as discussed in the previous chapter.

When pay-as-you-go measures are not adequate to fund proposed improvements, agencies may choose to borrow the money and pay it back over a period of time, usually twenty to thirty years. Bonds are issued (similar to a mortgage) and paid back through an existing revenue stream (such as utility payments) or through a voter-approved increase in ad valorem taxes for the life of the bond. The cities of Doral, Florida; Raleigh, North Carolina; and San Francisco all recently had multimillion-dollar parks and recreation bonds approved by voters. Raleigh, for example, is using its $92 million bond for parks and facility improvements, cultural resource projects, greenway projects, and land acquisition and development.

Appendix 3 lists the most common types of parks and recreation funding sources and can be used to estimate current and projected funding for parks and recreation improvements.

Comprehensive Plans

An important implementation action is to incorporate the parks and recreation master plan into the community's comprehensive plan. Yet many parks and recreation agencies do not participate in updates to their comprehensive plan, typically because of lack of awareness, lack of time, or resistance from other departments. As discussed previously, the comprehensive plan is the single most important guiding document in a community; it establishes the community vision, goals, objectives, and policies that guide all decision making. The parks and recreation vision should be integrated into the comprehensive plan as a vital element of the community's vision and included in the plan's goals, objectives, and policies. Parks and recreation actions (capital improvements, programs, etc.) should also be identified as implementation plan priorities.

In order to generate the most resiliency and sustainability benefits, the PRSMP must be integrated throughout the comprehensive plan, not just in a separate silo. For example, the outline for preparation of comprehensive plans in the Pennsylvania Municipalities Planning Code includes separate elements (sections) for land use, housing, movement of people and goods (transportation), community facilities and utilities (including parks and recreation), natural and historic resource protection, water supply, and energy conservation. Conversely, the Philadelphia 2035 comprehensive plan is organized around three integrating themes, as follows:

- Thrive: neighborhoods, economic development, land management
- Connect: transportation, utilities
- Renew: open space, historic preservation, environmental resources, public realm

The concepts of sustainability and resiliency are now driving many comprehensive plans. David Rouse, previous managing director of research and advisory services for the American Planning Association, noted that "planning for sustainability is the defining challenge of the 21st century. . . . Planning processes allow communities to look past immediate concerns, to evaluate options for how best to proceed, and to move towards a better future."[1] Comprehensive plans that reflect best practices for sustainability focus on a "livable built environment; harmony with nature; a resilient economy; interwoven equity; healthy communities; and responsible regionalism."[2] As mentioned in chapter 1, the 2035 comprehensive plan of the City of Portland, Oregon, is one of the best examples of an integrated public realm plan, integrating proposed parks and open space improvements with land use and transportation, transit, development centers and corridors, and neighborhoods. Because of this increased awareness of livability, sustainability, and resiliency, there has never been a better opportunity—or a more important time—to integrate parks and recreation needs, vision, and recommendations into a community's comprehensive plan.

Land Development Regulations

An equally important step toward implementation is to integrate the PRSMP into the community's land development regulations, codes, and ordinances. These regulatory documents ensure that the broad vision, goals, objectives, and policies established in the comprehensive plan will actually be implemented through new development. An encouraging current trend is to make these documents more prescriptive because historically they left much to the discretion of developers, planning staff, and elected officials. For example, some ordinances permit balconies, wetlands, and stormwater retention ponds to be counted as community open space. Many other ordinances include a fees-in-lieu clause that permits developers to pay fees in lieu of providing parkland, thereby foreclosing the opportunity to provide a park within a ten-minute walk of new residents and reducing the capacity of other nearby parks.

Nassau County, Florida, is working to strengthen its land development regulations by requiring new developments to provide two acres of developable parkland per one thousand residents in the form of six- to ten-acre local neighborhood parks; requiring homeowners' associations to assume responsibility for perpetual operations and maintenance; and granting fees in lieu of parks for only the smallest infill developments. The county has also developed prescriptive neighborhood park prototypes to specify the types of facilities and amenities that should be included in the park. In addition to providing small local parks for new residents, developers are charged park impact fees to help offset the costs of larger regional facilities needed by new residents, such as athletics fields, aquatics facilities, and indoor recreation centers.

Similarly, the 2018 parks ordinance for New Braunfels, Texas, prescribes specific park requirements including size, site suitability, access (one mile from all residences), relationship to schools, connectivity to trails, street frontage (no more than two sides of the park may abut the rear of homes), visibility, and protection of natural and historical resources. The ordinance also establishes the number of homes to be served per acre of parkland and establishes mechanisms for funding, operations, and maintenance.

Some communities are concerned about adding more regulations and costs to new residential developments, particularly small infill projects, because of the increasing demand for affordable housing or the fear of discouraging developers from building in their communities. During our work on the Public Spaces Master Plan for Arlington County, Virginia, for example, we discussed the inherent conflict in residents' needs for both open space and affordable housing. Ultimately, each community's land development regulations must reflect its residents' values, the community's needs, and the desired roles of government agencies and private developers in meeting those needs.

Staffing and Organizational Structure

Implementation can also take the form of changes in staffing and organization, particularly in the case of new or transitioning departments. For example, the Parks, Preserves and Recreation Strategic Master Plan for Sarasota County, Florida, recommended that the county focus on providing and maintaining large regional facilities and convey ownership and responsibility of smaller local facilities to several of the municipalities within the county. Implementation of the recommendation required organizational and staffing changes to both the county and municipal parks and recreation departments. For example, the City of Sarasota's parks and recreation department is proposing to add several new positions over the next few years to accommodate growth. The city has also created a new mission statement that focuses on community sustainability and youth development in addition to the traditional parks and recreation role, resulting in additional staffing and organizational recommendations.

The PIF

The PIF can be used to initiate discussions about these and other implementation techniques as early in the process as possible so that a feasible and acceptable implementation plan can be adopted by elected officials at the end of the process. Chapter 4 noted that strategic plans such as PRSMPs are based on political decision making;

there's a direct correlation between the relevance of the PRSMP regarding the issues that elected officials care about and successful adoption of the plan. A PIF acknowledges these issues at the beginning of the project, hypothesizes potential solutions and associated costs, and suggests how the solutions will be implemented, including the roles and responsibilities of various public and private agencies. Once captured in writing, the framework becomes a basis for discussion—and refinement—throughout the PRSMP process.

The Buckhead, Georgia, Greenspace Plan was one of our first projects to incorporate a PIF in the planning process. At our kickoff meeting with the client and the steering committee, we hypothesized that the plan recommendations would cost more than $200 million to implement, and we brainstormed how the plan would eventually be implemented. Key stakeholders included government agencies, nonprofit organizations, and private developers. Some of the PIF discussion topics included the following:

- Governance—which department or agency will be in charge of implementation, what will be the roles of the various organizations, and how will they collaborate?
- Funding—what sources of public and private funding will be available to implement the recommendations, and how much will be available?
- Operations, maintenance, and programming—once capital improvements are implemented, which agency or agencies will be responsible for operations, maintenance, and programming?

The PIF was refined throughout the planning process, resulting in successful initiation of the top-priority project, the GA 400 Trail, before the master plan was completed. The PIF phase of the project—and the thoughtful leadership of the client and the members of the steering committee, who continuously engaged in discussions about implementation—were the most important factors leading to successful implementation of the Greenspace Plan.

To illustrate how the preliminary implementation process can be applied to other PRSMPs, following are some key questions that could be raised regarding the most common dimensions discussed in chapter 2.

Accreditation

- How will the findings and recommendations from the PRSMP be incorporated into the CAPRA report?
- Which of the national accreditation standards will be addressed through the PRSMP process?
- Who is leading the accreditation process, and how will she or he be involved in the PRSMP process?
- What is the format for the accreditation report, and is it consistent with the format of the PRSMP?
- Who will be responsible for editing the sections of the PRSMP to meet the CAPRA requirements?
- What is the schedule for submittal of the CAPRA self-assessment report, and how does it align with the PRSMP schedule?

Bicycle and Pedestrian Access

- Who (which department, agency, or individual) will be responsible for implementing the bicycle and pedestrian recommendations from the PRSMP?
- Does the community have a current comprehensive transportation plan (CTP) that includes greenways, bikeways, trails, and sidewalks? If not, when will it be prepared or updated?
- Who will be responsible for preparing or updating the CTP? What is the schedule for the project?
- How will that department, agency, or individual be involved in the PRSMP?
- Can the needs assessments for the CTP and the PRSMP—particularly related to bicycle and pedestrian access—be completed concurrently?
- How will the findings from the needs assessments be integrated into both plans?
- How will the two departments or agencies collaborate on a long-range vision for bicycle and pedestrian access?
- How will the two departments or agencies collaborate on the identification and implementation of recommended capital improvements for bicycle and pedestrian access, particularly those related to access to parks and open spaces?

- Are there opportunities to leverage funding sources to generate multiple recreation and transportation benefits from proposed projects?
- Are there opportunities for public-private partnerships?

Social Equity

- How is social equity being defined for the purposes of the PRSMP? What criteria are being used? For example, the City of New York's criteria consider poverty, density, potential for growth, and level of public investment over the previous twenty years. How will the equity criteria be considered when determining community needs and responsibilities?
- What other agencies or departments are most involved in improving social equity in the community?
- How will those departments or agencies be involved in the PRSMP process?
- Are other plans being developed or updated to ensure social equity? How will the findings from the PRSMP be integrated with these other plans?
- Are there opportunities to leverage funding sources to generate multiple recreation and social equity benefits from proposed projects?
- Are there opportunities for public-private partnerships?

Comprehensive Plan

- Is the existing recreation and open space element (ROSE) of the comprehensive plan current? Does it reflect the issues, mission, vision, level-of-service (LOS) standards, and proposed initiatives of the parks and recreation department?
- When is the ROSE scheduled to be updated?
- Who will be leading the update?
- How will that department, agency, or individual be involved in the PRSMP?
- Can the ROSE be updated concurrently with development of the PRSMP?

- How will the findings from the PRSMP (including the needs assessment summary, long-range vision, LOS standards, and priority improvements) be incorporated into the ROSE?

Land Development Regulations

- Does the community anticipate significant growth in the coming years?
- Is there a political desire and willingness to require new development to provide neighborhood parks and open spaces to meet the needs of new residents?
- Do current land development regulations (LDRs) require developers to build and maintain new local (neighborhood) parks to meet the local park needs of new residents? For example, is a new six- to ten-acre park required within one-half mile (a ten-minute walk) of every new home?
- Do the current LDRs include a prototypical site plan illustrating the required minimum standards for a new neighborhood park?

Impact Fees

- Is there a political desire and willingness to require new development to contribute to the costs of new community or regional parks needed to meet the needs of new residents?
- In addition to building new neighborhood parks, are developers required to pay impact fees for larger community-wide facilities (i.e., parks and recreation facilities that are not normally constructed within new developments) such as athletics fields, indoor recreation centers, and aquatics centers?
- When was the last impact fee study completed or impact fees updated?
- Who is responsible for updating impact fees?
- How will that department, agency, or individual be involved in the PRSMP?
- If required, what is the schedule for preparing the impact fee study and proposing updated fees?
- Can the study and recommendations be completed prior to completion of the PRSMP, so that recommendations can be included in the PRSMP implementation strategy?

Funding

- Which of the funding sources (pay-as-you-go and borrowing) are supported by elected officials?
- Collectively, how much will those sources generate within the next year? Five years? Ten years? (See appendix 3. We often ask the sponsoring agency's finance director to estimate the funds that could be generated for various property tax millage, sales tax, and other sources.)
- What is the gap between estimated funding and estimated costs? (In order to estimate costs prior to completion of the PRSMP, we often use costs from PRSMPs of comparable-size communities. Or we develop a quick, hypothetical vision for the community—based on existing plans and documents and experience from other communities—to develop the basis for a preliminary estimate of costs. We also use a rule of thumb to estimate annual operations and maintenance costs, for example, 5 percent of estimated capital costs.)
- What is the likelihood that voters will approve a bond or sales tax referendum for proposed parks and recreation improvements? (Needs assessment surveys can include questions regarding willingness to support funding. And nonprofit agencies such as the Trust for Public Land will work with local communities to poll residents to determine the level of support for various conservation and open space ballot initiatives.)
- What other sources of funding could be used to fund proposed improvements? For example, are there opportunities for public-private partnerships to fund some of the initiatives, particularly those that generate revenue?
- How could implementation of the vision be phased over time, using estimated costs and funding?

Stormwater Treatment and Green Infrastructure

- Who will be responsible for implementing the stormwater recommendations from the PRSMP?
- Does the community have a current stormwater/green infrastructure master plan (SMP) that includes opportunities for

the colocation of parks, greenways, and stormwater treatment facilities? If not, when will it be prepared or updated?

- Who will be responsible for preparing or updating the SMP? What is the schedule for the project?
- How will that department, agency, or individual be involved in the PRSMP?
- Can the needs assessments for the SMP and the PRSMP—particularly related to the proposed locations of new parks and the enhancement of existing parks—be completed concurrently?
- How will the findings from the needs assessments be integrated into both plans?
- How will the two departments or agencies collaborate on a long-range vision for green infrastructure, including parks and stormwater facilities?
- How will the two departments or agencies collaborate on the identification and implementation of recommended capital improvements for parks, flood control, and stormwater treatment?
- Are there opportunities to leverage funding sources to generate multiple recreation and stormwater and flood control benefits from proposed projects?
- Are there opportunities for public-private partnerships?

Health and Wellness

- Have local health departments or agencies identified and published a summary of health-related issues facing the community?
- How will those departments or agencies be involved in the PRSMP process?
- Which health issues can be addressed, at least in part, through the PRSMP process?
- How will health and wellness be considered when determining community needs and responsibilities?
- What other health providers, such as hospitals and clinics, should be involved in the PRSMP process?
- Are other plans being developed or updated to promote health and wellness? How will the findings from the PRSMP be integrated with these other plans?

- Are there opportunities to leverage funding sources to generate multiple recreation and health benefits from proposed projects?
- Are there opportunities for public-private partnerships?

Recreation, Social, and Educational Programs

- In addition to the recreation programs offered by the sponsoring agency, what other providers offer recreation, social, and educational programs to the community, such as schools, Boys & Girls Clubs, YMCAs, churches, and social service agencies?
- How will those providers be involved in the PRSMP process?
- What planning processes have the other providers used to determine the needs of their constituencies and the roles of the provider in meeting these needs? Have they prepared strategic plans or master plans for their organizations?
- How will the findings from the PRSMP be incorporated into other agencies' plans?
- Can the PRSMP process be used to help better define the roles of the various agencies in providing recreation, social, and educational programs to the community?
- Are there opportunities to partner with other agencies to increase the level of service provided to the community by leveraging existing funds, staffing, equipment, facilities, and other resources?
- Are there opportunities for public-private partnerships?

Economic Development

- What local agencies are responsible for economic development in the community, such as the office of economic development and the chamber of commerce?
- Have these agencies developed strategic plans for economic development in the community, identified a summary of key economic issues facing the community, or both?
- How will those departments or agencies be involved in the PRSMP process?
- How has economic development been defined (e.g., job creation, increased tax values, job training, attracting new businesses, attracting new retirees)?

- Which economic development issues can be addressed, at least in part, through the PRSMP process?
- Have locations been identified where new or expanded parks could serve as catalysts for economic development?
- How will the findings from the PRSMP be integrated with economic development plans?
- Are there opportunities to leverage funding sources to generate multiple recreation and economic benefits from proposed projects?
- Are there opportunities for public-private partnerships?

On the basis of these and other discussions (depending on the specific dimensions of the PRSMP), the framework should be developed to clearly define how each dimension of the PRSMP is proposed to be implemented. The PIF should be circulated among the participants of the planning team, the steering or advisory committee, and elected officials for review and comment, and it should be continuously updated as more information becomes available. For example, the PIF for Nassau County—which focused on the role of private land development in parks and recreation—is now in its seventh iteration, has been expanded from five to twenty pages by both agency staff and consultants, and has been the basis for most of the project discussion. Based on a hypothetical long-range vision and estimate of costs—including local parks, regional parks, trails and greenways, and conservation lands—it has led to successful implementation of new LOS standards, land development codes, impact fees, and updates to the comprehensive plan. The PIF has also led to initiation of the county's first comprehensive parks and recreation system plan.

As in the initiation and planning phase, time spent developing the PIF early in the process will pay great dividends at the end. Early in my career, I made the mistake of stunning a city council with a proposed cost estimate and implementation strategy at the end of the PRSMP process, without having had the types of discussions suggested here. In hindsight, it's no surprise that the plan was rejected and never implemented. A PIF would have ensured that the proposed implementation strategy was fully vetted, refined, and approved prior to asking the council to adopt the plan.

PART III

EXECUTING THE NEW APPROACH

07 EXISTING CONDITIONS ANALYSIS

—

Before beginning this third and final part of the book, let's recap the big ideas presented thus far. First, part I established the philosophical foundation underlying the idea of generating multiple community benefits through the parks and recreation system planning process. This included the concept of parks and the public realm as an integrated system; the concept of alternative dimensions of parks and recreation systems that could be addressed through the planning process; and the concept of High-Performance Public Spaces.

Part II advocated for a more thoughtful and robust process for parks and recreation system planning, including the integration of methodologies from applied social research and strategic planning. It also proposed that planners spend more time initiating and planning the parks and recreation system master plan (PRSMP) process, including preparation of a readiness audit, project charter, project plan, and preliminary implementation framework.

Part III incorporates the ideas from parts I and II into a step-by-step guide to each major phase of the PRSMP process—analyzing the existing parks and recreation system, conducting a needs assessment, establishing level-of-service (LOS) standards, creating a long-range vision, and developing a realistic, actionable funding and implementation plan. This chapter focuses on the first phase, the existing conditions analysis.

Overview

The purpose of this phase of work is to evaluate existing conditions in order to identify implications for the parks and recreation system, the public realm, and community resiliency and sustainability. For example, the site evaluations may determine that the community has deferred maintenance on its parks and recreation facilities and should focus on correcting deficiencies before acquiring and developing new parkland. Research and discussions with the public works or engineering department may reveal new information, such as the need for additional stormwater treatment or floodwater storage in certain areas of the community or the opportunity to meet recreation needs and stormwater needs on the same site. Investigation into crime rates and safety issues could identify hot spots that might benefit from additional security, nighttime recreation programs, or design modifications in accordance with guidelines for crime prevention through environmental design (CPTED). Parking and transportation issues could be investigated to determine the potential role of parks in providing trail connections, bike-share stations, overflow parking, transit stops, or other multimodal transportation solutions. And discussions regarding housing and economic development could detect opportunities for parks and green spaces to stabilize neighborhoods, improve property values, and catalyze redevelopment. Planners must embark upon the analysis of existing conditions with an open mind in order to recognize real opportunities to increase community sustainability and resiliency; traditional plans, which focus solely on the conditions of the existing parks system, have often had a blind spot regarding such opportunities.

One of my colleagues coined this phase of work as the discovery phase, in which the planning team becomes immersed in discovering everything possible about the existing parks and recreation system as well as all the other dimensions of the project identified in the scope of work. The importance (and fun) of this discovery phase is nicely illustrated in an old episode of the ABC News show *Nightline* titled "The Deep Dive" (aired July 13, 1999; available on YouTube). The show explores how an innovative design process works by asking the global design company IDEO to redesign a shopping cart in a five-day period. Several takeaways from the show are directly applicable to the existing conditions analysis phase of a PRSMP.

First, IDEO assembled a multidisciplinary, collaborative team to address the shopping cart challenge, including an individual with a master's degree in business administration, a linguist, an engineer, a biologist, a marketer, and a psychologist; the company's philosophy was that a multidisciplinary team would provide a much more comprehensive and multidimensional evaluation than would a one-dimensional team. The team then conducted site visits, interviews, and research to better understand the existing uses of shopping carts and associated issues. They visited grocery stores to observe customers' shopping habits and use of carts, interviewed customers and store employees, and conducted research on shopping cart accidents, theft, and related issues. Team members then reconvened to share their findings and collaboratively identified alternative dimensions of shopping cart design, including child safety, shopping, checkout, location of store items, cart theft, privacy (from other shoppers), manufacturing costs, cart nesting, wind resistance (in parking lots), and life-cycle costs. The findings from this deep dive evaluation of existing conditions formed the foundation for the remainder of the shopping cart design process, which led to the revolutionary reinvention of the shopping cart in response to users' needs.

The exact scope of the existing conditions analysis phase of a PRSMP will vary depending on the dimensions included in the scope of work. It is important to remember that this phase is not just a perfunctory check-the-box exercise but is an effort to truly understand conditions, issues, and opportunities to meet residents' parks and recreation needs while also generating economic, social, and environmental benefits for the community, such as increased property values, improved health, and higher resistance to the impacts of climate change. The authors of *Management of Park and Recreation Agencies* refer to this as an "environmental scan" that includes demographic data, social problems, physical resources status and changes, economic data, technology, environmental quality, and political atmosphere.[1] Four of the most common dimensions to be evaluated, discussed in the sections that follow, are the existing and projected demographics; the existing parks and recreation system, including facilities, programs, staffing, and operations; other elements of the public realm, such as transportation, stormwater, utilities, and schools; and community-wide social, environmental, and economic issues.

Existing and Projected Demographics

The purpose of conducting a deep dive into demographics is to better understand the characteristics of the population to be potentially served by the parks and recreation system. This includes not only the current customers of the system but also those who may be underrepresented. Relevant demographic information may include ethnic heritage, age, gender, residence, occupation, income level, religious affiliation, education level, disabilities and health status, and family configuration. These demographics may have implications for residents' needs or preferences for parks and recreation opportunities.

It is important to distinguish between demographic data, projections, and analysis. Demographic *data* reflects existing conditions at the time the data was collected but does not—by itself—reflect trends, issues, or needs that may be relevant to the PRSMP. Most demographic data in the United States is collected by the US Census Bureau (USCB) through censuses, surveys, and estimates. For example, the Decennial Census is conducted every ten years; the Economic Census measures the nation's economy every five years; and the Census of Governments provides data about the nearly 90,000 state and local governments in the United States every five years.

Demographic *projections* try to predict future conditions, which are very important for a long-range PRSMP. The USCB, for example, publishes annual population estimates and demographic components of change, such as births, deaths, and migration, as well as estimates of population size and characteristics based on future demographic trends, including births, life expectancy, and migration patterns.

Several agencies and organizations also provide population projections, as well as an *analysis* or interpretation of the census data, including Esri (Environmental Systems Research Institute), local metropolitan planning organizations (MPOs), state demographers' offices, universities, social service organizations, and others. Also, many communities have planning departments, regional planning councils, and councils of governments that can provide local demographic data. For example, the Parks, Recreation and Cultural Resources System Plan for the City of Raleigh, North Carolina, included demographic projections and analysis from the USCB, the city's comprehensive plan, Esri, and the Capital Area MPO.

The demographics analysis may have significant implications for the parks and recreation system. For example, in one community we found that 14 percent of residents' incomes were below the 2015

Federal Poverty Level (FPL) of $11,770 for a family of four, and a majority of households (58 percent) earned less than the basic cost of living, known as the ALICE (Asset Limited, Income Constrained, Employed) threshold of $24,250. In other words, these were working households struggling to meet basic survival needs including housing, child care, food, transportation, and health care. The implications for the parks and recreation system included the following:

- A majority of residents did not have disposable income to spend on parks and recreation fees, so affordability would be important.
- A majority of residents did not have reliable private transportation, so walkable access to local parks and recreation facilities would be important.
- A majority of residents could not afford to take vacations, join fitness clubs, or attend private recreation facilities, so public parks and recreation facilities might be their only choice for staycations, exercise, and recreation.
- Many residents had a need for accessible social, educational, and health-care programs, so the parks and recreation department might wish to offer referrals to, or even provide space for, social service agencies in its recreation centers.
- Many residents had a need for affordable child care, so the parks and recreation department might wish to partner with other agencies, provide space in its recreation centers, or both, for child care.

These findings were incorporated into the existing conditions analysis and compared with the findings from the next phase of work, the needs assessment. Both the existing conditions analysis and the needs assessment then informed the community's long-range vision and implementation strategy. As a result, recommendations were made to provide more things to do at existing parks; offer discounted, subsidized recreation programs; provide affordable child care at the city's recreation center; and partner with workforce training agencies to offer job skills programs at city buildings. This is just one example of how a deep dive into demographic data can yield important information regarding community needs, which can then lead to recommendations for improving community resiliency and sustainability through the parks and recreation system.

Existing Parks and Recreation System

For most communities, the focus of the PRSMP is the existing parks and recreation system, including physical resources, programs, staffing, and operations. Many parks and recreation professionals believe that recreation *programs* are the most important component of the system because they determine the types and characteristics of facilities required. For example, swim lessons may require only a simple lap pool; competitive swimming and diving may require a diving well and a fifty-meter pool; and family recreation programs and activities may require a water park. Many landscape architects and planners, however, believe that the physical resources are the most important components of the system because they provide the basic infrastructure for recreation programs; require the greatest capital investment; and must be designed to accommodate rapidly changing trends, needs, and programs. Thus, an evaluation of the parks and recreation system must include both programs *and* resources—particularly for the purpose of identifying opportunities for greater resiliency and sustainability as well as operations, maintenance, and staffing.

Physical Resources

An evaluation of a system's physical resources—possibly including parks, civic spaces, recreation centers, aquatics centers, sports complexes, environmental lands, trails, or other lands and facilities owned and managed by the community—begins with the collection of available data and the development of a GIS (geographic information system) base map for the project. As an example, the Atlanta-based firm Perez Planning + Design requests the following list of base map data from its clients at the beginning of the discovery or existing conditions phase of PRSMP projects:

- Existing and future land-use map
- Water bodies, canals, rivers, streams, and creeks

- Water rise studies
- Streets
- Transit
- Bikeways and trails
- Rights-of-way
- Parcel data (preferably linked to land and building value data)
- Environmentally sensitive areas and conservation areas
- Flooding areas
- Areas of high crime
- Tree canopy
- Utility corridors
- Current inventory of parks and recreation facilities (including acreage and facilities)
- Current inventory of schools, churches, and nonprofits (Boys & Girls Club, YMCA, etc.)
- Current inventory of private recreation facilities
- Current inventory of vacant and derelict sites
- Historic and cultural resources

Most of this data is available from local municipal or county parks and recreation agencies, planning departments, property appraisers' offices, the MPO, the Federal Emergency Management Agency (FEMA), and other local, state, or federal agencies.

The basic evaluation of the parks and recreation system begins with creation of an evaluation form and scoring method, based on agreed-upon evaluation criteria. Parks and recreation facility evaluation criteria usually include categories such as aesthetics, functionality, maintenance, access, comfort, and uses. Depending on the dimensions selected for the project, additional evaluation criteria should be included related to community resiliency and sustainability. For example, our typical evaluation form includes criteria related to stormwater treatment, energy efficiency, transit, economic development, and community health (see appendix 4).

Typically, the planning team visits each site to complete the site evaluation forms, using the agreed-upon scoring method. To illustrate, we use a scoring scale of 1 (needs improvement) to 5 (exceeds expectations). It is important to note that expectations may vary widely among systems; we're working with one community, for example, that believes that a $50,000 prefabricated restroom building is acceptable, while another community just constructed a custom-designed, $300,000 restroom building of the same size! Because staff and consultants can be unconsciously biased in their evaluations, it is often helpful to invite members of the project steering committee, members of the public, or both to participate in the evaluations, as seen, for example, in the flyer for the Hunter's Creek Community Park in figure 7-1. This has the added benefit of building support and credibility for the project from the very beginning.

The findings from the site evaluations can be charted and mapped to show the cumulative scores for each facility and each criterion as well as differences in scores between geographic areas. Figure 7-2 shows the scoring and mapping of the PRSMP site evaluations for the City of Smyrna, Georgia, conducted by Perez Planning + Design. The vertical columns indicate the scores of individual parks, identifying areas for improvement within each park; the horizontal

Figure 7-1: Hunter's Creek Community Park Evaluation Event, Orange County, Florida

(Photo *A* courtesy of David Barth; *B* courtesy Hunter's Creek Community Association, Inc.)

(Figure 7-1 *continued*)

B

Chart Legend

1.0 Needs Improvements

5.0 Exceeding Expectations

Parks · Park System Benchmark

Evaluation Criteria

	Lake Court Park	Liberty Park	North Cooper Lake Park	Ridgeforest Park	Riverline Park	Rose Garden Park	Spring Road Linear Park	Taylor Brawner Park	Tolleson Park	Twentieth Century Veterans Memorial	Village Green + Community Center	Ward Park (Lattanzi Field)	Whitfield Park	AVERAGE
TOTAL SYSTEM AVERAGES	**2.6**	**3.4**	**2.7**	**2.5**	**2.4**	**2.5**	**2.5**	**3.6**	**2.3**	**3.6**	**4.4**	**1.9**	**2.4**	**2.6**
PROXIMITY, ACCESS, AND LINKAGES	**2.0**	**3.2**	**2.0**	**2.3**	**2.0**	**2.6**	**3.0**	**3.3**	**1.5**	**4.4**	**4.0**	**2.0**	**2.4**	**2.4**
Visibility from a distance	2	5	2	2	2	4	3	2	1	5	5	2	4	2.9
Ease in walking to the park	2	5	3	3	2	3	5	2	2	5	5	3	4	3.3
Transit Access	-	-	1	1	1	-	5	2	1	-	1	2	-	1.9
Clarity of information/signage	2	1	2	1	2	2	2	4	1	3	3	1	2	1.8
ADA Compliance	2	4	3	4	3	2	2	5	2	5	5	2	1	2.5
Lighting	2	1	1	3	2	2	1	5	2	4	5	2	1	1.9
COMFORT AND IMAGE	**2.4**	**4.3**	**2.7**	**2.9**	**2.7**	**2.4**	**2.7**	**4.4**	**2.1**	**3.9**	**4.8**	**1.6**	**2.6**	**2.8**
First Impression / overall attractiveness	2	4	3	3	3	2	3	5	2	5	5	2	2	2.8
Feeling of safety	2	5	4	3	3	2	2	4	2	5	5	2	3	3.0
Cleanliness/overall quality of maintenance (Exterior Site)	2	4	3	3	3	2	3	5	2	5	5	2	3	3.0
Cleanliness/overall quality of maintenance (Facilities Interior)	3	-	-	-	3	2	-	5	2	-	5	1	-	2.8
Comfort of places to sit	2	-	2	3	1	2	3	3	2	2	4	1	2	2.2
Protection from bad weather	2	-	1	1	2	5	1	5	2	1	5	1	2	2.1
Evidence of management / stewardship (Exterior Site)	3	4	3	4	3	2	4	5	3	5	5	1	3	3.1
Evidence of management / stewardship (Facility(ies) Interior)	3	-	-	-	3	2	-	5	2	-	5	1	-	3.1
Ability to Easily Supervise and Manage the Park or Facility (Interior)	-	-	-	-	3	-	-	2	1	-	5	3	-	2.5
Condition and Effectiveness of any Equipment or Operating Systems	3	-	3	3	3	3	-	5	3	4	4	2	3	3.2
USES, ACTIVITIES, AND SOCIABILITY	**2.6**	**3.0**	**3.0**	**2.0**	**2.8**	**3.2**	**1.8**	**3.2**	**3.3**	**2.8**	**4.7**	**1.5**	**2.0**	**2.4**
Mix of uses/things to do	3	-	3	2	3	4	1	3	5	2	5	1	2	2.6
Level of activity	3	-	2	2	3	3	3	4	4	2	5	1	2	2.7
Sense of pride/ownership	3	3	3	3	4	3	3	5	3	5	5	2	3	3.0
Programming Flexibility	3	-	4	2	3	4	1	3	4	4	5	1	2	2.4
Ability of Facility to Effectively Support Current Organized Programming	-	-	4	-	2	4	-	2	3	-	3	3	-	2.9
Marketing or Promotional Efforts for the Facility or Activities	1	-	2	1	2	1	1	2	1	1	5	1	1	1.3
ENVIRONMENTAL SUSTAINABILITY	**2.3**	**3.0**	**3.0**	**2.7**	**2.3**	**2.3**	**2.5**	**3.0**	**2.3**	**3.3**	**4.0**	**2.3**	**2.5**	**2.7**
Stormwater Management	3	-	4	3	3	2	3	4	3	4	4	3	3	3.2
Multi-modal Capacity	1	3	2	3	2	2	2	3	2	4	5	3	2	2.5
Facility Energy Efficiency	3	-	3	2	2	3	-	2	2	2	3	1	-	2.3
BUILDINGS AND ARCHITECTURE	**3.5**	-	-	-	**2.4**	**2.0**	-	**4.3**	**2.1**	-	**4.4**	**2.1**	-	**2.9**
Image and Aesthetics	2	-	-	-	2	1	-	5	2	-	5	2	-	2.7
Clarity of Entry and Connections to Park	2	-	-	-	2	2	-	5	3	-	4	3	-	2.8
Interior Layout	5	-	-	-	3	2	-	5	3	-	5	3	-	3.2
Interior Finishes and Furniture and Equipment	5	-	-	-	3	2	-	5	1	-	5	1	-	3.0
Functioning Dimensions of spaces	3	-	-	-	2	2	-	3	2	-	4	2	-	2.7
Building Enclosure	4	-	-	-	2	2	-	4	2	-	5	2	-	3.2
Building Systems	4	-	-	-	3	3	-	4	3	-	4	2	-	3.4
Energy and Sustainability	3	-	-	-	2	2	-	3	1	-	3	2	-	2.3

Figure 7-2: City of Smyrna, Georgia, site evaluations summary and map (Perez Planning + Design)

(Figure 7-2 *continued*)

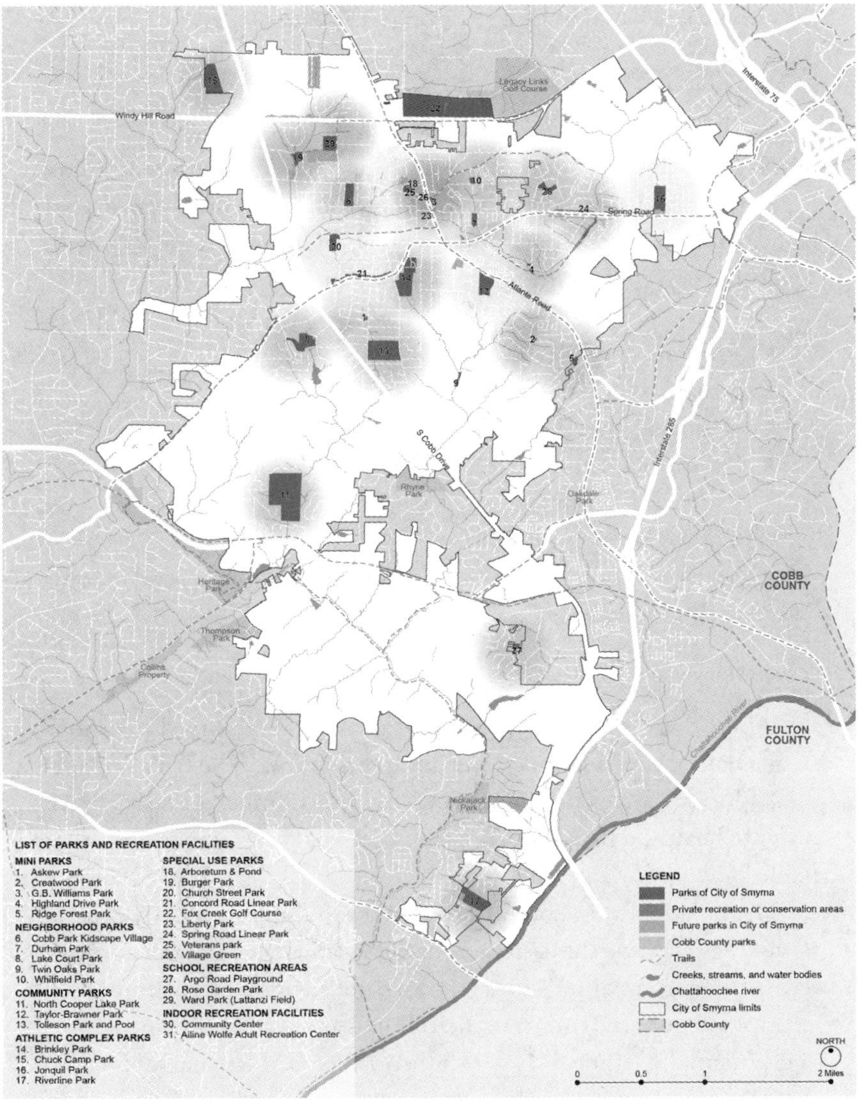

rows show the scores for each specific criterion, identifying how well the entire parks system is performing as a whole.

Programs

Similar to the evaluation of physical resources, the programming evaluation begins with the collection of data, most of which should be available from the parks and recreation agency or department. Typical program data includes the following:

- Program guides
- Participation rates
- Resident versus nonresident data
- Satisfaction surveys
- Costs and revenues
- Cost recovery goals
- Participation trends (e.g., increase or decrease in attendance for each program)

Program data should also be collected from other agencies, including data related to resiliency and sustainability dimensions such as social services and job training programs. The City of Sarasota, Florida, for example, partners with a number of agencies to provide health, education, and social service programs to residents (table 7-1).

The breadth and depth of program evaluation is directly related to the organizational mission, as discussed further in the next chapter; if the organization's mission does not include job training, for example, should the program include existing job training programs and potential partners? This reinforces the need to clearly state the extent of the program evaluation in the project's scope of services.

In addition to collecting data regarding existing programs, it is helpful to research local and national programming trends. PROS Consulting, for example, often references the Sports and Fitness Industry Association's annual *Sports, Fitness, and Leisure Activities Topline Participation Report*, which includes data regarding national trends in sports and fitness participation, core versus casual participation, and activities by generation. PROS also uses local sport and

Table 7-1
Health, Education, and Social Service Programs Offered at the Robert L. Taylor Community Complex, Sarasota, Florida

Organizations	Services
Brothers and Sisters Doing the Right Thing	Tutoring, homework help
Senior Friendship Center	Senior programming including transportation, group exercise, and free lunch five days per week
SRQCommit Men	Men's group offered weekly
Newtown–North Sarasota Redevelopment Office (NRO), Community Redevelopment Agency (CRA)	Monthly CRA board meetings
Community Health Action Team (CHAT)	Community gardening and healthy eating programming for community members
Greater Newtown Centennial Steering Committee	Planning sessions for Newtown Centennial Celebration activities
Career Entrepreneur Opportunity (CEO)	Ten-week free Introduction to Business classes
Sarasota County Technical Institute (SCTI)	Ceremony for graduates of GED course at SCTI
Safe Children Coalition	Fostering and adoption information fair, Child Abuse Awareness Month Proclamation Ceremony
Law Enforcement/Ministerial Focus Group	Meets first Wednesday of each month to discuss community issues and plan community events
Caretakers Focus Group	Meets second Wednesday of each month to discuss issues of caregiving in the community
Goodwill (Community Expo)	Annual Community Health Expo in the spring
UN Women	Holds free movie nights; also hosted International Women's Day Tea
NAACP	Hosts Youth Council Breakfast and Men of Valor Breakfast
SMA (Basketball)	Hosts Boys and Girls varsity and junior varsity home games
United Way Suncoast Vita Program	Free tax preparation service
Brotherhood of Men	Mentoring program for boys
City of Sarasota	Community engagement
We Are For Kids	Works with the HARD:NOC teen program
Booker High School	Speech on underage drinking prevention
All Faiths Food Bank	Free healthy cooking classes for kids
SCF Collegiate School	Information night concerning new courses at State College of Florida

(*continued*)

Table 7-1 *(continued)*

Organizations	Services
Visible Men Academy	Free school for young men
Sarasota County Emergency Services	Hurricane planning media event
Sarasota County Area Transit (SCAT)	Ten-year Transit Development Plan/public forum
Eternal Bread of Life	Provides free food and Thanksgiving dinners to the community
Florida Department of Juvenile Justice	Community conversation
Newtown Beautification Committee	Planted trees and flowers in the community
SRQ County Health District	Affordable Care Act Navigators helped community access health-care website
Asolo Repertory Theatre	Free live presentation of *Romeo and Juliet*
Amaryllis Park Neighborhood Association	Community conversation and information sessions
Sarasota Police District	New Beginnings II/Partners in Blue
Newtown Historic District	Community conversation and information sessions
Florida League of Cities	Florida League of Cities, hosted by the City of Sarasota
Big Brothers/Big Sisters	Recruiting and meet and greet sessions for students and mentors
Sarasota Scullers Rowing Team	Community Rowing Program at Nathan Benderson Park, teaming with the HARD:NOC Teen Program

Source: City of Sarasota Parks and Recreation District.

leisure market data provided by Esri, which analyzes the likelihood that residents will participate in certain activities when compared with national averages. The National Recreation and Park Association (NRPA) also regularly publishes articles and reports about parks and recreation trends.

Criteria for evaluating existing programs will vary depending on the mission and values of the agency. For example, cost recovery—the amount of costs recovered through participation fees—may be important for one community but not for another (see figure 7-3). Similarly, increased or decreased participation in individual programs may or may not be significant. Other program evaluation criteria may include a program life-cycle analysis (see figure 7-4) and evaluation of core versus secondary and tertiary programs. However,

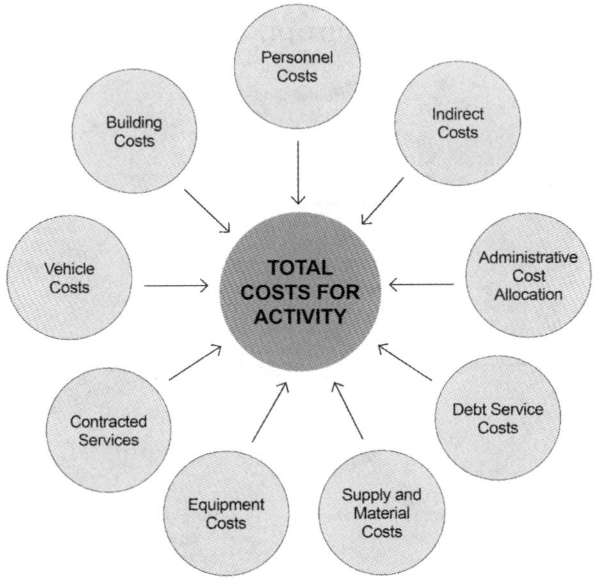

Figure 7-3: Cost recovery evaluation (PROS Consulting, Inc.)

full evaluation of existing programs cannot be completed without collecting data from the needs assessment phase of the PRSMP—including resident surveys, interviews, focus groups, and public meetings—as discussed in the next chapter.

Other Elements of the Public Realm

The extent of data collection and evaluation of other elements of the public realm—such as streets, bikeways and trails, stormwater facilities, and utilities—will depend on the dimensions selected for the PRSMP process and the scope of work outlined in the project plan. At a very minimum, planners should review secondary data—such as master plans, reports, and studies—that may have implications for the PRSMP. These may include comprehensive transportation master plans, stormwater master plans, climate change studies, public school master plans, health assessments, sustainability and resiliency plans, sea-level and climate change studies, and others. By understanding the existing conditions and challenges facing other elements of the public realm, parks planners can identify opportunities to generate greater community-wide benefits through the PRSMP.

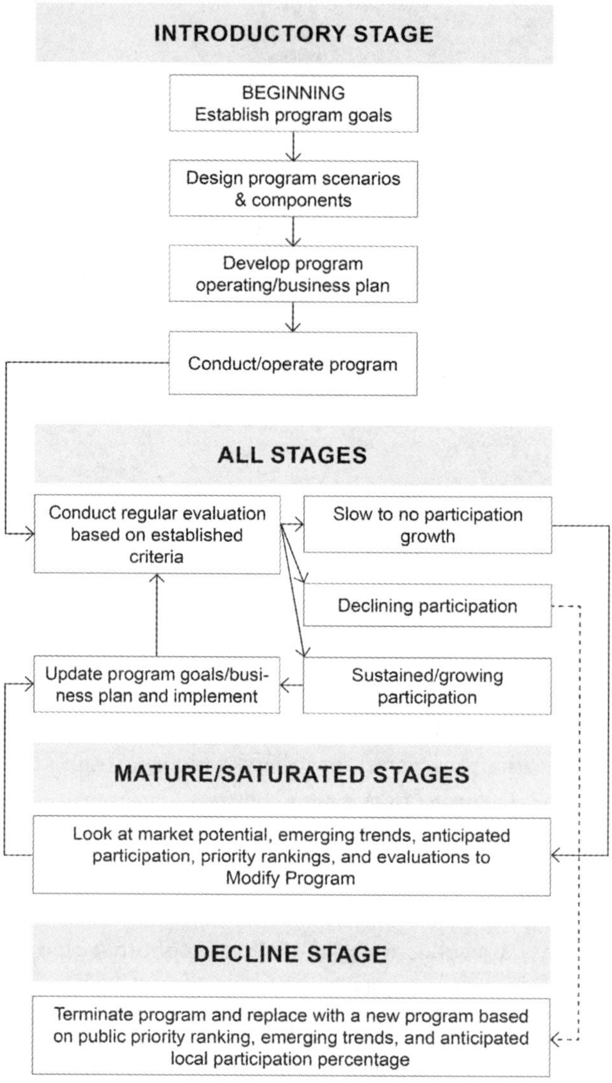

Figure 7-4: Program life-cycle analysis (PROS Consulting, Inc.)

To illustrate, in one community we determined that large community parks could serve as trailheads for the community bikeways and trails network; many parks could be restored to provide native wildlife habitat; and other parks could be used to relieve flooding in low-lying neighborhoods or treat stormwater before it is released to coastal waters. We also found that some parks could play a role in mitigating the anticipated impacts of climate change and sea-level rise through shoreline stabilization, wetland protection, additional tree planting, reduction of pervious surfaces, shade structures, and additional flood storage.

In addition to collecting and reviewing reports and studies, it is also helpful to meet with engineers, planners, and other subject matter experts to gain a deeper understanding of the other elements of the public realm and their potential relationship with the parks and recreation system. These experts could also be invited to serve on the steering or advisory committee, attend the project kickoff meeting, and participate in the planning process.

Community-wide Social, Environmental, and Economic Issues

Gaining an in-depth understanding of community-wide environmental, economic, and social issues is critical to identifying opportunities to generate multiple benefits for the community. As with the data collection process for other elements of the public realm, much of the necessary information can be gleaned by reading reports and studies and speaking with subject matter experts.

Many universities offer economic and business data from research centers, such as the University of Florida's Bureau of Economic and Business Research. Health-related data is usually available from the local city or county health department; crime and safety information can be obtained from local law enforcement agencies; and stormwater or flooding maps and data may be available from the local engineering or public works department. Online blogs, newspapers, and magazine articles provide a wealth of information regarding local trends and issues such as sea-level rise, habitat loss, population growth, income disparities, transportation challenges, and homelessness. For example, we found numerous articles in the local Sarasota newspapers that chronicled the city's transportation, homelessness, and development issues, all of which had implications for the city's PRSMP. Government and nonprofit agencies also issue reports regarding various community-wide issues, such as the United Way's ALICE report (mentioned earlier in the chapter) and reports issued by local health departments.

A case in point is Seattle's 2017 Parks and Open Space Plan, which—in addition to evaluating demographics, the city's parks and recreation system, and recreation demand, participation, and trends—evaluated community satisfaction, walkability, equity and health, income and poverty, and bus and transit access to parks and open space. The plan states:

> There are many citywide plans that directly relate to recreation, community and environmental goals. . . . The *2011 Development Plan* and the *2014 Parks Legacy Plan* (PLP) developed goal statements to embody the values of access, opportunity, and sustainability. Seattle's *Climate Action Plan* provides a framework for meeting Seattle's climate protection goals, such as the goal of becoming carbon neutral by 2050, and urban forest restoration goals are outlined in the *Green Seattle Partnership Strategic Plan*.[2]

Similarly, because of the city council's strategic goals and priorities, a proposal for North Carolina's Asheville Parks, Recreation, Cultural Arts and Greenways Master Plan included a health impact assessment, an economic impact assessment, and a sustainability and green infrastructure assessment in the existing conditions analysis phase. Other PRSMPs have also evaluated stormwater drainage and flooding, vulnerability to sea-level rise, education, crime rates and safety, homelessness and affordable housing, workforce training, natural resource management, and many of the other dimensions listed in chapter 2.

Interim Summary Report

The findings from the discovery or existing conditions phase should be summarized in a succinct interim report that discusses the implications for the PRSMP. In other words, what are the big ah-ha's from the analysis—what meaningful and useful information have you learned that will inform the next phases of the planning project? Applied social science research methods tell us that it is important to note the differences between the data, findings, and conclusions. The *data*—such as the population and historical growth rate of a community—tells us only the existing conditions at a single point in time. The *findings* from the data—such as the potential need for additional parks or indoor recreation centers to serve the needs of a growing population of seniors—merely suggest a possible interpretation or implication. But planners have to be careful not to rush to *conclusions* at this early stage in the process; the initial findings will have to be tested and explored more fully through the needs assessment, visioning process, and other phases of the project.

A potential outline for the interim report might include the following:

1. Introduction, methodology
2. Dimensions of the analysis
3. Demographics analysis
4. Parks and recreation system findings
    - Existing parks and recreation facilities
    - Programs
    - Maintenance
    - Staffing and organization
    - Accreditation
5. Findings regarding other elements of the public realm
    - Streets
    - Bikeways and trails
    - Stormwater treatment facilities
    - Utilities
    - Schools
    - Libraries
6. Community-wide issues
    - Social
    - Educational
    - Economic
    - Health
    - Transportation
    - Stormwater, flooding
    - Sea-level rise, climate change
7. Preliminary implementation framework (PIF)
8. Appendixes

I like to include the PIF in the existing conditions analysis because this is typically the first interim report prepared by the planning team, and it offers the opportunity to initiate discussions about implementation. For example, I recently presented the interim findings from a PRSMP existing conditions analysis and PIF at a city council meeting, which led to discussions about how the community could help solve and fund community resiliency and sustainability issues through the parks and recreation system. These early discussions enriched and informed our work during the long-range visioning phase of the project and helped build support for the eventual adoption and implementation of the PRSMP.

The appendixes of the report should include references, links, and, if applicable, copies of critical data or reports collected throughout the first phase of the PRSMP. Because of the sheer volume of the data collected, it should all be filed in an accessible location such as Dropbox or another cloud-based file hosting service. While such data collection, management, and analysis are very time-consuming, they will provide the foundation for the eventual recommendations that will contribute to greater community resiliency and sustainability.

This includes an inventory of facilities, an organizational chart, a department strategic plan, a program guide, capital and operations budgets, cost recovery goals, LOS standards, policies, and existing partnerships. (Much of this data is required for accreditation or reaccreditation by CAPRA—the Commission for Accreditation of Parks and Recreation Agencies—if that is a desired dimension of the PRSMP.)

If the evaluation of existing conditions is analogous to taking a deep dive, then I think of the interim existing conditions report as the first opportunity to come up for air in the PRSMP process. It's a time to reflect on the initial findings and conclusions; make adjustments to the approach, if necessary; and prepare for the needs assessment, the next phase of the project. Don't be surprised if the existing conditions analysis reveals significant new dimensions of the PRSMP that have not yet been considered; examples from previous projects have included issues related to race relations, affordable housing, schools, transportation, and interagency conflicts. In response, planners may wish to broaden the scope of the PRSMP, particularly the needs assessment, as discussed in the next chapter.

08 THE NEEDS ASSESSMENT

Once you've done the hard work of building a foundation with the analysis of existing conditions and, it is hoped, discovered some new, interesting dimensions to the role parks and recreation resources can fill in a community, it's time to move on to the needs assessment. This is the heart of the parks and recreation system master plan (PRSMP) process and is typically the catalyst for most plans. Elected officials and staff want to know, "What do our residents want or need from our parks and recreation system?" The answer might include parkland, programs, athletics facilities, indoor recreation centers, aquatics facilities, trails and bikeways, natural areas, water access, and other elements of the public realm.

Timing is a special consideration for the needs assessment. As discussed in chapter 1, the new approach to PRSMPs proposes that, ideally, parks and recreation needs assessments be conducted simultaneously with other public realm needs assessment processes—such as comprehensive transportation plans and stormwater master plans—to create a plexus or integrated system. Most public realm needs assessment processes use the same types of quantitative and qualitative techniques, and an integrated needs assessment process may lead to more collaborative planning. However, if an integrated process isn't possible, representatives from the other subsystems of the public realm should be invited to participate in the PRSMP.

As with the evaluation of existing conditions, the needs assessment process should solicit public input regarding the entire public realm system as well as community-wide resiliency and sustainability needs. Many communities have established broad citywide goals in their comprehensive plan or strategic plan, which could form the basis for inquiry. For example, the needs assessment process for Germantown, Tennessee, solicited input regarding community values, safety, education, heritage and culture, cleanliness, health, transportation, sustainability (ecological, fiscal, and social equity), volunteerism, partnerships, and other topics in addition to typical parks and recreation needs. The City of Sarasota, Florida, included questions in its surveys about community challenges that could potentially be addressed through the city's parks and recreation system, including the following:

- Community safety
- Flooding
- Homelessness
- Lack of workforce housing
- Limited access to healthy foods such as fresh fruits, vegetables, and whole foods
- Limited access to multimodal transportation options (e.g., sidewalks, bikeways, trails, transit)
- Limited adult education
- Poor health
- Poverty
- Preservation of natural areas
- Attracting and retaining youth and young families
- Sea-level rise
- Substandard childhood education
- Traffic congestion
- Water quality

The specific scope and dimensions of the needs assessment should be determined during development of the project plan, as discussed in chapter 5.

Needs Assessment Methodology and Techniques

Regardless of the scope of the needs assessment process, the new approach to parks and recreation system planning proposes a more rigorous, scientific methodology than that used by many communities. Needs assessments are often scrutinized by the public, stakeholders, and elected officials; parks planners need to be able to defend their methodology, data collection process, and findings. As mentioned in chapter 4, if done correctly, a needs assessment is a type of applied social research that involves developing a research design, gathering and analyzing the data collected from various sources, and using the results to inform policy and program development.

Also as mentioned in chapter 4, in our practice we use a mixed-methods, triangulated approach to needs assessments, which compares the findings from quantitative, qualitative, and secondary research techniques and data to identify top priorities. At the risk of oversimplification, quantitative research focuses on measuring or calculating the data (numbers), while qualitative research focuses on the meaning of the data (words); both types of research generate primary data collected directly from the target population. Most types of research yield both qualitative and quantitative data—although one type may predominate—as illustrated in figure 8-1.

Once the data is collected and analyzed, we compare the findings from various needs assessment techniques to identify top priorities. For example, we compare the findings from a mail survey—the most

● = Predominant
○ = Minor

	Quantitative Technique	Qualitative Technique
PRIMARY DATA		
Statistically-Representative Mail Survey	●	○
Level-of-Service Analysis	●	○
On-line Survey	●	○
Site Evaluations	○	●
Interviews	○	●
Focus Groups	○	●
Public Meetings	○	●
Interactive Web Site	○	●
SECONDARY DATA		
Census Data	●	○
Comprehensive Plans	○	●
Previous Studies	○	●

Figure 8-1: Research techniques typically used in parks and recreation needs assessments (Barth Associates, LLC)

statistically valid quantitative technique available—with the findings from workshops, interviews, focus groups, level-of-service (LOS) analyses, and other techniques to recognize consistent priorities.

Following is a discussion of each of the most common types of needs assessment techniques used in PRSMPs. Many of these techniques can be used to determine not only parks and recreation needs and priorities but also priorities for other elements of the public realm and community-wide issues.

Primary Data—Predominantly Qualitative

The qualitative needs assessment techniques used most often in parks and recreation planning include site evaluations of parks and recreation facilities; stakeholder interviews and focus group meetings; public meetings; and interactive websites. Following are discussions of each technique.

Site Evaluations

Site evaluations, discussed in the previous chapter, can also be used as a needs assessment tool; they are primarily a qualitative technique, based on the subjective opinions of the evaluators. In addition to helping planners understand existing conditions, they can be used to hypothesize the potential need for improvements to existing parks and recreation facilities. For example, a lack of shade or weather protection may indicate the need for additional trees, shelters, or shade covers. An overabundance of fenced and locked athletics fields may indicate the potential need for more multipurpose open lawn areas. The other needs assessment techniques can be used to confirm or disprove the findings from the site evaluations.

Interviews and Focus Groups

Interviews and focus group meetings provide the opportunity for parks planners to speak directly with key stakeholders about parks and recreation issues and priorities. Typical stakeholders include elected officials, department heads, business leaders, sports association representatives, youth and seniors' groups, environmental and health advocates, and others with insights regarding community needs and priorities. Effort should also be made to be as inclusive as possible, involving youth groups, seniors, ethnic minorities, and other typically underrepresented populations. The Raleigh, North Carolina, PRSMP process included focus groups for Hispanics (including a translator), the arts, culture and history, outdoor adventure, sustainability, and other areas of interest to the community.

The process begins with identification of the key stakeholders to be interviewed. Leon Younger of PROS Consulting, for instance, advocates for identifying "the one hundred most influential people in the community" to get their input and to raise broad community awareness and support for the process. Another approach is to identify all potential partners who may be involved in the eventual implementation of the plan. Good resources for identification of prospective participants include elected officials, senior management, department heads, steering committee or board members, and subject matter experts for each dimension of the PRSMP.

Once a list of prospective participants has been identified, they can be designated for either one-on-one interviews or focus group meetings. The one-on-one interviews are typically reserved for elected officials, senior administrators, or others who (1) can't legally meet at the same time without public notice or (2) may wish to discuss politically sensitive or confidential information during the interview. Focus group participants are those with similar interests, such as business groups, youth athletics groups, seniors, and teens.

Each participant should be personally invited via e-mail, phone, or mail. A good practice is to set up a schedule in one-hour increments—which is enough time to gather information needed without taking up too much of participants' valuable time—and fill in the time slots as participants confirm their attendance. Whenever possible, the interviews and focus group meetings should be scheduled in a single location, such as a city hall or community center, to make the most efficient use of planners' time.

Our typical interview questions roughly parallel the PRSMP process, beginning with questions about the planning process and concluding with questions about funding and implementation.

1. *Review of scope and schedule:* Do you have any questions about the project scope or methodology? Are there any additional meetings, workshops, presentations, or other outreach efforts that we should consider for your community?
2. *Needs and priorities:* On the basis of what you know, see, and hear about the community, what do you believe are residents' parks and recreation needs? Of these needs, what are your top three priorities?
3. *Broader issues:* What broader social, environmental, or economic issues could be addressed through your parks and recreation system?
4. *Vision:* Describe your long-range vision for your parks and recreation system and public realm.
5. *Comparable communities:* Are there any parks and recreation systems that you've visited that are good examples of your vision?
6. *Funding and implementation:* Assuming that the parks and recreation master plan will identify hundreds of millions of dollars in desired and needed improvements, which of the following funding source or sources would you support?

   Pay-as-you-go
   - General fund or capital improvement program
   - Sales tax
   - Park impact fees
   - Grants
   - User fees
   - Special assessments
   - Other (please specify)

   Borrowing
   - General obligation bonds
   - Revenue bonds
   - Other (please specify)

The interviews are rarely linear, however, and we often digress to discuss parks planning principles and trends, community issues, funding philosophies, and other tangential information. I am constantly impressed with the amount of thoughtful and insightful

Figure 8-2: Focus group meeting (Photo courtesy of David Barth)

information gleaned from interviews and focus group meetings. In addition to identifying needs and priorities, the information can be used to help define the survey questionnaire; continue to refine the preliminary implementation framework; and form the foundation for the long-range vision.

Public Meetings

Public meetings have long been the traditional technique for gathering community input. However, they are potentially one of the least reliable techniques for determining needs, primarily because (1) they are often poorly attended; (2) attendees rarely represent a cross section of the community; and (3) those who do attend are often lobbying for a particular special interest, such as youth athletics fields, pickleball courts, hunting lands, dog parks, or aquatics facilities.

One of my favorite stories is about a public meeting that was held in a local senior center. It was attended primarily by the seniors who were already at the center, participating in the evening programs, and a group of individuals from other cities who were representing a local rodeo organization. Unsurprisingly, the top two parks and recreation priorities from the meeting were a new food-warming table for the senior center and a new rodeo ground for the nonresidents! Another meeting was dominated by local hunters (dressed in full camouflage), seeking the right to hunt on public parkland; and senior pickleball players, requesting additional pickleball courts. Therefore, it is important to compare the findings from the public meetings with the more broadly representative techniques such as the mail survey, online survey, and LOS analysis in order to discern the community's true spending priorities.

Public meeting formats have changed dramatically over the past decade or two. Residents do not have the time or inclination to listen to long presentations; instead they want to show up, voice their opinions, and leave. Therefore, the open house format has gained in popularity, allowing participants to spend as little or as much time as they wish. Our typical open house format generally includes a sign-in table; a brief orientation, often repeated throughout the open house; and three to five interactive stations, such as the following:

- Facility priorities
- Program priorities
- Priority benefits
- Citywide issues and challenges
- Individual park improvements
- Travel preferences to parks (transit, auto, bike, pedestrian)
- Parks that are used most often, and why
- Preferred distance or travel time to different facility types
- Spending priorities
- Support for various funding initiatives including sales tax, bonds, and user fees
- Open stations ("whatever else is on your mind")

Workshop materials should be available in multiple languages, depending on community demographics, and translators should be available when needed.

Public meetings may also include smaller, more personal venues such as homeowners' association meetings, church meetings, condominium association meetings, and other small group gatherings. Planners may also wish to set up booths at festivals and special events. We conducted a teen focus group at a local café, for example, and staffed a booth at a weekly food truck rally. It is important to note, however, that the needs identified at these meetings may be more applicable to a specific neighborhood or geographic area rather than the entire community.

One of the most comprehensive public meeting needs assessment processes was conducted by Los Angeles County, California, in 2016. Led by the firm PlaceWorks, the process involved a forty-person steering committee; eighty-six cities within the county; 3,023 parks; and 178 community engagement workshops. The project's executive summary outlines the extensive preparation for a process of this magnitude.

> A Countywide education and awareness effort informed residents about the Parks Needs Assessment and encouraged them to attend a community workshop in their Study Area. The effort included a robust media component, informational meetings, and a dedicated online presence.
>
> The lead agency in each Study Area was responsible for advertising its local workshop. . . . Each lead agency submitted a community engagement plan describing the efforts they would make to attract participants to its workshop and was given resources such as flyers, logos, and social media hashtags to assist.
>
> Translations of workshop and outreach materials were available in Spanish, Chinese, Korean, and Armenian and were strongly recommended for use in all Study Areas where 15% or more of the population is linguistically isolated. These four languages were selected because they are the dominant languages spoken by the linguistically isolated populations within the Study Areas meeting that criteria.
>
> Workshop facilitators attended an intensive training session and received a 50-page Facilitator Toolkit with Study Area-specific results of the analysis of the five park metrics, community profile information, templates, and other resources needed to host a successful workshop.[1]

Figure 8-3: Public open house (Photos courtesy of David Barth)

While the findings from the workshops were not compared with those from statistically valid surveys, quantitative techniques in the process included LOS metrics for park condition, park access, park amenities, and park acreage. The results of the analysis of the park metrics were combined to determine an overall park need level for each study area, creating a framework for assessing park needs from a countywide perspective.

Interactive Websites

Many communities supplement public workshops by hosting interactive online forums to broaden the opportunities for public input. As with public workshops, the data collected from such forums will not be statistically representative of the community but may provide insights into residents' issues and needs. The data can also be geographically based. Popular interactive sites include MetroQuest, Social Pinpoint, and mySidewalk.

Primary Data—Predominantly Quantitative

While the qualitative techniques yield useful information, they do not generate the type of data analysis desired by many communities in order to determine priority needs. The most commonly used quantitative techniques in parks and recreation planning are mail surveys, online surveys and interactive websites, and LOS analysis, as discussed in the following sections.

Mail Surveys

The mail survey is the most statistically representative needs assessment technique because it is based on a random sample of the target population. For most parks and recreation surveys, the target population is the residents of a town, city, or county. Since surveying all of the residents is prohibitively expensive for most communities, a random sample is an affordable way to determine residents' needs and priorities. The statistical validity of random sampling has long been established.[2]

Random sampling ensures that each member of the population has an equal chance of being selected for the survey. The random sample is generated from a list of all residents' addresses, and surveys are mailed to those selected. Respondents are typically given the option of responding by mail, by telephone, or online.

The most frequently asked question about surveys is "How many responses are needed for statistical validity?," and the answer often surprises people. According to the survey firm ETC Institute, the optimal sample size for most communities in the U.S. is 400–500 completed surveys, resulting in a 95 percent level of confidence and a margin of error between 4.9 percent (for 400 completed surveys) and 4.4 percent (for 500 surveys). This means that the survey will generate the same findings 95 out of 100 times, within ±5 percent; additional survey responses will reduce the margin of error only slightly. A sample size of 800-1000 completed surveys may be required for larger communities with a population over 250,000.

Typically, mail surveys are completed by private survey firms or organizations such as universities. For example, appendix 5 is a sample of a mail survey questionnaire from ETC. Rather than copy a previously prepared survey, however, it is vitally important to take the time to develop a survey instrument (questionnaire) that reflects the specific issues and dimensions that are important to the community. Ron Vine of Ron Vine and Associates notes that "even a statistically valid survey won't be helpful if it doesn't ask the right questions." He recommends that planners first conduct the qualitative needs assessment techniques—such as the interviews, focus group meetings, and public workshops discussed earlier—in order to identify the most important topics or issues for the survey. In other words, "What specifically do we want to learn from the survey?" Such qualitative feedback from residents and stakeholders, he says, provides valuable insights that can be incorporated into the survey questions and will help build credibility for the validity of the survey findings. In applied social research, this is referred to as a deductive approach: "the researcher, on the basis of what is known about a domain [e.g., parks and recreation needs], deduces a hypothesis . . . that must then be subjected to empirical scrutiny" through quantitative techniques such as surveys and LOS analysis.[3]

The steps to prepare the questionnaire, in accordance with the applied social research approach discussed in chapter 4, are as follows:

1. Identify the issues to be researched, including those related to parks and recreation, the greater public realm, and community resiliency and sustainability.
2. Review literature and studies related to these issues, as well as the findings from the qualitative research techniques, such as interviews, focus group meetings, and public workshops.
3. Formulate the general research questions to be asked.
4. Decide on sample size, as discussed earlier.
5. Decide whether the instrument will also be used for other modes of administration, such as face-to-face interviews and focus groups or online surveys.
6. Develop specific survey questions (the survey agency will assist with this step).
7. Review questions and assess "face validity"; that is, do the survey questions adequately reflect "the content of the content in question"?[4]
8. Conduct a pilot test (typically completed by the survey agency).
9. Revise questions as needed; finalize survey instrument.[5]

Ron Vine notes that the order of questions in the survey is important and that the questionnaire should "flow like chapters in a book." For example, questions regarding funding alternatives should not be placed before questions that identify needs; otherwise the survey respondents won't understand what's being funded.

Once the instrument is completed, the survey agency will administer the questionnaire; follow up with nonrespondents; complete a second mailing if the response rate is not adequate to be statistically valid; transform the completed questionnaires into data; enter the data into a statistical analysis program; analyze the data; and provide a survey report that summarizes the data and interprets the findings. It is important that the findings be presented in an easily understood graphic format, to avoid confusion and to strengthen credibility.

To illustrate, ETC generates a chart from its survey findings that is particularly useful in the needs assessment process (figure 8-4).

The chart is generated by combining the findings from three questions to generate a numerical ranking.

1. Please indicate if you or any member of your household has a need for each of the parks and recreation facilities or programs listed.
2. If Yes, please rate all of the facilities and programs on a scale of 5 to 1, where 5 means the needs of your household are 100% met and 1 means 0% met.
3. Which FOUR amenities from the list are most important to your household?

The combined scores for need and importance provide the basis for determining the priority rankings. If a facility or program is important to residents but needs are mostly being met, then the priority is low. Similarly, if the facility or program is not important to most residents—even though the need may be high for a small constituency—the priority is also low. Highest priority is given to facilities or programs that are both important to and needed by the highest percentage of residents.

We worked with ETC and AECOM, an engineering and planning firm, on one of the most ambitious parks and recreation mail surveys conducted in the United States, the Community Leisure Interests Survey for Miami-Dade County. The project was initiated with a staff workshop to determine what staff specifically wanted to find out from the survey, that is, "What do we want to learn that we do not already know?" Staff priorities for the survey included resident input regarding lifestyle (quality-of-life benefits); priorities (parks and recreation facilities and programs); and performance (value of parks for daily life, barriers to participation).

Once the survey team developed a preliminary survey instrument based on staff input, we pilot-tested the survey through four public workshops to ensure that the survey questions were clear to residents. This step is rarely used in needs assessments but generated great benefits. Residents identified questions that were unclear, misleading, or unnecessary. They also helped us identify additional questions that should be asked.

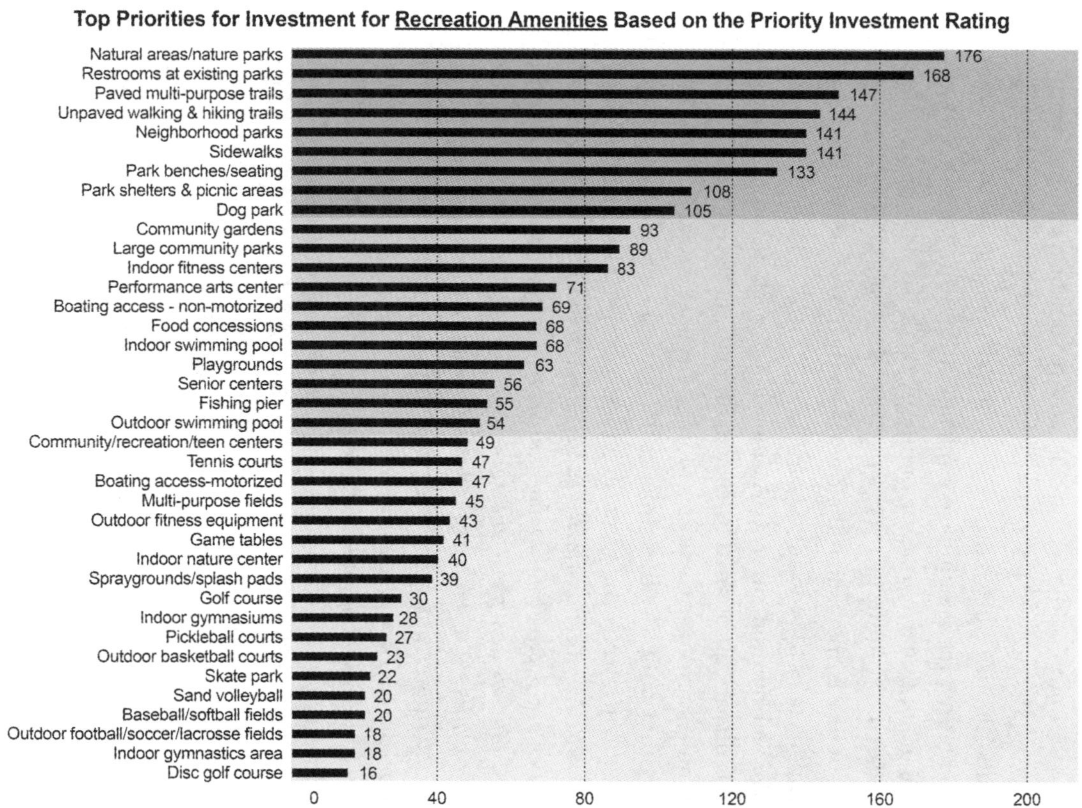

Figure 8-4 Summary chart from a mail survey illustrating top priorities (ETC Institute)

Because of Miami-Dade County's vast size (over 2,400 square miles) and diverse population (almost 2.8 million people), county staff decided to "geo-code" the survey data into 70 neighborhoods, 23 communities, and 8 regions. To ensure statistical validity, a minimum of 100 survey responses were required for each of the 70 neighborhoods. This ultimately required mailings to over 72,000 households, which could be completed in English, Spanish, or Creole by mail, by telephone, or online. A total of 7,888 surveys were completed, resulting in a 95 percent level of confidence; a margin of error of ±1.1 percent at the county level; and a margin of error of ±4.8 percent at the community level.

A final note on surveys: As mentioned earlier, sometimes survey results are questioned by elected officials, staff, residents, or special interest groups when the findings are not consistent with their needs, for example, when athletics fields are shown as a low priority. A frequently occurring scenario goes something like the following.

Results from a statistically valid survey indicate that youth sports facilities are a low priority for most community residents. However, elected officials and parks and recreation agencies are constantly pressured to build more athletics fields by growing youth athletics organizations and travel teams whose members may or may not live in the town, city, or county. Therefore, elected officials and stakeholders may conclude that the survey findings must be wrong.

However, national studies indicate that participation in youth sports is declining in many communities as a result of increasing costs, specialization, and lack of qualified coaches,[6] and far more residents participate in passive recreation activities than in organized sports. For example, a 2013 statewide survey in Florida showed that only 11–15 percent of residents participated in baseball, softball, football, or soccer, while far more people viewed wildlife (49 percent), biked on paved trails (40 percent), picnicked (40 percent), visited historical or archaeological sites (39 percent), or fished (48 percent).[7]

Therefore, it is important to reemphasize that the purpose of surveys and other needs assessment techniques is to collect and analyze data regarding residents' needs, and it is up to elected officials and other policy makers to determine how to use the data. Sometimes this is not a matter of survey validity but a matter of community values and policy. Regardless of needs assessment findings, community leaders may wish to invest in certain facilities because of the perceived benefits. For example, youth sports are an important part of American culture and have long been perceived as being important for youth development.[8] In addition to athletics fields, communities around the United States have invested in hockey rinks, equestrian arenas, tennis complexes, gymnastics centers, and other sports and special use facilities regardless of general public need or demand. One elected official reminded me that the needs and priorities of "his voters" were more important to him than those of the general population.

Online Surveys and Interactive Websites

A modified version of the mail or telephone survey can be conducted using an online survey platform such as SurveyMonkey or through an interactive platform such as MindMixer. While the costs of internet surveys are significantly lower than for other survey methods, the reliability and validity of online surveys are not as high. Internet surveys are not based on a random sample of the target population; anyone with a computer can participate, regardless of where they live, and others may be excluded because of lack of access to a computer. Special interest groups can also influence survey results by encouraging like-minded people to respond. That being said, we often find that the results are similar between mail or telephone and online surveys. Whenever possible, we use both types of surveys, consistent with our mixed-methods, triangulated approach to needs assessments.

LOS Analysis

An LOS analysis can be a useful needs assessment technique if done carefully and thoughtfully. The purpose of the LOS analysis is to determine *potential* deficiencies in parks and recreation facilities on the basis of agreed-upon metrics for park acreage, recreation facilities, access, and other LOS measures. The problem with the technique is that there are no universally accepted LOS standards; each community must establish its own metrics. The National Recreation and Park Association's (NRPA's) *Park, Recreation, Open Space, and Greenway Guidelines*, last published in 1996, notes that "the LOS is merely a quantification of the park and recreation delivery philosophy and policy of a community."[9] However, very few communities update their LOS standards regularly; some LOS metrics have been embedded in community comprehensive plans for years, with little or no backup data or institutional knowledge to explain how or why the metrics were established.

Today, most communities use LOS metrics as a tool to benchmark themselves against similar communities rather than as absolute standards. Two commonly used sources of benchmarks are NRPA Park Metrics (https://www.nrpa.org/publications-research/ParkMetrics/), and the Trust for Public Land ParkScore index (https://parkscore.tpl.org/#sm.0000bnm94owlgctn103afxo2wtump). A more detailed discussion of alternative LOS metrics is provided in the following chapter.

Secondary Data

As mentioned at the beginning of this chapter, our triangulated, mixed-methods approach to needs assessments also includes the use of secondary data (information that has already been gathered by others) in addition to primary qualitative and quantitative data.

Comprehensive plans are one important source of secondary data because they typically include previously determined parks and recreation principles, goals, objectives, and LOS metrics. For example, a common finding is that a community is not meeting the acreage or facilities level of service established in its comprehensive plan. If the primary data indicates a high-priority need for more parkland or facilities, then the comprehensive plan metrics help support those findings.

Comprehensive plans are also often the repository of the community-wide vision, mission, and needs of other elements of the public realm. For example, New York City's plaNYC includes six sections that all have implications for parks, recreation, and the public realm.

- Land, including housing, open space, and brownfields
- Water, including water quality and water network
- Transportation, including congestion and state of good repair
- Energy
- Air quality
- Climate change

Census data is another source of secondary data, providing insights into residents' needs using demographics such as age, ethnicity, and level of income. However, as discussed in the previous chapter, it is important not to make assumptions based solely on census data and projections; this can lead to stereotypical conclusions such as "We need more shuffleboard courts because our senior population is increasing." A better use of census data is to hypothesize needs (similar to the use of site evaluations as a needs assessment tool); help validate other needs assessment findings, such as the need for additional youth programs or bilingual marketing materials; or as a basis for further analysis. For example, when combined with market segmentation data such as Esri's Tapestry Segmentation, census data can be used to "understand customers' lifestyle choices, what they buy, and how they spend their free time."[10]

Previously prepared plans and studies can also provide insight into needs, including long-range transportation plans, previous parks and recreation master plans, community-wide strategic plans, climate change vulnerability reports, community health reports, economic development studies, and others. While such studies may not identify specific parks and recreation needs, they often identify community issues or needs that can be addressed—at least in part—through the parks and recreation system. The premise of High-Performance Public Spaces, discussed in chapter 3, is that each public space has the potential to help meet one or more community needs such as flood control, stormwater treatment, neighborhood stabilization, social equity, increased adjacent property values, or others. For example, the City of Fort Lauderdale's PRSMP envisions the use of parks for storage of floodwaters caused by sea-level rise through the use of swales, bioretention, sunken multiuse fields, permeable paving, and grass parking.

Summary

Once data has been collected using the various needs assessment techniques—including primary data from both qualitative and quantitative methods and secondary data from existing sources—the findings can be charted or graphed as shown for the City of Sarasota (figure 8-5). Each dot on the chart indicates the finding of a priority need from a particular needs assessment technique. Needs identified from multiple techniques, including the statistically representative survey, are considered the highest-priority needs for the community. For example, the chart indicates that residents' top amenity priorities for Sarasota residents are nature areas and nature parks, restrooms at existing parks, paved multipurpose trails, unpaved walking and hiking trails, neighborhood parks, and park shelters and picnic areas. Programming priorities include community special events, adult fitness and wellness programs, and nature and environmental education programs. Residents' greatest barrier to usage is not knowing where parks are located, and the top three community-wide challenges that could be addressed by the public realm include traffic congestion, homelessness, and community safety.

At this stage of the PRSMP process, it is critical to build consensus regarding the findings and conclusions from the needs assessment process before moving into subsequent phases; you don't want people questioning the needs assessment methodology, process, or findings during the subsequent visioning or implementation phases. Therefore, we conduct a series of presentations to solicit feedback before proceeding, including meetings with staff, the project steering committee, the public, and elected officials. If there are significant questions or concerns regarding the needs assessment process—or a lack of consensus regarding the findings—then the project should be put on hold until consensus is reached and the key parties all agree to move forward.

Be aware that reaching consensus may require additional research. In one community, for example, we conducted an additional online survey to verify and clarify findings from the mail survey. In another community, parks and recreation staff conducted a series of neighborhood and condominium association workshops to vet the findings from the needs assessment. Regardless of the additional time and effort required, a PRSMP process will not be successful if members of the community—particularly elected officials and key stakeholders—do not believe in the validity of the needs assessment methodology and findings, and the credibility of the conclusions.

	Mail/Telephone Survey	Online Survey (50%+ "need more")	Public/CCNA Workshops (20% or more participants)	Commission Interviews	Level-of-Service Analysis	Site Evaluations
AMENITY PRIORITIES						
Natural areas/nature parks	●	●			●	●
Restrooms at existing parks	●	●	●	●		●
Paved multi-purpose trails	●	●	●	●		
Unpaved walking and hiking trails	●	●	●	●		
Neighborhood parks	●	●	●	●	●	
Sidewalks	●	●				
Park benches/seating	●	●		●		●
Park shelters and picnic areas	●		●	●	●	●
Dog parks	●					
Community gardens		●				
Large community parks		●				
Water access (non-motorized)		●	●			
Community/recreation/teen centers		●			●	●
Improved maintenance				●		●
Safety, better lighting				●		●
Shade				●		●
PROGRAMMING PRIORITIES						
Community special events	●	●				
Adult fitness/wellness	●	●	●			
Nature programs/environmental education	●	●	●			
Movies in the park	●	●				
Outdoor dining	●	●				
Music programs						

Figure 8-5: City of Sarasota Needs Assessment Summary Charts *(continued)*

Figure 8-5 *(continued)*

	Mail/Telephone Survey	Online Survey (50%+ "need more")	Public/CCNA Workshops (20% or more participants)	Commission Interviews	Level-of-Service Analysis	Site Evaluations
BARRIERS TO USAGE (TOP FIVE)						
Not knowing where parks are located	●	●				●
Not feeling safe at parks/facilities	●	●				
Household uses private facilities	●	●				
Lack of parking	●	●				
Facilities are not well-maintained		●				●
COMMUNITY-WIDE CHALLENGES (TOP FIVE)						
Traffic congestion	●	●	●			
Homelessness	●	●	●	●		●
Community safety	●	●	●			
Preservation of natural areas	●	●				
Jobs and job training, economic development			●	●		
Flooding and sea level rise			●	●		
Limited access to multi-modal transportation		●	●			●

09 LEVEL-OF-SERVICE ALTERNATIVES

Of all the needs assessment techniques discussed in the previous chapter, none are as obscure or confusing as parks and recreation level-of-service standards. Unlike LOS standards for other elements of the public realm—such as those in the *Highway Capacity Manual*, published by the Transportation Research Board (see figure 9-1)—there are no universally accepted LOS standards for parks and recreation. The 1996 *Park, Recreation, Open Space, and Greenway Guidelines* from the National Recreation and Park Association (NRPA) states that "we must realize an open space standard is not so much an exemplary measure to be used in some form of comparison or judgement of adequacy or accomplishment, but is an expression of a community consensus of what constitutes an acceptable level of service."[1]

The problem lies, in part, with the "fuzzy language" that we use in parks and recreation planning. I've witnessed staff and citizen committees spend countless hours trying to define meanings and metrics for passive recreation versus active recreation, nature parks versus preserves, open space versus parkland, developable versus undevelopable parkland, and other commonly used—but poorly defined—parks and recreation terms. A related challenge is the lack of consistency in the use of terms; a neighborhood park in one community, for example, may be considered a community park in another. And a third challenge, as suggested earlier, is that no two communities are alike; a community focused on youth sports, for example, could have very different LOS standards from a community concentrating on adult health and wellness.

A case in point are the Blue Zone communities in the United States, which focus on longevity and well-being. The Blue Zones Project, working with *National Geographic*, found that the healthy lifestyle habits shared by people who've lived the longest include

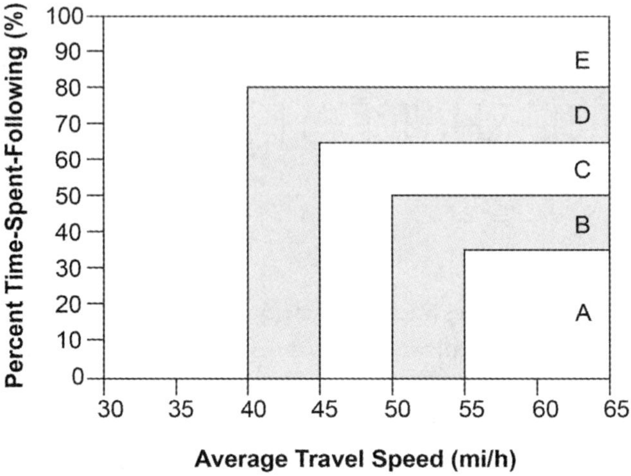

Figure 9-1: Roadway level-of-service (LOS) standards (Transportation Research Board. 2000. *Highway Capacity Manual 2000*. Adapted and reproduced with permission from the National Academy of Sciences, Courtesy of the National Academies Press, Washington, D.C.)

moving naturally, having a purpose, having a routine to reduce stress, using alcohol moderately and regularly, having a predominantly plant-based diet, belonging to a faith-based community, and putting family first.[2] Metrics related to these habits could include the average amount of alcohol consumed by residents, the percentage of residents who eat plant-based diets, the percentage who regularly attend a faith-based service, and the percentage who have active lifestyles. Such metrics are very different from conventional parks and recreation LOS metrics, such as the percentage of residents who play team sports or the number of ball fields per one thousand residents, but they are entirely appropriate for communities focused on sustainability or resiliency-based goals.

Additional challenges to creating any type of absolute LOS standards are variations in population density (the number of people living per square mile), which significantly impact the availability of land and alternative modes of transportation; geography, for example, warm-weather versus cold-weather activities and needs; variations in the popularity of certain sports or activities, often based on community demographics; and differences in urban, suburban, and rural land development patterns and lifestyles. For instance, it is doubtful that residents living on twenty-acre ranchettes would have the same need for dog parks as those living in downtown apartments!

In spite of these challenges and the lack of universal standards, there remains a keen interest in many communities for establishing quantifiable LOS metrics to help determine priority needs. Recently, for example, a city councilman asked me to define the exact LOS for athletics fields that need to be constructed in a community where most residents are fifty-five or older. After we explained all the variables outlined here, however, he still asked us to define a specific number as a basis for decision making!

While parks and recreation LOS metrics cannot be used as absolute standards, they can be helpful in determining if there is a deficiency in parkland or facilities and if parkland, facilities, programs, and funding are distributed equitably across geographic, political, and socioeconomic boundaries. In long-range planning, LOS standards can also help planners determine the general size and location of proposed new parks and recreation facilities needed to accommodate anticipated growth, and they can be incorporated into land development codes and policies (comprehensive plans, impact fees, etc.) to help determine the fair share of parks and recreation capital and operating costs to be borne by the developers of new residential or mixed-use projects. And—as suggested by the Blue Zones example—LOS metrics can be used to measure a community's progress toward sustainability and resiliency goals.

The key to developing useful LOS metrics is first to define community values and philosophies, as suggested in the strategic planning approach discussed in chapter 4, and then to develop the appropriate metrics through a comprehensive planning process, including a robust public review process. As with the mail survey, the metrics should be informed by findings from qualitative techniques such as interviews, focus groups, and public workshops. Preliminary metrics and standards should be reviewed and discussed with agency staff, the project advisory or steering committee, and elected officials in order to build consensus regarding how parks and recreation levels of service should be defined, measured, and counted. Planners should make sure to schedule sufficient time in the process of developing a parks and recreation system master plan (PRSMP) to develop the LOS metrics. This step usually takes a few weeks, but it can take much longer. One of our project steering committees, for example, took several months to discuss, debate, and build consensus regarding the most appropriate LOS metrics for their community.

Common LOS Metrics

Table 9-1 outlines the traditional metrics used to define parks and recreation LOS. Most communities use multiple metrics to determine needs because each metric may be necessary but not sufficient to establish needs by itself. For example, a community may have enough park acreage, but it may not be equitably distributed to be accessible to all residents. Or the park acreage may be equitably distributed, but there may not be enough recreation facilities to serve residents' needs.

Acres per Capita

The "acres of parkland per 1,000 residents" metric is the most common technique for determining whether a community has enough parkland. It is also known as a community's acreage level of service. Acreage LOS is often used as a basis for benchmarking, or comparing a community's parks and recreation system with that of another community, for determining how much parkland should be provided in a new development to meet the needs of new residents, or as a basis for calculating parks and recreation impact fees.

The acreage LOS metric was established in the 1930s by George Butler of the National Recreation Association, who proposed a standard of "10 acres of park and open space per 1,000 population within each city, plus an equal area in parkways, large parks, forests, and the like, either within or adjacent to the city."[3] Butler acknowledged that the standard may vary according to location and other factors and that each community must determine its own standards based on local history, culture, demographics, density, development patterns, and other factors. Acreage LOS often does not address the equitable distribution of the parkland, the capacity or quality of the facilities, or the level of programming provided.

Table 9-1
Traditional Parks and Recreation Level-of-Service Metrics

Metric	Purpose
Acres per capita	To help determine if a community has enough parkland To help determine if parkland is equitably distributed based on population and geography
Facilities per capita	To help determine if a community has enough recreation facilities such as athletics fields, playgrounds, tennis courts, swimming pools, etc. To help determine if the facilities are equitably distributed based on population and geography
Building square footage per capita	To help determine if a community has enough indoor recreation space such as recreation centers, community centers, senior center, or gymnasiums To help determine if the indoor space is equitably distributed based on population and geography
Access distance or time (bike, pedestrian, car, transit)	To help determine if parkland and facilities are easily accessible to residents via preferred modes of transportation including driving, transit, bicycling, or walking
Quality of facilities and experience	To help determine if park facilities are consistent and equitably distributed across geographies
Operating expenditures per acre managed	To help determine if adequate funding is being provided for effective operations and maintenance
Operating expenditures per capita	To help determine if adequate funding is being provided for effective operations and maintenance
Revenue per capita	To help determine if a community is recovering enough costs to meet expectations and goals
Revenue as a percentage of operating costs	To help determine if a community is recovering enough costs to meet expectations and goals

Source: Barth Associates, LLC.

As mentioned earlier, the conundrum with acreage LOS is "What should be counted?" Some communities include public golf courses and beaches, while others include publicly accessible lakes and wetlands. Some cities and counties include public parkland owned by other agencies, such as state parks and national forests. Some communities also count private recreation areas owned and managed by homeowners' associations because these areas help meet residents' local recreation needs.

Since the primary purpose of acreage LOS is to measure and monitor a community's supply of parkland, I believe that communities should count only developable, publicly accessible parkland within their jurisdiction. Undevelopable lands such as conservation areas, wetlands, water bodies, golf courses, and beaches cannot help a community meet its needs for parks, playgrounds, athletics fields, open play space, recreation centers, and other basic parks and recreation facilities. Public parkland owned by another jurisdiction (such as county-owned parks within a municipality) is already counted by that jurisdiction for its own LOS and should not be included in a community's acreage calculation. Several of my clients disagree with this approach, however, insisting that a nearby regional park or beach (owned and managed by another agency) should count toward their own acreage LOS.

Many communities have also established LOS metrics for various park types based on the 1996 NRPA park classifications, such as miniparks, neighborhood parks, school parks, community parks, and the like. These classifications—which include location and size criteria—no longer reflect the complexities of parks and recreation planning, particularly in urban or urbanizing areas. For example, there may not be a vacant parcel large enough to provide the thirty to fifty acres prescribed for a new community park, but a well-designed ten-acre urban park with on-street parking may meet residents' needs just as well.

The book *Eden by Design: The 1930 Olmsted-Bartholomew Plan for the Los Angeles Region*—which republished the ambitious, far-sighted, but ill-fated parks and recreation system plan for Los Angeles—offers a refreshingly simple basis for establishing modern parks LOS. It states that there are only two classes of parks and recreation functions and facilities.

1. Those that serve mainly *local* needs and can be reduplicated in small and easily accessible units in every part of the region
2. Those that serve mainly *regional* needs, which people can reasonably be expected to travel rather long distances to reach and which cannot be reduplicated locally[4]

As a result, we've been encouraging our clients to establish different acreage LOS metrics. For example, a local or neighborhood park LOS could include both public and private parks; the purpose would be to ensure that all residents have access to a significant local park within easy access of their home (see the discussion of access LOS in the next section). A separate LOS could also be established for larger community or regional parks.

Regardless of nomenclature or classifications, acreage LOS remains a useful and meaningful metric for analyzing whether a community has enough public parkland. The key is to spend enough time discussing and analyzing the data to make sure that the metric truly reflects the community's values and goals.

Access LOS

Access LOS is expressed as the distance or amount of time a resident or visitor must travel to a park or facility. It should be used in conjunction with other LOS metrics such as acreage and facilities. For example, the analysis of acreage LOS may indicate that a community has enough parkland, but the access LOS analysis may reveal that it is distributed inequitably. As communities have become more densely populated and congested, it has become more important to ensure equitable access. Many residents of urban areas do not drive cars—either by choice or by necessity—and residents are encouraged to take transit, bicycle, or walk to save energy, reduce pollution and congestion, and improve health. Thus, access is an important measure of service.

As with the other LOS metrics, there are no standard criteria for access LOS. Each community must determine its own, based on land development patterns; street, bicycle, and pedestrian networks; transit access; and demographics. Depending on the area's values, a standard for a neighborhood park may be a five-minute or quarter-mile walk, while a standard for a community park may be one to five miles. For example, the City of Denver (see figure 9-2) set a goal of a green space within six blocks or a ten-minute walk of every resident, and the City of St. Petersburg, Florida, has a goal of a playground within a half-mile of every resident.

The "Denver Parks and Recreation 2017 Game Plan Update" discusses the interrelation between park acreage and access metrics, as well as the nuances of each.

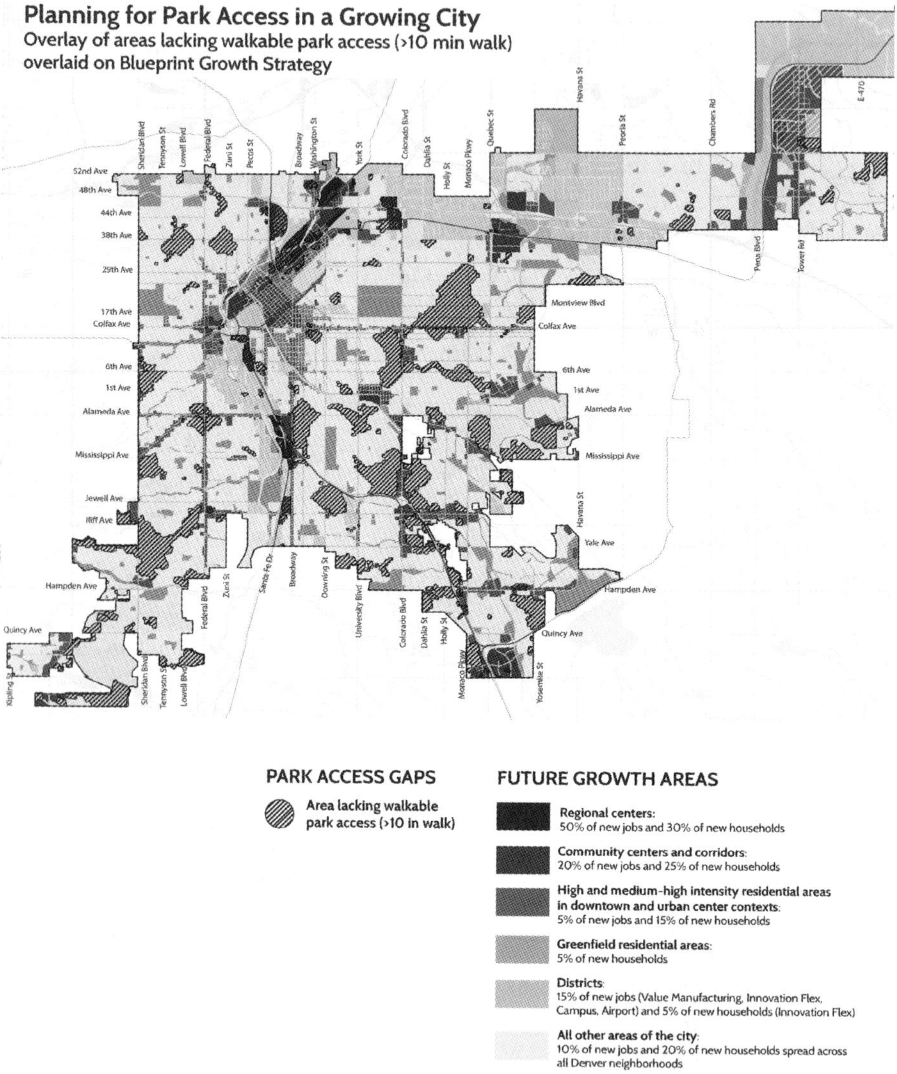

Figure 9-2: Denver, Colorado, park access map (City of Denver, *Blueprint Denver*, 2019, p. 57)

Overall 86% of Denver's residents have access to a park within a half mile, placing Denver about 20% above the national median. At 5,957 acres of urban parkland, Denver sits just above the national median in terms of overall park acreage; however, Denver is below the median in terms of parkland per capita, at 8.97 acres per 1,000 residents. This is due primarily to two factors: first, Denver's

> urban park acreage does not include its extensive Mountain Parks system, and second, Denver's population continues to grow without park acquisition being able to match the city's rate of growth and densification. Parkland per capita cannot include the Mountain Parks system because, although it is an incredible resource for the people of Denver, it is not accessible to all residents. Currently public transit is limited to a few mountain parks along major routes, so one must have access to a car or group bus trip to visit most of the mountain parks. Given Blueprint Denver's prediction that the city will continue to grow at a similar rate over the coming decade, Denver's park acres per capita will be an important metric to monitor. It will continue to decline unless the city can find ways to carve out additional parkland in densifying neighborhoods.[5]

This analysis underscores several important points about parkland and access LOS metrics: (1) acreage LOS will vary depending on what is counted, for example, urban parks versus mountain parks; (2) although a community may have enough acreage, it may not be accessible to all residents; (3) multimodal transportation access can help improve access and partially compensate for lack of parkland in close proximity to residents; and (4) it will continue to be increasingly more difficult to maintain the same LOS standards in high-density urban areas as in lower-density suburban areas because of the scarcity and cost of vacant urban land. As a result, communities may also wish to establish differential access LOS standards for specific facilities based on existing or desired land development patterns. For example, in urban core areas that encourage walkability, an access LOS of a quarter-mile may be desirable for playgrounds, basketball courts, plazas, and other types of urban spaces or facilities. Conversely, a three- to five-mile service area may be acceptable in suburban or rural communities for facilities such as soccer fields and swimming pools.

Communities should conduct a spatial analysis of the parks and recreation system to identify the existing access LOS for both parklands and facilities. The analysis can also identify gaps in transit, roadway, bicycle, and pedestrian networks. Access to a landlocked park, for example, may be increased by creating new roadway, bicycle, or pedestrian connections, thereby reducing or eliminating the need to purchase additional parkland. At the same time, access improvements can create new recreational amenities such as sidewalks, bike lanes, and trails.

Facilities LOS

Facilities LOS addresses the oft-asked question "Do we have enough recreation facilities?," such as athletics fields, swimming pools, playgrounds, and tennis courts. As discussed earlier, the number of facilities needed can vary widely because of a number of variables among communities including population density, climate, demographics, development patterns, and recreation trends. For example, cold-weather communities often have a higher demand for indoor recreation facilities than do warm-weather communities, and a community with a high percentage of senior citizens might have a much lower need for athletics fields than a community with a high percentage of youth. Also, some communities' facility needs are influenced by their culture or traditions, as with the equestrian heritage of Germantown, Tennessee.

When calculating current facilities LOS, a community may wish to develop a first-tier and a second-tier LOS. The first-tier LOS should count only the community's own publicly accessible recreation facilities to develop an accurate baseline LOS. The second-tier facilities LOS calculation could include additional facilities that help meet residents' needs, such as publicly accessible school athletics fields and gymnasiums, homeowners' association pools and playgrounds, and nonprofit facilities such as YMCA pools and Boys & Girls Club gymnasiums. During the needs assessment process, the community can discuss whether the second-tier facilities are actually meeting residents' needs, thereby potentially reducing the need to build additional first-tier facilities.

Building Square Footage per Capita

In addition to calculating the number of indoor facilities in the facilities LOS, a community should calculate the total square footage of indoor facilities. Recreation and community centers can range from less than one thousand square feet to more than three hundred thousand square feet, so a simple calculation of the number of facilities (rather than actual square footage) is not sufficient to analyze the true level of service for indoor recreation space. As with the facilities LOS calculations, a community may wish to create a first-tier facilities LOS of its own indoor facilities and a second-tier LOS of other publicly accessible facilities to enable more thoughtful discussion during the needs assessment process.

Quality LOS

Quality LOS standards are used to measure whether parks and recreation facilities are meeting the design and maintenance criteria established by the local community. Even though a community may be meeting its acreage, facilities, and access LOS standards, it cannot be meeting residents' needs if it provides poorly designed or maintained facilities. A quality LOS analysis can have implications beyond traditional recreation usage; it may also identify socioeconomic issues such as equity, vandalism, homelessness, neighborhood stability, community pride, and sense of place.

Very few communities have established quality LOS standards for their parks and recreation facilities. Again, each community should develop its own quality criteria based on community values and priorities. I often ask residents and elected officials if parks, recreation, and civic facilities (such as a city hall or public library) represent their values and desired community image. Basic quality LOS criteria may include aesthetics, architectural character, quality of construction materials, frequency of maintenance, safety inspections, cleanliness, and others. Those interested in developing quality LOS metrics may wish to begin by reviewing basic parks and recreation industry publications such as the NRPA's Commission for Accreditation of Parks and Recreation Agencies (CAPRA) standards and *Management of Park and Recreation Agencies*. Similarly, a wide variety of organizations publish park design guidelines, including the Project for Public Spaces and the Landscape Architecture Foundation.

Once the community has established its quality LOS criteria, parks and recreation facilities can be evaluated and mapped to illustrate the distribution of different levels of quality throughout the community. For example, Washington, DC, mapped the quality of its recreation centers according to their condition (deferred maintenance), size, and capacity (see figure 9-3). The analysis indicated an inequitable distribution of high-quality recreation centers throughout the community based on size (square footage of interior space), level of maintenance, program offerings, and opportunities for expansion. Existing centers were also compared with a desired

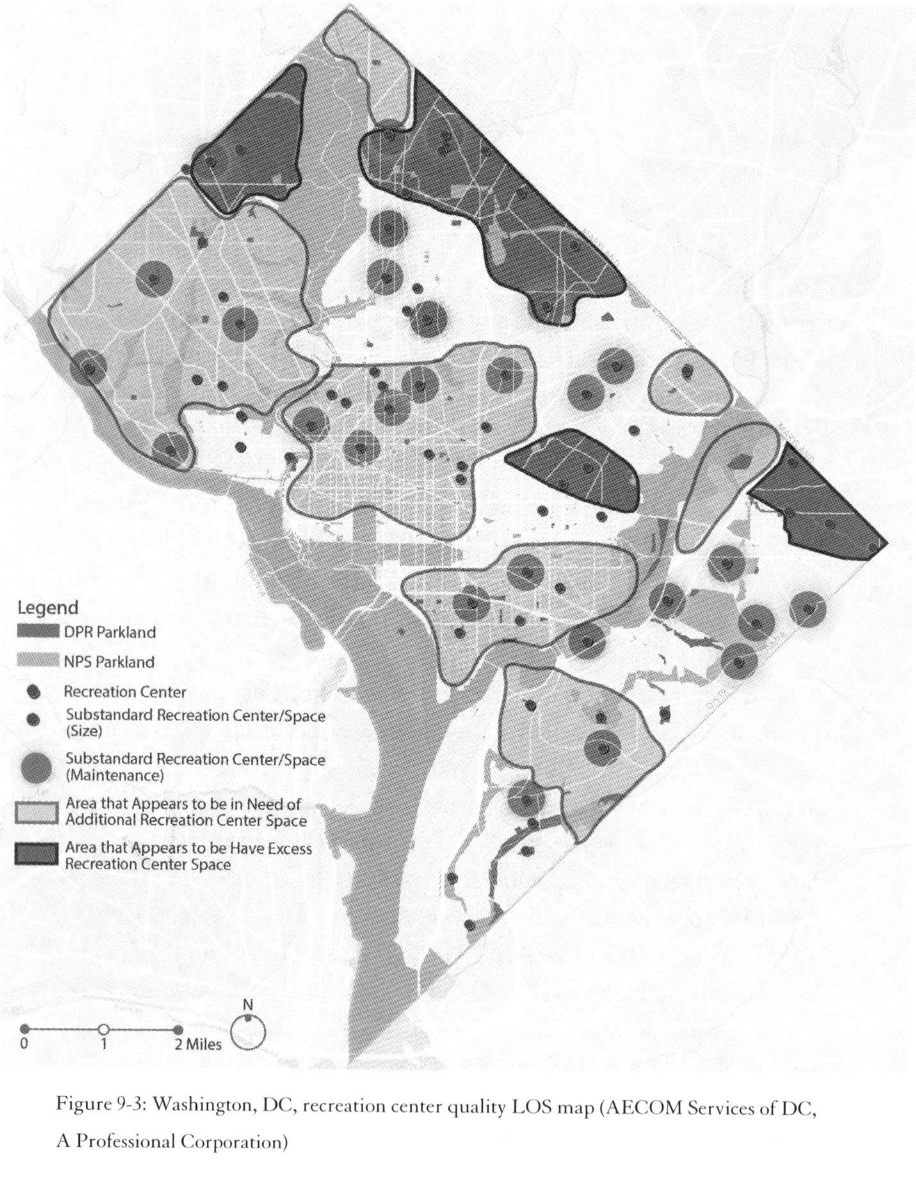

Figure 9-3: Washington, DC, recreation center quality LOS map (AECOM Services of DC, A Professional Corporation)

future recreation center prototype that we developed during the PRSMP process. As a result, the quality LOS analysis allowed planners to identify which of the existing centers should be demolished, repurposed, renovated, or expanded.

Operating Expenditures per Acre and per Capita

Two metrics that can help gauge whether a community is adequately funded to manage, operate, and maintain its parks and recreation areas are operating expenditures per acre managed and operating expenditures per capita. The first metric, operating expenditures per acre managed, is calculated by dividing total operating expenditures by total parkland acres managed by the agency. The second metric, operating expenditures per capita, is calculated by dividing total operating expenditures by the population of the jurisdiction served by the agency.

Operating expenditures include all of the costs of providing parks and recreation services to the community, including personnel salaries and benefits, utilities, equipment, and materials. Operating expenditures may also include debt service if it is paid out of the annual operating budget, as well as any expenditures incurred as part of a special or enterprise fund (such as a golf course) managed by the public agency.

It is important to note that operating costs can vary widely among communities because of differences in parks and recreation facility standards, types of equipment, repair and replacement schedules, types and topography of parkland, degree of maintenance required, levels of use, and other variables. Operating costs and efficiencies can also vary with the number of acres managed and the size of the population served. For example, a community that manages extensive conservation lands will have a lower ratio of expenditures to acreage than will a community that primarily manages developed parkland. Communities that benchmark operating expenditures (see the discussion of benchmarking later in the chapter) should conduct follow-up research to analyze and document the specific reasons for differences in operating expenditures. For example, it may be helpful to visit and photograph the facilities at benchmarked communities and meet with agency staff to document key differences in facility quality or level of maintenance. It may also be helpful to determine if a community is serving a population larger than its own residents. Elected officials, managers, and residents may be more supportive of increased operation budgets if they clearly understand the reasons for variations in funding among communities and the implications of different funding levels.

Revenue per Capita and as a Percentage of Total Operating Expenditures (Cost Recovery)

Two metrics that can be used to track revenues and compare revenue generation with that of other agencies are revenue per capita and revenue as a percentage of total operating expenditures. The first metric, revenue per capita, is calculated by dividing the total revenues generated by the agency by the population of the jurisdiction served by the agency. The second metric, revenue as a percentage of total operating expenditures (also known as cost recovery), is calculated by dividing the total revenues generated by the agency by the total operating expenditures of the agency. A community's parks and recreation revenues (also known as annual direct revenues) include all of the monies generated directly from parks and recreation classes, programs, memberships, concessions, permits, rentals, and other nontax sources. Revenues do not include funding from taxes, grants, foundations, bonds, assessments, or other indirect sources.

In addition to revenue tracking and benchmarking, these metrics can be used to establish cost recovery policies and goals. This is typically a policy decision determined by the agency department head, the city or county manager, elected officials, or all of these. Some communities have established different cost recovery policies for senior, adult, and youth programs, while others have established overall cost recovery goals as a percentage of operating expenses. For example, a community may wish to subsidize youth programs to encourage accessibility but require 100 percent cost recovery for adult sports leagues. Databases such as NRPA Park Metrics can help agencies determine reasonable and realistic cost recovery goals based on data from other agencies.

Additional LOS Metrics for the New Approach to Parks and Recreation System Planning

The new approach to parks and recreation system planning proposes that planners supplement traditional parks and recreation system metrics with additional LOS metrics that reflect the various dimensions discussed in chapters 2 and 3. These types of metrics are closely related to sustainable development indicators (SDIs), used by many communities since the late 1980s to measure and monitor progress toward sustainability goals, and more recent metrics established to measure resiliency. For example, many of the twenty-five criteria for High-Performance Public Spaces discussed in chapter 3 are based on SDIs and could be expressed as LOS metrics.

As with the common LOS standards, there are no universally agreed-upon SDIs to help measure and monitor progress toward sustainability. These metrics tend to be more aspirational in nature, based on community-wide values, principles, goals, and long-range vision. Denver's parks and recreation master plan (the Game Plan) does a great job of explaining the difference.

> Aspirational goals differ from the performance goals . . . in that they are higher level and touch on many other goal areas. Equity, engagement and sound economics are really on the levels of core values for the department rather than physical or programmatic elements. As such, their aspirational goals aren't exactly "achievable" in the traditional sense: there isn't a box to check when these goals are met, because in many ways we are always striving to do more and do better in these categories.[6]

In addition to common parks and recreation metrics, Denver's Game Plan establishes metrics for water use, healthy waterways, urban tree canopy, waste and recycling, reduced heat island effect, and adaptation to climate change. The City of Philadelphia's Green City, Clean Waters plan has established a monitoring plan and metrics for its goals to reduce localized flooding, reduce combined sewer overflows, and improve water quality. And the City of Portland, Oregon, has established metrics for each of the five goals in its comprehensive plan, which are economic prosperity, human health, environmental health, equity, and resilience. Each of these communities has established LOS metrics for its parks and recreation system that include the community's goals for resiliency and sustainability, in addition to traditional parks and recreation metrics.

Several of the dimensions discussed in chapter 2 could be measured through new, aspirational LOS metrics, including bicycle and pedestrian access, green infrastructure and stormwater treatment, health and wellness, social and educational programs, and economic development. These types of metrics are generally recalculated annually to track progress. Table 9-2 provides examples of potential metrics related to some of these dimensions.

How to Calculate Parks and Recreation LOS Metrics

The process for developing parks and recreation LOS metrics will vary according to the values, goals, and outcomes being measured. The LOS calculation process outlined in the 1996 NRPA guidelines is fairly complex and laborious, but the basic steps are still applicable to most types of metrics, including alternative dimensions related to sustainability and resiliency.

1. Determine which park or facility classifications (or other dimensions) for which an LOS will apply.
2. Determine the criteria for each park or facility type (or other dimensions), such as size or service area access.
3. Determine which metric or metrics should be used to calculate LOS.
4. Determine the existing inventory (supply) of the park or facility classification (or other dimensions) and the existing LOS.
5. Determine the demand for the park or facility classification (or other dimensions), based on the needs assessment (including residents' priorities and benchmarking against other communities).
6. Calculate the LOS required to meet the community's needs, based on parks and recreation guiding principles, service delivery models, and long-range vision (or other dimensions).

Table 9-2
Examples of Resiliency and Sustainability Metrics

Dimension	Potential Metrics
Bicycle and pedestrian access to parks, open spaces, natural areas, civic sites, and other elements of the public realm	Miles of paved multiuse trails
	Percentage of the long-range bicycle and pedestrian network vision completed
	Percentage of parks and open spaces with bicycle and pedestrian access
	Percentage of complete streets
Green infrastructure and stormwater treatment	Percentage of community tree canopy coverage
	Improvement in water quality of key water bodies
	Percentage of stormwater treatment projects incorporating green design practices
Health and wellness of community residents	Percentage of residents considered obese
	Participation in fitness and wellness programs
	Reduction in chronic health conditions such as type 2 diabetes and heart disease
Social and educational programs	High school graduation rate
	Local unemployment rate
	Percentage of households considered by the United Way to be Asset-Limited, Income-Constrained, Employed (ALICE)
Economic development	Increase in property values adjacent to new or improved parks and open spaces
	Increase in number of businesses opened in response to new or improved parks and open spaces
	Increase in public and private sector jobs created through parks and open spaces

Source: Barth Associates, LLC.

The NRPA process for the last step—calculating the new, aspirational LOS—is particularly complex and formula driven. A simpler, commonsense approach is to ask the following questions after completion of steps 1–5:

- Does the existing LOS for park acreage, access, and facilities appear to meet residents' needs? If the answer is yes, adopt the LOS for that particular metric.
- Did the needs assessment process—such as the interviews and focus group meetings—identify obvious solutions to meeting needs? For example, did the youth athletic association estimate the additional number of fields needed to meet current demand for soccer, or did stormwater engineers estimate the acre-feet of stormwater ponds required to treat stormwater runoff? If so, add the number of facilities required to meet needs to the existing inventory, and calculate the proposed new LOS.
- Have guiding principles or a long-range vision been established for the parks and recreation system? (See chapter 10.) For example, a principle or vision may be that all residents should have access to a park and playground within a ten-minute walk of their home. If such a vision has been developed, a new aspirational LOS could be established based on the number of acres or facilities proposed.
- Does the long-range vision include aspirational desired future conditions (DFCs) related to resiliency or sustainability? If so, what is the gap between existing and desired conditions? What metrics or indicators of success can be tracked to measure progress toward the DFC?

It is important to note that LOS calculation is not an exact science and there are no right or wrong answers; as stated earlier, an LOS is ultimately a reflection of a community's values, goals, and philosophy regarding the delivery of parks and recreation services. For example, I was recently engaged in a healthy debate with a board of city commissioners regarding what should be counted toward their city's park acreage calculations, including natural areas, county parks and preserves, greenways and trails, and private amenity areas maintained by homeowners' associations. We also discussed whether undevelopable public lands—such as beaches, lakes, wetlands, and golf courses—should be counted as public parkland. As discussed at the beginning of this chapter, LOS variables could also include ownership, definitions, land development patterns, population densities, climate, and others.

LOS Data Sources

Several sources of parks and recreation–related data are available to assist planners in LOS research and benchmarking.

- Park metrics: NRPA Park Metrics was developed to replace outdated standards (formerly known as PRORAGIS) with a database that allows parks and recreation agencies to benchmark their parks and recreation systems against similar systems across the country. It is the largest collection of parks and recreation operating data in the United States. NRPA Park Metrics is typically used in concert with other parks and recreation system planning tools such as mail or telephone surveys, service area analyses, and stakeholder interviews. Its reporting functions provide the ability to perform side-by-side comparisons based on filtered searches including jurisdictional population, department budget, employee number, location, and acres managed. These comparisons allow agencies to benchmark and evaluate performance against most similar agencies and aggregated data from across the country.
- Statewide comprehensive outdoor recreation plans (SCORPs): States must prepare and regularly update SCORPs in order to be eligible for federal Land and Water Conservation Fund grants from the National Park Service and the US Department of the Interior. Most SCORPS address the supply of and demand for local, state, and federal recreation resources; identify needs and new opportunities for recreation improvements; and establish implementation programs to meet plan goals. Many SCORPs also include regional and statewide parks and recreation LOS standards or data that can be used for benchmarking.
- The Trust for Public Land ParkScore index and City Park Facts: The Trust for Public Land (TPL) is a national nonprofit organization working to create and improve neighborhood parks. TPL's ParkScore index measures how well the seventy-five largest US cities are meeting the need for parks, providing in-depth data to guide local park improvement efforts. TPL's City Park Facts is an annually published almanac of the

parks and recreation systems of the one hundred most populous cities, which can be used for benchmarking.

- Sustainability and resiliency metrics initiatives such as those developed at the United Nations Conference on Sustainable Development; the Sustainable Sites Initiative, administered by Green Business Certification Inc. (GBCI); and the Landscape Architecture Foundation's Landscape Performance Series Case Study Briefs, a searchable database of over one hundred exemplary built projects with quantified environmental, economic, and social benefits.

Some cities and counties also conduct their own research to benchmark themselves against communities with similar demographics, geography, or climate. Other communities select aspirational benchmarks using cities or counties they wish to emulate. Both Park Metrics and TPL reporting functions provide the ability to perform side-by-side comparison based on filtered searches including jurisdictional population, department budget, employee number, location, and acres managed. These comparisons allow agencies to benchmark and evaluate performance against the most similar agencies and aggregated data from across the country.

Findings from LOS benchmarking can be compared with findings from surveys, focus groups, and other needs assessment techniques to determine if the existing LOS is adequate. For example, if the facilities LOS benchmarking for athletics fields indicates that the community provides a lower number of fields per capita than comparable communities—and the statistically valid survey indicates a high unmet need for athletics fields—then the community may decide to establish a higher facilities LOS standard to reflect demand and need.

Embracing the Freedom of the Parks and Recreation LOS

In spite of the inexact methodology for calculating LOS for parks and recreation services, a thoughtful, meaningful set of LOS standards can be very useful to communities for long-range planning, needs assessments, and growth management. There are very few, if any, state or federal mandates that dictate which metrics must be used; communities are free to develop the LOS metrics and standards that best serve their needs and reflect their values, priorities, and policies.

Key considerations for selecting LOS metrics include the following:

- Do the metrics reflect the values, needs, and DFCs that are most important to residents?
- Are the LOS standards, metrics, and definitions logical and easy to understand?
- Is accurate data available for each metric and relatively easy to collect?
- Do the metrics truly represent the actual LOS provided?
- Collectively, do the metrics and standards provide a comprehensive perspective of LOS, including quantity, quality, and access to facilities and programs, as well as other factors that are important to the community?
- Do the metrics reflect all of the various dimensions of the PRSMP, including sustainability and resiliency aspirations in addition to traditional parks and recreation LOS?

Most important, LOS standards should not be viewed as absolute or static. They should be reviewed and recalculated annually and updated every five years, at a minimum, in conjunction with a needs assessment process to ensure that they remain reflective of the community's needs, values, and goals. A comprehensive set of LOS standards, tested and updated regularly, helps ensure that a community is truly meeting residents' needs and generating the greatest benefits from its parks and recreation system.

10 DEVELOPING A LONG-RANGE VISION

The visioning phase is the most exciting and thought-provoking phase of the planning process. It occurs midway between the needs assessment and the implementation strategy, providing a time to reflect on the findings to date and a time to look toward a desired future condition. In strategic planning terms, the focus of the long-range vision is to formulate and evaluate alternative strategies to address issues and needs. For a traditional parks and recreation system master plan (PRSMP), these alternatives are typically expressed in terms of proposed new or enhanced parks, conservation lands, bikeways and trails, civic spaces, athletics and other special use facilities, recreation centers, programs, staffing, level-of-service (LOS) metrics, or other improvements. For other dimensions of a PRSMP, the long-range vision may also describe desired future conditions (DFCs), strategies, and initiatives to improve social equity, community health, water quality, climate resilience, and other aspects of community resiliency and sustainability. The scope of the long-range vision should initially be determined in the initiating and planning phase of the PRSMP and then refined according to the findings from the needs assessment phase. Because there is no single prescribed methodology for creating a compelling long-range PRSMP vision, a discussion of various aspects to consider is presented here.

Collaborative and Concurrent Visioning

The new approach to parks and recreation system planning proposes that the parks and recreation vision be developed concurrently with development of visions for the other elements of the public realm, such as streets, bikeways and trails, civic spaces, stormwater treatment facilities, and utilities. Unfortunately, this does not appear to be occurring in many communities. Although many parks and recreation agencies collaborate regularly with other departments and agencies to design and construct specific projects, I have not been able to identify any that collaboratively and concurrently plan their entire public realm.

Communities could employ a number of strategies to increase collaboration at the visioning and planning levels. First, each public realm department or agency could notify others of the proposed schedule and process for updates to their individual subsystem plans, including the PRSMP, comprehensive transportation plan (CTP), stormwater master plan, utilities master plan, climate change action plan, comprehensive plan, and other long-range planning initiatives. Department heads could also discuss upcoming planning initiatives at senior staff meetings and identify opportunities to collaborate.

Second, departments and agencies could conduct joint existing conditions analyses and needs assessment processes—including site visits, interviews, focus group meetings, public workshops, and surveys—and share the findings and conclusions with other agencies and departments. Imagine the benefits of a public works director hearing firsthand about the need for more bus shelters or bike racks at parks or a parks director hearing about neighborhood flooding issues adjacent to a city park. These are just two examples of endless opportunities to generate multiple benefits from collaborative actions.

A related idea is to schedule concurrent visioning phases of various subsystem master plans. Collaborative brainstorming by people with different perspectives and backgrounds—as illustrated by the "Deep Dive" story in chapter 7—can often yield far more innovative and imaginative ideas than can visioning that involves only those of similar mind-sets. Similarly, multiagency and multidepartmental reviews of proposed capital improvements and programs could be scheduled to identify opportunities for partnerships, collaboration, or joint use. The collective visions for the public realm could be published in a single document, similar to the Citywide Systems Plan of Portland, Oregon.

Elements of a Long-Range Vision

Regardless of whether or not the PRSMP visioning process is conducted concurrently with other public realm subsystems, a good long-range parks and recreation vision should be both comprehensive and compelling. Consistent with the principles of strategic planning, it should answer the question "Where do we want to go?" in response to community needs and issues. The basic elements of a long-range PRSMP vision include a mission statement, reaffirming the purpose and role of the visioning agency; the guiding principles or best practices that have influenced the vision; and an illustrated description of proposed service delivery models, facility classifications, land acquisition, capital improvements, recreation programs, and other initiatives. The vision should also include estimates of costs for both capital and operations and proposed staffing and organizational changes. Additional elements, depending on the dimensions selected at the outset of the project, may include the role of the agency in addressing larger community-wide issues, opportunities to collaborate with other agencies and organizations, LOS metrics, and recommendations for revisions to the comprehensive plan, land development regulations, and impact fee ordinance. Figure 10-1 illustrates the basic framework for a long-range vision.

Figure 10-1: Framework for a long-range parks and recreation system vision (Barth Associates, LLC)

Foundational Values

The first step in the visioning process is to define the common values of the team, department, and community. The best definition of values that I've heard is "what you really care about the most." For example, in *Dare to Lead*, author Brené Brown lists over one hundred values, from accountability to wisdom (see box 10-1). We recently incorporated this list into a visioning workshop exercise, asking participants to select three to five values from the list that they cared most about. We then discussed the implications of their common values for the long-range vision, forming the foundation for a robust and compelling vision based on what they cared about the most.

Mission Statement

I used to dismiss mission statements as empty rhetoric that sounded good but meant very little. While many mission statements still fit this description, I've come to recognize the powerful benefits of a well-crafted mission statement that clearly defines the reason why an organization exists, based on common values. This is particularly important for parks and recreation agencies aspiring to transcend their traditional roles and make more significant contributions to community resiliency and sustainability. John Bryson, author of the well-regarded *Strategic Planning for Public and Nonprofit Organizations*, notes that "an organization's mission, in tandem with mandates, provides its raison d'être, the social justification for its existence. For a governmental agency . . . , this means there must be identifiable social or political needs that the organization seeks to fill. Viewed in this light, organizations must always be seen as a means to an end, not an end to themselves."[1]

Bryson notes a number of benefits that "flow from clarifying and agreeing on an organization's mission," including the following:

- A habit of focusing on what is truly important.
- Clarification of organizational and community purpose, including organizational structures and systems and the resource allocation system.

Box 10-1

List of Values from *Dare to Lead*

Accountability	Friendship	Peace
Achievement	Fun	Perseverance
Adaptability	Future generations	Personal fulfillment
Adventure	Generosity	Power
Altruism	Giving back	Pride
Ambition	Grace	Recognition
Authenticity	Gratitude	Reliability
Balance	Growth	Resourcefulness
Beauty	Harmony	Respect
Being the best	Health	Responsibility
Belonging	Home	Risk-taking
Career	Honesty	Safety
Caring	Hope	Security
Collaboration	Humility	Self-discipline
Commitment	Humor	Self-expression
Community	Inclusion	Self-respect
Compassion	Independence	Serenity
Competence	Initiative	Service
Confidence	Integrity	Simplicity
Connection	Intuition	Spirituality
Contentment	Job security	Sportsmanship
Contribution	Joy	Stewardship
Cooperation	Justice	Success
Courage	Kindness	Teamwork
Creativity	Knowledge	Thrift
Curiosity	Leadership	Time
Dignity	Learning	Tradition
Diversity	Legacy	Travel
Environment	Leisure	Trust
Efficiency	Love	Truth
Equality	Loyalty	Understanding
Ethics	Making a difference	Uniqueness
Excellence	Nature	Usefulness
Fairness	Openness	Vision
Faith	Optimism	Vulnerability
Family	Order	Wealth
Financial stability	Parenting	Well-being
Forgiveness	Patience	Wholeheartedness
Freedom	Patriotism	Wisdom

Source: "List of Values" from DARE TO LEAD: BRAVE WORK. TOUGH CONVERSATIONS. WHOLE HEARTS. by Brené Brown, copyright © 2018 by Brené Brown. Used by permission of Random House, an imprint and division of Penguin Random House LLC.

- Explicit attention given to philosophy, values, and culture, which are rarely discussed directly.
- Clarification of goals to be pursued, or problems addressed, prior to exploring solutions. "Agreement on purpose . . . gets an organization to pursue the following sequence of conflict resolution activities: agree on purpose, identify problems, and then explore and agree on solutions."[2]

Bryson's fourth point, regarding the sequence of activities, is particularly relevant to the parks and recreation system planning process. A stakeholder at a recent visioning workshop asked whether the community's needs assessment process should include facilities or programs that may not be consistent with the agency's mission; in other words, which comes first—mission or needs? If your mission does not include greater multimodal connectivity, should you ask community members if they have a need for bikeways and trails? (These are often the number one priority.) Conversely, if the needs assessment indicates a need for bikeways and trails, should your mission include connectivity? There is no right or wrong answer to this question; as in many other aspects of parks and recreation system planning, each community must determine its own mission for the parks and recreation system, often based on the values and priorities of those in leadership positions.

Guiding Principles and Best Practices

Guiding principles and best practices are also an important component of a long-range vision, replacing standards as a basis for decision making. While the mission statement defines the raison d'être of the agency, the guiding principles and best practices provide high-level guidance for developing a compelling vision for the parks and recreation system. Following are several examples of guiding principles, drawing on the foundation of forward-thinking processes discussed throughout the book. They include the concept of an integrated system or plexus, described in chapter 1; the concept of High-Performance Public Spaces (HPPSs), discussed in chapter 3; Peter Harnik's seven measures of an excellent city park system; the

Project for Public Spaces' Power of Ten+; and the 10-Minute Walk Campaign of the Trust for Public Land (TPL), the National Recreation and Park Association (NRPA), and the Urban Land Institute.

Parks as Plexus

First, the principle of a plexus literally forces participants to transcend individual organizational silos and collaborate on the development of an integrated system. Imagine how we would plan and design parks differently if we thought of them as stormwater treatment areas within a larger stormwater and flood control system; as trailheads and training areas within a bicycle and pedestrian network; as exercise and fitness facilities within a community-wide wellness initiative; as wildlife habitat and tree canopy within a larger ecological system; as neighborhood stabilizers, job creators, and property value enhancers within a greater economic development initiative; as indoor and outdoor classrooms within the community's education and job training systems; as unique visitor destinations, with exceptional dining and recreation experiences, within a greater tourism development initiative; or as exhibition sites within the community's system of museums and botanical gardens. Viewing the parks and recreation system as an integral element of these other systems leads to much more creative, thoughtful, and collaborative visioning.

High-Performance Public Spaces

The concept of the HPPS—the idea of generating multiple benefits that contribute to a more sustainable and resilient community—is another innovative principle that can guide the development of the long-range vision. Each of the twenty-five HPPS criteria can be used as an aspirational goal for every existing and proposed park, trail, natural area, sports complex, and civic space in the system. Meeting the criteria often requires collaboration with other public realm providers. For example, meeting the first criterion—"the space creates and facilitates revenue-generating opportunities for the public sector, the private sector, or both"—may require a public-private partnership working in conjunction with numerous public agencies (e.g., public works, utilities, planning) to provide the required approvals and infrastructure. One of our clients has integrated the HPPS criteria into her project kickoff meeting checklist in order to (1) make sure that all team members are aware of the aspirational goals of the project and (2) encourage team members to develop innovative design solutions that will generate multiple resiliency and sustainability benefits.

The Excellent City Park System

Peter Harnik provides additional guiding principles in *The Excellent City Park System*,[3] which states that there are seven measures of an excellent system.

1. A clear expression of purpose
2. Ongoing planning and community involvement
3. Sufficient assets in land, staffing, and equipment to meet the system's goals
4. Equitable access
5. User satisfaction
6. Safety from physical hazards and crime
7. Benefits for the city beyond the boundaries of the parks

Each of these measures could provide guidance for the development of a long-range vision.

Placemaking

The Project for Public Spaces (PPS) defines the guiding principle of placemaking as "both a process and a philosophy." First, "it is centered around observing, listening to, and asking questions of the people who live, work, and play in a particular space in order to understand their needs and aspirations for that space and for their community as a whole. With this knowledge, we can come together to create a common vision for that place." Second, "placemaking inspires people to collectively reimagine and reinvent public spaces as the heart of every community. . . . More than just promoting better urban design, placemaking facilitates creative patterns of use, paying particular attention to the physical, cultural, and social identities that define a place and support its ongoing evolution."[4]

One of PPS's tools for placemaking is the Power of 10+, the idea that

> places thrive when users have a range of reasons (10+) to be there. These might include a place to sit, playgrounds to enjoy, art to touch, music to hear, food to eat, history to experience, and people to meet. Ideally, some of these activities will be unique to that particular place, reflecting the culture and history of the surrounding community. . . .
>
> Further, when cities contain at least 10 of these destinations or districts, their public perception begins to shift amongst both locals and tourists, and urban centers can become better equipped for generating resilience and innovation.[5]

Therefore, the Power of 10+ can be used as the guiding principle for an entire city or region, the public realm, a parks and recreation system, or an individual park or place, as illustrated in figure 10-2.

10-Minute Walk Campaign

Another potential guiding principle is the ten-minute walk. The 10-Minute Walk Campaign (https://10minutewalk.org/) is promoted by TPL in partnership with the NRPA and the Urban Land Institute to ensure that "there's a great park within a 10-minute walk of every person, in every neighborhood, in every city across America." This is actually a level-of-service metric (access LOS) that can be used as a guiding principle.

Other Sources of Guiding Principles

Other organizations, such as the American Planning Association (APA), the American Society of Landscape Architects, and the NRPA, conduct and publish research that can be used as guiding principles for a community's parks and recreation system. For

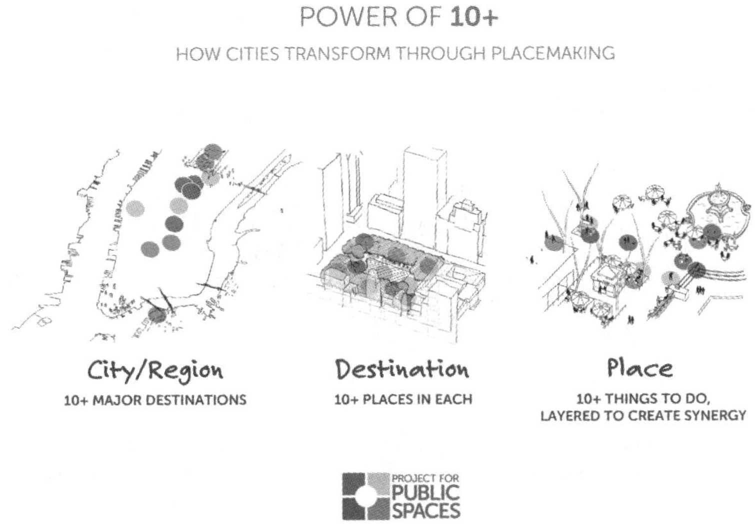

Figure 10-2: Power of 10+ (Project for Public Spaces)

example, the APA is one of six key partners behind a new effort called Naturally Resilient Communities. The program

> promotes the role nature-based solutions can play in helping reduce flood risk for communities while providing other benefits, such as improved water quality and enhanced recreational opportunities and wildlife habitat—all of which positively impacts local economies. Together, we collectively represent county governments, professional engineers, community planners, floodplain managers and conservationists.
>
> Online at NRCSolutions.org, the partners have created a guide of nature-based solutions and related case studies of successful projects to help communities learn more and identify those solutions that might work best for them.[6]

Numerous other organizations and agencies publish guiding principles that are applicable to other dimensions of PRSMPs. Table 10-1 provides examples of principles for some of the most common dimensions addressed in chapter 2.

Table 10-1
Examples of Guiding Principles for Common Parks and Recreation System Planning Dimensions

Dimension	Principle	Source
Bicycle and pedestrian access	All streets should be designed, built, and operated to enable safe use by everyone, regardless of age, ability, or mode of transportation.	Michelle Lieberman, "Complete Streets Policies + Bicycle + Pedestrian Plans: Key Tools for Supporting Healthy Communities," November 2018, https://www.saferoutespartnership.org/sites/default/files/resource_files/completestreets-bicyclepedplans.pdf.
Social equity	Residents of all races, economic means, and abilities are welcome and equipped to participate in all aspects of community life.	Mid-America Regional Council, "Creating Sustainable Places: Guiding Principles," https://www.marc.org /Regional-Planning/Creating-Sustainable-Places/Creating-Sustainable-Places/Guiding-Principles.
Stormwater treatment to protect natural streams	Postdevelopment balance of evapotranspiration, streamflow, and infiltration should mimic the predevelopment balance, which typically requires keeping significant runoff volume from reaching the stream.	Christopher J. Walsh et al., "Principles for Urban Stormwater Management to Protect Stream Ecosystems," *Freshwater Science* 35, no. 1 (March 2016): 398–411, https://www.journals.uchicago.edu/doi/10.1086 /685284.
Green infrastructure	Green infrastructure should include an interconnected network of a wide range of landscape elements that support native species, maintain natural ecological processes, sustain air and water resources, and contribute to the health and quality of life for communities and people.	Green Infrastructure Center, "Green Infrastructure Principles and Planning Tools," http://www.gicinc.org/PDFs/Richmond_Regional_Workshop_Show_mini_workshop.pdf.

(*continued*)

Relationship to Needs

While guiding principles can form the framework for a long-range vision, the findings from the needs assessment define short-term priorities. Needs assessments should be updated at least every five years to reflect changes in community trends, demographics, and policies, and the long-range vision will need to be updated accordingly.

Table 10-1 *(continued)*

Dimension	Principle	Source
Health and wellness	Healthy communities decrease dependence on the automobile by building homes, businesses, schools, churches, and parks closer to one another so that people can more easily walk or bike between them; provide opportunities for people to be physically active and socially engaged as part of their daily routine; and allow persons, if they choose, to age in place and remain all their lives in a community that reflects their changing lifestyles and changing physical capabilities.	Centers for Disease Control and Prevention, National Center for Environmental Health, Division of Emergency and Environmental Health Services, "Healthy Community Design," fact sheet, June 2018, https://www.cdc.gov/healthyplaces/docs/Healthy_Community_Design.pdf.
Economic development	Economic development should focus on strengthening assets that enable distinctive industries to flourish and grow from within rather than rely primarily on marketing to recruit individual firms from elsewhere.	Fred Drews, "5 Principles for Remaking Economic Development to Generate Growth, Prosperity, and Inclusion," Brookings Institution, March 23, 2016, https://www.brookings.edu/blog/brookings-now/2016/03/23/5-principles-for-remaking-economic-development-to-generate-growth-prosperity-and-inclusion/.
Climate change adaptation	Responses should be sensitive to the wider context in which climate change is experienced, including multiple stressors.	Siri Eriksen et al., "When Not Every Response to Climate Change Is a Good One: Identifying Principles for Sustainable Adaptation," *Climate and Development* 3 (2011): 7–20, https://www.cakex.org/sites/default/files/sustainable.pdf.

Source: Barth Associates, LLC.

Staff and stakeholders often ask whether a long-range vision should include needs that are not currently financially feasible, for example, a new multimillion-dollar water park or athletics complex. We believe that even if funding is not available in the near future, the long-range vision should reflect residents' needs and priorities. Often a compelling vision can attract funding from unexpected sources. Many innovative and transformative parks and open space projects—such as the Path 400 Greenway in Atlanta, Georgia, identified as a priority through the Buckhead Greenspace PRSMP—are funded only when they appear as part of a compelling long-range vision that responds to residents' priority needs. For example, once the Path 400 Greenway was announced, it attracted funding from many sources. Atlanta's city council voted to allot $5 million in local sales tax funding to the project, and the Atlanta Regional Commission included $7.42 million in its transportation improvement program project list that allocates funding from the Federal Highway Administration. The private, nonprofit PATH Foundation chipped in as well.

Visioning Workshop

As mentioned earlier, there is no prescribed method for when and how a parks and recreation agency discusses its response to community needs. Some conduct these discussions as part of a strategic planning process, while others may use the CAPRA (Commission for Accreditation of Parks and Recreation Agencies) accreditation process for such discussions.

In our practice, we kick off the visioning phase of the project with a visioning workshop in which we discuss how best to respond to the top priorities from the needs assessment and implications for the agency's values, mission, guiding principles, subsystems, service delivery models, and classifications. The workshop is divided into sessions lasting one and one-half to two hours, each dealing with a different topic or priority need. For example, the visioning topics at a recent, typical workshop included the following:

- Values and mission statement
- Improvements to existing parks
- Development of a bikeways and trails system
- Aquatics and recreation centers
- New local and community parks
- Homelessness
- Economic development
- Flooding
- Crime reduction

- Youth development
- Athletics fields

Other visioning topics have included LOS metrics, programs, organizational structure, public art, historic preservation, boating access, civic spaces, cultural programs, special events, and others. Generally, we wait until completion of the needs assessment—and the identification of top-priority needs—before we establish the visioning workshop agenda. Otherwise, we might preconceive a vision for the community, based on our own perspectives and biases, that doesn't respond to the specific needs, desires, and concerns of the community. The scientific process reminds us to analyze the results from the needs assessment, report the findings, form conclusions, and then determine alternative responses for consideration.

Each visioning session may be attended by different participants. For example, a session on bikeways and trails may include parks and recreation staff, public works and engineering staff, representatives of the local metropolitan planning organization (MPO), and local bicycling, hiking, and trails advocates. We try to involve community residents, stakeholders, and agency representatives who are the most knowledgeable about each topic.

Discussions for each topic follow a similar outline, beginning with a summary of residents' needs and followed by discussions regarding alternative service delivery models, facility classifications, alternative roles of various agencies, preferred alternatives, a desired long-range vision, and interim recommendations. Each session is led by an experienced facilitator, recorded, and transcribed. The notes from the session—along with the guiding principles and priority needs—serve as the basis for writing and illustrating the long range-vision.

Subsystems and Service Delivery Models

While values, mission, guiding principles, and needs help inform the long-range vision for a community's parks and recreation system, service delivery models (SDMs) and classifications define how the vision will actually be implemented. SDMs are useful not only for traditional PRSMP visions but for other dimensions as well.

First, a typical parks and recreation system is made up of numerous subsystems, such as aquatics, athletics, bikeways and trails, conservation lands, and other elements of the public realm. A multidimensional system, focused on community sustainability and resiliency, could also include such subsystems as green infrastructure, climate change adaptations, homeless services, educational and social programs, economic development, and others. Each subsystem has its own unique constituents, facilities, programs, amenities, and issues; therefore, services may be delivered differently among subsystems. Each subsystem also provides different opportunities to generate benefits for the community; for example, parks may provide the greatest opportunity for stormwater treatment, while bikeways and trails provide opportunities to increase fitness and multimodal connectivity. Parks and recreation system planners should identify the primary subsystems of their parks and recreation system and the benefits that they wish each subsystem to generate.

Many service delivery models have evolved organically, without much forethought given to possible alternatives. A more beneficial result is likely to come from approaching the process with greater intention. Five common alternative SDMs may be useful in developing a long-range vision: the centralized model, the decentralized (equity) model, the hub-and-spoke model, the venues model, and the activities model. These models apply not only to parks and recreation programs and facilities but also to other dimensions; examples include distribution of social services, economic development initiatives, and conservation land programs.

First, the centralized SDM (figure 10-3*A*) assumes that residents and visitors throughout the community will drive to the central facility. This model typically applies to regional or signature facilities and subsystems, such as an aquatics center, a sports complex, a social services center, an urban festival park, a town center, or a cultural center.

The decentralized (equity) SDM (figure 10-3*B*), on the other hand, focuses on the equitable distribution of services, measured in terms of distance (access LOS) or population served (facility or acreage LOS). The decentralized SDM assumes that facilities or parks will be distributed equitably throughout the community, for example, one facility per quadrant, as opposed to a single centralized facility. It is often used as a basis for the delivery of local parks, community parks, sports fields, and recreation centers. It could also be used as a basis for determining strategic satellite locations for the delivery of social services, grocery stores (in food deserts), and neighborhood retail centers.

The hub-and-spoke SDM (figure 10-3*C*) combines the centralized and decentralized (equity) models. A common example is a large centralized community or recreation center supplemented by several smaller satellite facilities. Or it might be a central location to provide workforce training or homeless services, supplemented by smaller computer labs or food banks in community centers or libraries.

The venues SDM (figure 10-3*D*) is a variation of the centralized model; it assumes that the system is composed of specialized facilities that will serve the entire community, regardless of access distance or population densities. For example, the City of Naples, Florida, has a tennis complex, a downtown urban festival park, a sports park, a dog park, an environmental preserve, a cultural arts park, a boat ramp park, a city beach, a city pier, and an aquatics and community center. Each facility was planned and designed as a first-class venue to serve the needs of residents citywide.

Finally, the activities SDM (figure 10-3*E*) focuses on providing desired recreation opportunities throughout the community without regard to the type of park or recreational facility. This model is most common in large urban sites where land is at a premium. A dog park or tennis courts may be located on top of a parking deck; a playground may be provided through a local church; and an athletics field may be provided through partnerships with local schools. For example, the City of Seattle built the I-5 Colonnade, an urban mountain bike skills park, under Interstate 5; and the City of New York tows a seven-lane swimming pool barge down the East River—dubbed the "Floating Pool Lady"—to serve the residents of the Bronx each summer (figure 10-4). The emphasis is not on park or facility types but on providing access to recreational opportunities wherever and however they can be provided.

As previously mentioned, each subsystem may deliver services using a different SDM. For example, an aquatics subsystem may deliver services through a single large, centralized multipurpose

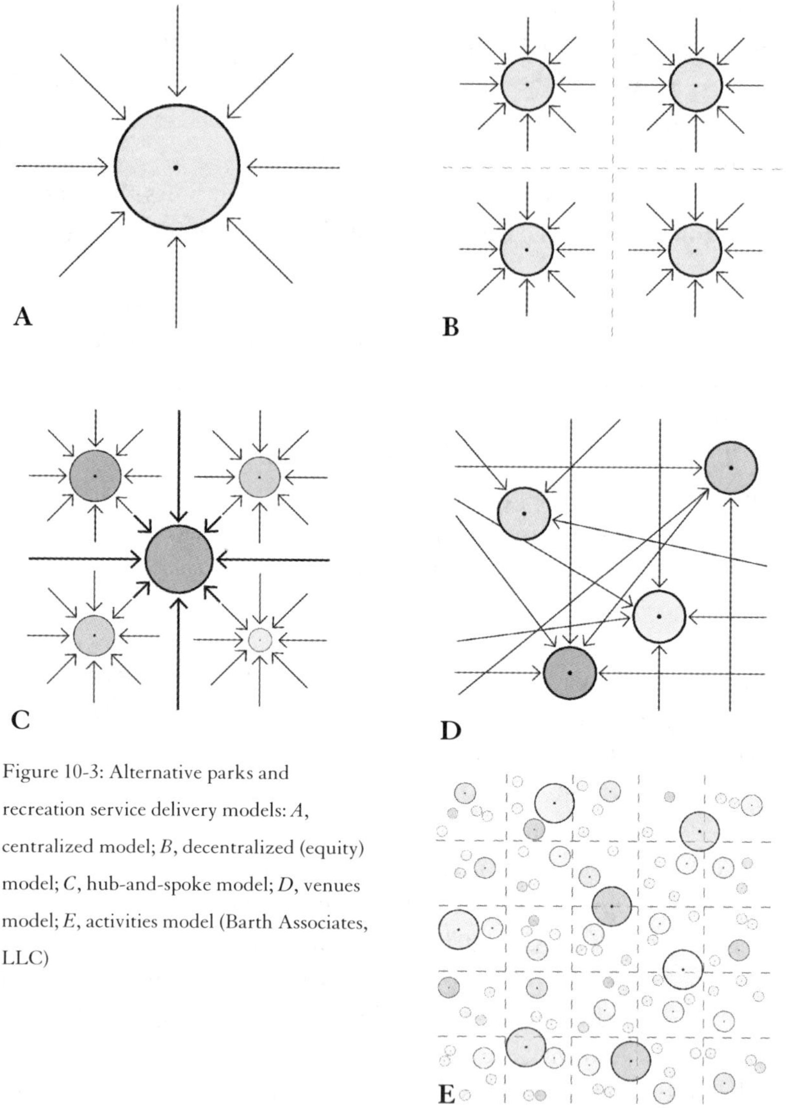

Figure 10-3: Alternative parks and recreation service delivery models: *A*, centralized model; *B*, decentralized (equity) model; *C*, hub-and-spoke model; *D*, venues model; *E*, activities model (Barth Associates, LLC)

aquatics complex that includes a family water park, a lap pool, and a competitive pool. A neighborhood parks subsystem, on the other hand, may deliver services through an equitably distributed decentralized model in which every neighborhood has access to a small public or private recreation area that includes a picnic shelter, a playground, basketball courts, and a multipurpose lawn. SDMs could be defined for other dimensions of a long-range vision as well, such

Figure 10-4: New York City's Floating Pool Lady (Photo by Jeffrey Bary, "Floating Pool Lady Deck," Creative Commons/https://www.flickr.com/photos/70118259@N00/711351365)

as the delivery of health and wellness services, workforce training, computer training, before- and after-school programs, homeless services, and others.

Facility Classifications

Traditional parks and recreation classifications have included mini-parks, neighborhood parks, school parks, community parks, large urban parks, regional parks, natural resource areas, greenways, sports complexes, and special use facilities.[7] Classifications are typically defined by acreage, service areas, and the types of facilities offered. I have found these classifications—particularly those related to parks—to be overly cumbersome and complex; few people can clearly define the differences between mini-neighborhood, community, urban, and regional parks, and the classifications have no practical use. Similarly, there is no clear definition of "active" versus "passive" parks or the alternative "user-based" versus "resource-based." These classifications do not recognize the wide variety of facilities and spaces found in modern parks systems, including dog parks, skate parks, splash pads, festival grounds, mountain bike parks, and others. They also do not reflect variations in levels of amenities and maintenance among facilities within the same subsystem. Therefore, many communities are developing their own classification systems to better reflect their needs and priorities.

As mentioned in the previous chapter, *EDEN by Design: The 1930 Olmsted-Bartholomew Plan for the Los Angeles Region* offers a much simpler and more compelling parks classification: local parks and regional parks. I have found that most communities' parks fall into one of these two categories. The primary exceptions are special use facilities, such as aquatics centers, sports complexes, and other single-purpose facilities, which also typically serve a regional population.

Another idea is to abandon traditional park classifications altogether and focus on differentiating parks and recreation facilities within each subsystem. We recently developed a three-tier classification system based on various levels of attributes including amenities, maintenance, staffing, and cost recovery goals. Figure 10-5 illustrates that base-tier facilities are the most common, with the lowest levels of attributes, while top-tier facilities are the least common.

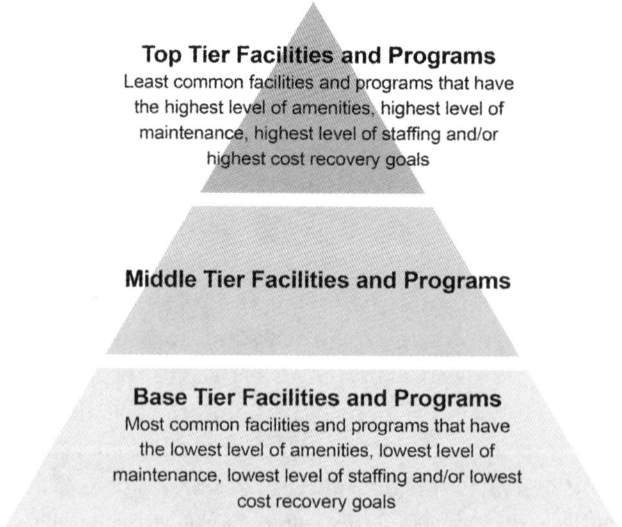

Figure 10-5: Three-tier classification system (Barth Associates, LLC)

Table 10-2
Sarasota County, Florida, Classification System

Subsystem	Top Tier	Middle Tier	Base Tier
Parks	Signature, special use	Community	Local
Natural areas and preserves	Destination	Enhanced	Accessible
Trails	Paved, multiuse, regional	Paved with amenities	Unpaved within parks and preserves
Beaches	Destination	Beach parks	Natural
Athletics	Signature	Competition	Recreation
Indoor recreation centers	Signature	Community	Neighborhood
Water access	Deep water, motorized	Small boats	Pier, dock, bank fishing

Source: Barth Associates, LLC.

The three-tier classification system can be applied to each subsystem within the parks and recreation system; table 10-2 lists proposed classifications for Sarasota County, Florida.

There are several benefits to such a classification system. First and foremost, it offers a descriptive alternative to the obsolete traditional classification system. Second, it is very flexible, easily customized to fit any system to reflect actual subsystems and SDMs. Finally—and most important—the three-tier system provides a basis for meaningful discussions about the allocation of resources among facilities, including amenities, programming, and maintenance, including the alternative dimensions of a PRSMP. Communities interested in establishing a new classification system may wish to use the following sequence:

1. Define subsystems for each dimension.
2. Define regional versus local parks, facilities, programs, or initiatives within each subsystem.
3. Define the three tiers of attributes for each type of park, facility, program, or initiative within each subsystem.

Oklahoma City's PRSMP took a slightly different approach. The city chose to use its traditional parks classification system but added tiers to differentiate levels of amenities, as shown in table 10-3 and figure 10-6.[8]

Table 10-3
Oklahoma City Classification System

Local Parks	Regional Parks	Other Parks
Serve the needs of nearby neighborhoods	Serve the needs of nearby neighborhoods and regional needs	Integral to the park and recreation system but do not have a defined level of service
Neighborhood parks	District parks	Greenspaces
Community parks	Metropolitan parks	Greenways
School parks		Nature parks
		Special use parks

Source: Oklahoma City Parks Master Plan, https://www.okc.gov/home/showdocument?id=1526.

SUMMARY OF AMENITIES

	Local Parks			Regional Parks		Other Parks			
	Neighborhood Parks	Community Parks	School Parks	District Parks	Metropolitan Parks	Greenspaces	Greenways	Nature Parks	Special Use Parks
PASSIVE RECREATION									
Informal Practice Fields/Open Space	●	●	●	●	●	○	○	●	●
Internal Walking Trails	●	●	●	●	●	○	○	●	●
People Watching Areas	●	●	●	●	●	○	○	○	○
Unique Landscape/Features	●	●	●	●	●	●	○	●	●
Nature Interpretation Areas	○	●	●	●	●	○	○	●	●
Arboretum/Botanical Garden	○	●	●	●	●	○	○	●	●
Ornamental Gardens	●	●	●	●	●	○	○	○	●
Community Gardens	●	●	●	●	●	○	○	●	●
ACTIVE RECREATION									
Biking Trails	○	●	●	●	●	○	●	●	●
Outdoor Fitness/Exercise Facilities	●	●	●	●	●	○	●	●	●
Play Structures	●	●	●	●	●	○	○	●	○
Creative Play Attractions	●	●	●	●	●	○	○	○	○
Large Play Structures	○	●	●	●	●	○	○	○	○
Court Games	●	●	●	●	●	○	○	○	○
Tennis Courts	●	●	●	●	●	○	○	○	○
Volleyball Courts	●	●	●	●	●	○	○	○	○
Regulation Playfields/Game Fields	○	○	○	●	●	○	○	○	○
Regulation Sports Courts	○	○	○	●	●	○	○	○	○
Splash Pad/Spray Grounds	○	●	●	●	●	○	○	○	○
Outdoor Swimming Pools	○	○	●	●	●	○	○	○	○
Disc Golf Areas	○	○	○	○	●	○	○	○	○

Figure 10-6: (right and top of page 213) Oklahoma City's three-tier classification system ("Oklahoma City Parks Master Plan," August 2013, prepared for the City of Oklahoma City and Oklahoma City Community Foundation by Wallace Roberts & Todd, LLC, https://www.okc.gov/home/showdocument?id=1526)

Figure 10-6 (*continued*)

SUMMARY OF AMENITIES

	Local Parks			Regional Parks		Other Parks			
	Neighborhood Parks	Community Parks	School Parks	District Parks	Metropolitan Parks	Greenspaces	Greenways	Nature Parks	Special Use Parks
FACILITIES									
Individual Picnic/Sitting Areas	●	●	●	●	●	○	○	●	●
Group Picnic/Sitting Areas	●	●	●	●	●	○	○	●	●
Park Shelters	●	●	●	●	●	○	○	●	●
Facilities for Plays or Concerts	○	●	●	●	●	○	○	○	●
Aquatic Center	○	○	○	●	●	○	○	○	○
Multi-Generational Center	○	○	○	●	●	○	○	○	○
Senior Wellness Center	○	○	○	●	●	○	○	○	○
Indoor Fitness/Exercise Facilities	○	○	○	●	●	○	○	○	○
Nature Center	○	○	○	○	●	○	○	●	●
Boating Amenities	○	○	○	○	●	○	○	○	○

Classifications and terminology for parks, trails, programs and services, and other elements of the public realm vision should be as simple (the fewer the better) and self-explanatory as possible in order to avoid confusion, to provide the greatest flexibility possible, and to facilitate meaningful discussions.

Compelling Graphics

Regardless of the specific dimensions of the PRSMP, the vision must also include graphic maps to illustrate big ideas and bold initiatives; for example, the Miami-Dade County Master Plan poster (figure 0-1) conveyed the idea of a "50-Year, Unifying Vision for a Sustainable Miami-Dade County" through five subsystems—great parks, great public spaces, great natural and cultural places, great streets, and great greenways, trails, and water trails. The Washington, DC, parks master plan (figure 10-7A) illustrates seven elements (subsystems) and targets to revitalize the parks system in order to meet the parks and recreation department's mission to encourage residents to "move, grow, and be green." Denver's plan illustrates the elements of a healthy city. And Portland's comprehensive plan shows the interrelationships between parks, natural areas, trails and greenways, land use, and transportation.

In addition to compelling maps, a good vision includes graphics and illustrations to convey important concepts. For example, our New Port Richey, Florida, PRSMP included before-and-after images of the city's riverside drive to create a multimodal, activated greenway through the heart of the city (figures 10-7 C,D). And our plan for the City of Sarasota includes park prototypes and before-and-after images to illustrate the concepts of HPPSs, activation, and the Power of 10+.

Executive Summary

In my experience, few elected officials or key stakeholders have time to read an entire PRSMP report, which is why every plan should include a stand-alone executive summary. A well-written four-page summary, with plenty of compelling photos and graphics, can easily summarize the existing conditions, needs assessment, and long-range vision. It can also include the estimated costs and proposed implementation strategy, as discussed in the next chapter.

Challenges and Tips for a Successful Vision

The new approach to developing a long-range PRSMP vision described in this chapter—especially if it includes multiple dimensions related to resiliency and sustainability—can be incredibly time-consuming. Few public agency staff can put their regular duties on hold during the visioning phase, and they may feel as if they're working two jobs for a while. However, the investment of time is absolutely necessary to realize the types of community benefits discussed here, and many parks and recreation professionals have reported being educated, energized, and even exhilarated by a comprehensive and robust PRSMP visioning process.

Some keys to increasing the probability that a long-range vision will be adopted and implemented are as follows:

- Be as inclusive and collaborative as possible. My colleague Carlos Perez often repeats a quotation (source unknown) used by Jesús Aguirre, former agency director for the Washington, DC, Department of Parks and Recreation: "Bring me in early, and I am your partner; bring me in late, and I am your judge!"
- Develop a detailed schedule with key milestones during the planning and initiation phase of the project, so key team members and stakeholders can block out sufficient time to participate in the visioning process.
- Spend the necessary time to become knowledgeable about critical topics prior to the visioning phase, as discussed in chapter 7 (the deep dive).
- Make sure that the vision responds to residents' needs and desires, especially the priorities of elected officials and other decision makers.
- Schedule frequent opportunities to review and discuss the proposed vision with elected officials and decision makers before, during, and after the visioning process to build consensus prior to requesting approval and adoption. Nonvoting workshops and one-on-one meetings are the best venues for meaningful discussion.

It is especially gratifying when elected officials develop a greater appreciation for the role of parks and recreation systems in achieving greater community resiliency and sustainability, new funding is made available, and key innovative elements of the vision are adopted and implemented!

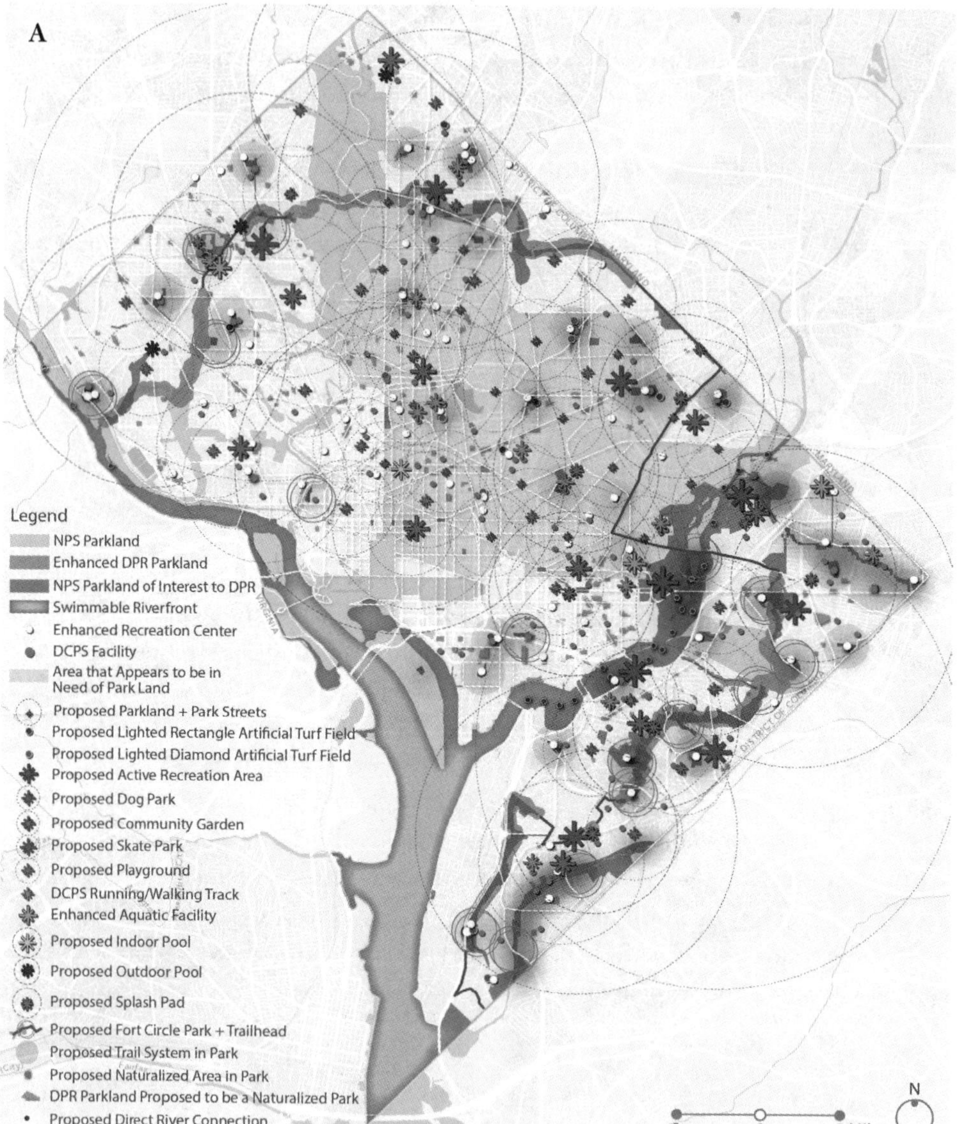

Figure 10-7 A: Examples of compelling maps and graphics in parks and recreation system master plans: District of Columbia (Washington, DC) Parks + Recreation Master Plan (AECOM Services of DC, A Professional Corporation);

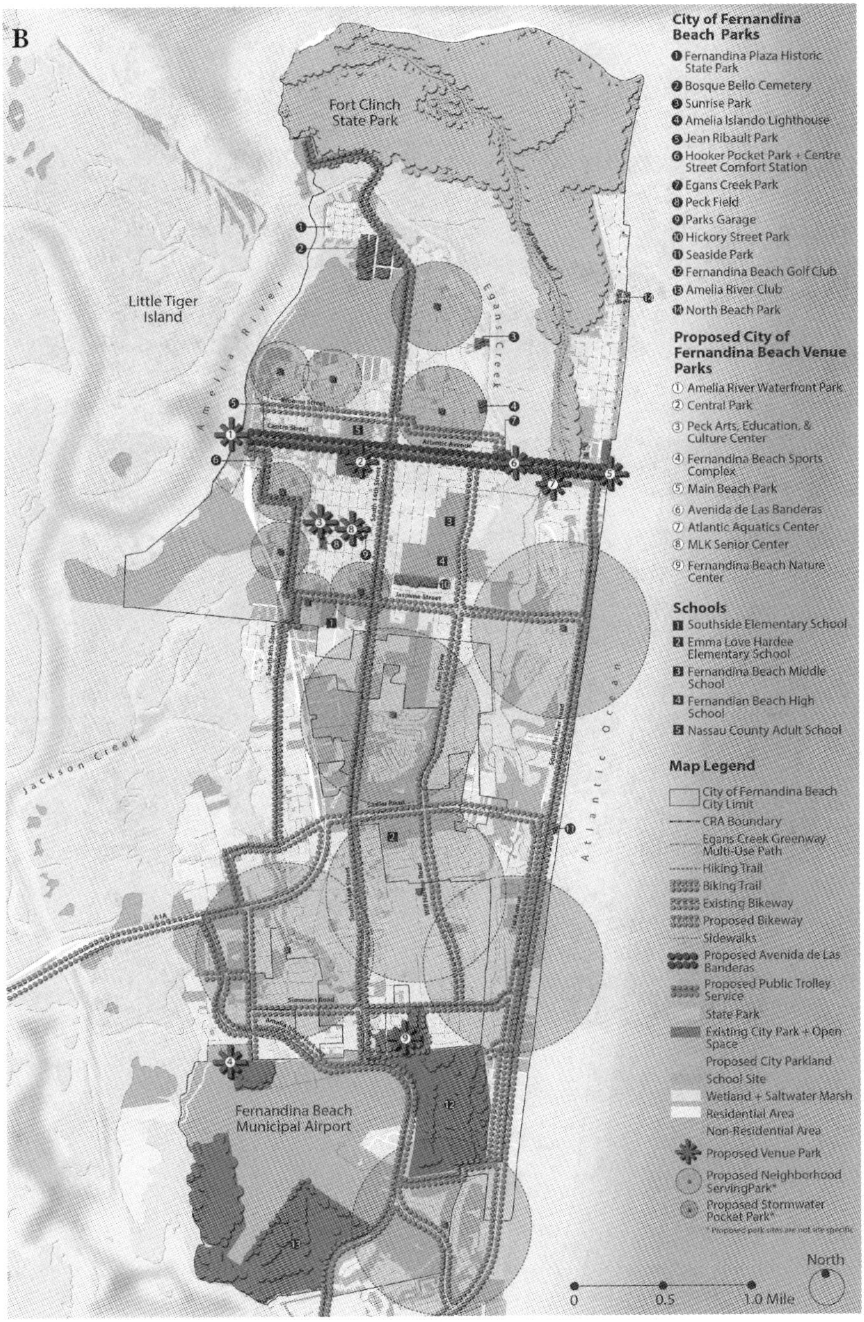

Figure 10-7 B: City of Fernandina Beach Parks + Recreation System Framework (Barth Associates, Perez Planning + Design);

Figure 10-7 C,D: City of New Port Richey Parks and Recreation Master Plan (Barth Associates, Perez Planning + Design)

11 IMPLEMENTATION STRATEGY

The implementation phase of the parks and recreation system master plan (PRSMP) represents the culmination of all the analyzing, planning, ideating, discussing, meeting, surveying, thinking, and visioning activities described in the previous ten chapters. During this phase, the process comes full circle from the hypothetical preliminary implementation framework, or PIF (chapter 6), to develop a realistic, feasible implementation strategy based on the findings from the needs assessment and visioning phases.

Consistent with the previous phases of the PRSMP process, the new approach to parks and recreation system planning emphasizes a collaborative approach to implementation involving community leaders, elected officials, multiple departments and agencies, businesses, and other key stakeholders. Each can play a significant role in implementation as a champion, facilitator, partner, funder, or supporter.

Implementation is not just about funding; the final implementation strategy may also include other forms of implementation discussed in chapter 6. These may include updates to the comprehensive plan, land development regulations, level-of-service (LOS) metrics, and impact fees; changes in staffing and organizational structure; development of service delivery models (SDMs) and prototypes; and creation of public-private partnerships or joint use memoranda. Parks system planners need to collaborate with numerous individuals, departments, and agencies to form a truly comprehensive strategy depending on the dimensions, breadth, and depth of the parks and recreation system vision. An effective implementation strategy requires that participants transcend the silos of their departments or agencies; identify opportunities for partnerships or joint use; leverage available resources, regardless of the source; and actively look for ways to generate multiple benefits for the community through implementation of projects, programs, and initiatives.

Estimate of Costs

The first step in developing the implementation strategy is to estimate the costs of all of the proposed land acquisitions, capital improvements, programs, and other initiatives identified in the long-range vision, including any new sustainability or resiliency initiatives. The estimate must also include the recurring annual operating and maintenance costs required to staff and maintain the improvements and programs once they're implemented. Many elected officials are more concerned about ongoing operations and maintenance (O&M) costs than capital costs.

It should be noted—and publicly stated!—that PRSMP cost estimates are planning-level, order-of-magnitude costs that should not be used as budgets for specific projects. Such specificity requires more detailed feasibility and design studies, which are far beyond the scope of a typical PRSMP. The purpose of the PRSMP order-of-magnitude estimate is to (1) establish realistic expectations for the magnitude of potential costs to implement and maintain the long-range parks and recreation vision and (2) provide the foundation for a realistic funding, phasing, and implementation strategy.

Funding Projections

While estimating anticipated costs, it is equally important to estimate projected revenues. The funding projections identified in the PIF (discussed in chapter 6) need to be refined to reflect funding realities. Ideally, the preliminary funding sources and projections will have been discussed throughout the PRSMP process—particularly during interviews and interim presentations—to gauge the community's level of interest in funding parks and recreation improvements. Some communities desire to use only pay-as-you-go sources such as ad valorem taxes, sales taxes, grants, sponsorships, and fees; others are interested in leveraging funds through bonds. Regardless of the funding source, all funding projections should be developed in concert with the agency's finance or budget director in order to be as accurate as possible.

For example, we recently presented preliminary funding charts (tables 11-1*A* and 11-1*B*) at an interim presentation of the needs

Table 11-1*A*

Potential Twenty-Year Phasing and Funding Scenario

Phase One Improvements						
Year	CIP[a]	Grants	Existing Millage	MSTU[b]	Bonds	Totals
1		$1M				$1M
2		$1M	$2M			$3M
3		$1M	$2M			$3M
4		$1M	$2M			$3M
5		$1M	$2M	$1.6M		$4.6M
6	$4M	$2M	$2M	$1.6M	$10M	$19.6M
7	$4M	$2M	$2M	$1.6M	$10M	$19.6M
8	$4M	$2M	$2M	$1.6M	$10M	$19.6M
9	$4M	$2M	$2M	$1.6M	$10M	$19.6M
10	$4M	$2M	$2M	$1.6M	$10M	$19.6M
						$112.6M

Source: Barth Associates, LLC.
[a]Capital improvement program.
[b]Municipal service taxing unit.

Table 11-1*B*

Potential Twenty-Year Phasing and Funding Scenario

Phase Two Improvements							
Year	CIP[a]	Grants	Existing Millage	MSTU[b]	Bonds	Sales Tax	Totals
11	$4M	$2M	$2M	$1.6M	$10M	$7.5M	$27.1M
12	$4M	$2M	$2M	$1.6M	$10M	$7.5M	$27.1M
13	$4M	$2M	$2M	$1.6M	$10M	$7.5M	$27.1M
14	$4M	$2M	$2M	$1.6M	$10M	$7.5M	$27.1M
15	$4M	$2M	$2M	$1.6M	$10M	$7.5M	$27.1M
16	$4M	$2M	$2M	$1.6M	$10M	$7.5M	$27.1M
17	$4M	$2M	$2M	$1.6M	$10M	$7.5M	$27.1M
18	$4M	$2M	$2M	$1.6M	$10M	$7.5M	$27.1M
19	$4M	$2M	$2M	$1.6M	$10M	$7.5M	$27.1M
20	$4M	$2M	$2M	$1.6M	$10M	$7.5M	$27.1M
							$271M

Source: Barth Associates, LLC.
[a]Capital improvement program.
[b]Municipal service taxing unit.

assessment findings to a city council showing potential funding sources (totaling over $380 million) for a hypothetical two-phase, twenty-year improvement program to respond to residents' needs and priorities.

The council was not willing to support such an ambitious program, however, so the projections were refined during the visioning phase of the project. As a result, the final implementation strategy included a much more modest ten-year, approximately $49 million program based on the funding projections in table 11-2.

This reinforces the importance of the PIF as a tool for early discussions in the planning process. Had we not presented the more ambitious approach during the needs assessment phase but instead waited to discuss funding at the conclusion of the visioning phase, we might have lost credibility and the support of the council. By discussing it early, we were able to use the process to build consensus regarding a feasible, realistic strategy.

Table 11-2
Ten-Year Phase One Funding Scenario

Year	CIP[a]	Grants	MSTU[b]	Other Sources	Totals
1	$1M	$1M		$1M	$3M
2	$1M	$1M		$1M	$3M
3	$1M	$1M		$1M	$3M
4	$1M	$1M		$1M	$3M
5	$2M	$1.6M	$1.6M	$1M	$6.2M
6	$2M	$1.6M	$1.6M	$1M	$6.2M
7	$2M	$1.6M	$1.6M	$1M	$6.2M
8	$2M	$1.6M	$1.6M	$1M	$6.2M
9	$2M	$1.6M	$1.6M	$1M	$6.2M
10	$2M	$1.6M	$1.6M	$1M	$6.2M
					$49.2M

Source: Barth Associates, LLC.
[a]Capital improvement program.
[b]Municipal service taxing unit.

Partnerships

Potential partnerships also need to be identified during the implementation phase of the project. For example, the PRSMP implementation strategy for the City of Raleigh, North Carolina, included a chart (table 11-3) of potential partnerships with other government agencies, nonprofits, and businesses to provide innovative solutions to a growing list of complex community needs.

It is important to note that different subsystems or dimensions of the vision may involve different partners. For example, potential partners in developing Raleigh's parks included the school system and private developers, while potential partners for the arts included nonprofit arts organizations and the State of North Carolina.

Implementation Workshop

An important milestone event in our planning practice is to convene a half-day implementation workshop to develop the PRSMP phasing and implementation strategy. Key stakeholders might include city or county managers, finance and budget directors, and existing and potential partners, as discussed earlier. Our typical agenda for an implementation workshop includes the following sequence of topics:

1. Review of the long-range vision
2. Review of estimated costs for both capital and operations
3. Review of funding projections
4. Review of priority needs
5. Establishment of prioritization criteria
6. Establishment of phases

The progressive discussion ultimately leads to the development of a proposed phasing plan, as illustrated in figure 11-1.

Development of the prioritization criteria is particularly important; few communities have the resources to immediately implement all of the projects and initiatives within a long-range plan. The criteria for a recent PRSMP, for example, included the following:

- The project or initiative will help accomplish one or more of the community's strategic goals.
- The project or initiative will help accomplish one or more of the commission's or council's priorities.
- The project or initiative will help meet one or more of residents' top-priority needs.

Table 11-3
City of Raleigh Existing and Potential Partnerships

Existing and Potential Partnerships			
Parks	**Natural Environments**	**Greenways**	**Athletics**
Wake County Public School System	Wake County Public School System	Wake County Public School System	Wake County Public School System
City of Raleigh Planning and Development	City of Raleigh Planning and Development	City of Raleigh Planning and Development	City of Raleigh Planning and Development
City of Raleigh Public Works	City of Raleigh Public Works	City of Raleigh Public Works	Greater Raleigh Convention and Visitors Bureau
Wake County	Wake County	Wake County	Wake County
Adjacent local governments	Adjacent local governments	Adjacent local governments	Private businesses
City of Oaks Foundation	City of Oaks Foundation	City of Oaks Foundation	City of Oaks Foundation
Private developers	Private developers	Private developers	Private recreation providers
Private recreation providers	Universities and colleges	Capital Area Metropolitan Planning Organization (CAMPO)	
	State of North Carolina	Public transit providers	
	Advocacy groups	Advocacy groups	
	Private schools		

EXISTING AND POTENTIAL PARTNERSHIPS

Programs and Services	Arts	Historic Resources	Growth Centers
Wake County Public School System	Wake County Public School System	Wake County Public School System	Wake County Public School System
City of Raleigh Public Works	City of Raleigh Planning and Development	City of Raleigh Planning and Development	City of Raleigh Planning and Development
City of Oaks Foundation	State of North Carolina	Greater Raleigh Convention and Visitors Bureau	State of North Carolina
Public transit providers	Wake County	Wake County Historical Society	Public transit providers
Universities and colleges	Universities and colleges	Raleigh Chamber of Commerce	Downtown Raleigh Alliance (DRA)
Local churches	Local arts service organizations		
Local activity centers	Arts partners and grantees		
Private schools			

Source: City of Raleigh, Parks, Recreation and Cultural Resources System Plan, 2014, https://raleighnc.gov/SupportPages/parks-recreation-and-cultural-resources-system-plan.

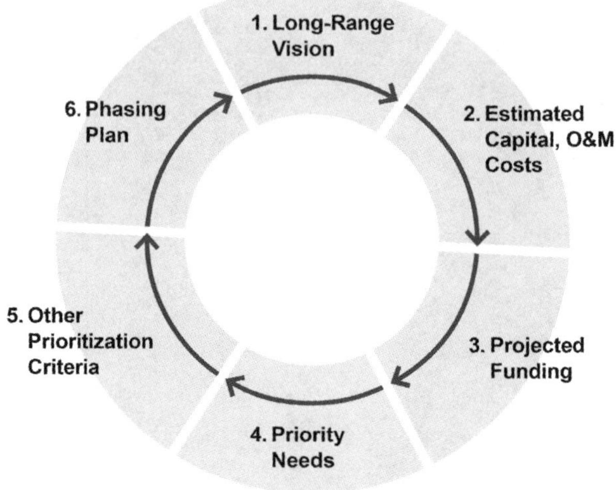

Figure 11-1: Prioritization process (Barth Associates, LLC)

- The project or initiative will provide a significant return on investment (ROI) economically, socially, environmentally, or all three.
- The project or initiative is exciting and compelling.

Other criteria may relate to public safety, protection of existing assets, availability of matching funds or grants, and benefits to youth and seniors. As with the LOS standards and long-range vision, each community must determine its own prioritization criteria based on community values and priorities.

Once the prioritization criteria are established, the planning team can score and rank each project. Some agencies choose to weight certain criteria; for example, they may determine that a score for youth development should count twice as much as a score for public safety. The preliminary scoring criteria should be reviewed by the project advisory committee and elected officials before being finalized; this will help build support and credibility for the final recommendations.

The final step in refining the implementation strategy is to reconcile the prioritized projects with available funding, which is a fairly simple exercise. Let's say, for example, that $200 million in expenses for projects and initiatives have been identified during the visioning process, but only $100 million in funding is projected to be available over the next ten-year period. The first phase of implementation would include the $100 million for projects and initiatives that received the highest ranking based on the prioritization criteria. Phasing is often further refined into small increments, such as one- and five-year strategies, but the process is the same.

Construction Delivery Methods

Few PRSMPs delve into the methods used to actually construct projects, but the topic warrants a brief mention because of the implications for project phasing. The three primary construction delivery methods include the conventional design-bid-build process, in which contactors bid on documents prepared by design professionals; the design-build process, in which contractors bid on preliminary design criteria documents and hire their own design team to work out the details; and the construction manager at risk (CM-at-Risk) process, in which a professional construction manager works alongside the client and the design team to develop the construction documents and provides a guaranteed maximum price once the project design has been solidified.[1] Each process has its pros and cons, which can be discussed during the implementation workshop.

The reason for discussing the alternatives during the PRSMP process is that certain construction delivery methods may be more appropriate for certain types of projects and can influence the way they are phased. For example, I prefer the CM-at-Risk method for large, complex projects where the contractor's expertise can be particularly valuable during the design process, potentially resulting in improved quality and significant cost savings. However, these projects can take a significant amount of time in construction manager selection, design team selection, and preparation of multiple design and bidding packages, such as site work, architecture, and landscape. The design-build process, on the other hand, can be a very cost-effective and time-saving method for implementing simpler projects, particularly when there are fewer complex design decisions to be made. A case in point is the implementation strategy for the Wild Spaces and Public Places program of Gainesville, Florida, which was funded through a sales tax initiative based on our Parks,

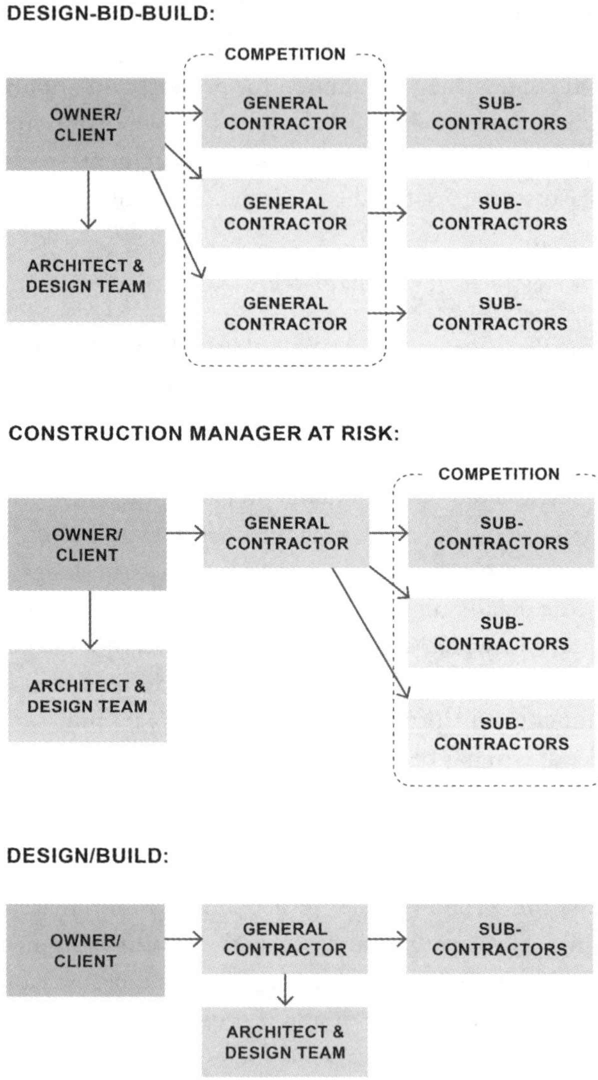

Figure 11-2: Alternative construction delivery methods (FGM Architects, Inc., used with permission; retrieved from http://www.jacksongalloway.com/news/2016/4/12/comparing-three-popular-construction-contracting-methods-designbuild-design-bid-build-and-construction-manager-at-risk)

Recreation, and Cultural Affairs Master Plan. The city is using a design-build contract to make basic site improvements on several projects simultaneously, including playgrounds, site furnishings, and trails.

Finalizing the Implementation Strategy

Following the implementation workshop, we typically memorialize the conclusions in a preliminary implementation strategy for review and approval. For example, table 11-4 shows the proposed first phase of capital improvements for the City of Sarasota, Florida.

The estimated costs include sustainability and resiliency initiatives within the parks such as rain gardens and stormwater facilities, trailhead development, and shoreline stabilization. Other recommendations, such as homeless services coordination and a sustainability liaison, are included in staffing and organizational recommendations.

Not all PRSMPs include full estimates of capital and operating costs, especially ambitious, far-reaching plans with multiple sustainability and resiliency initiatives. The costs of some recommendations may be too difficult to estimate with any accuracy, and others may require significant collaboration among residents, businesses, and multiple agencies and organizations. Some agencies prefer simply to focus on the first phase of implementation; for example, the City of Denver, Colorado, established a three-year action plan for its PRSMP.

> The 3 Year Action Plan is a framework for keeping the Game Plan for a Healthy City a "living" document over the course of its 15–20 year planning horizon. As such, it is intended to be renewed and updated every 3 years for the life of the Game Plan.
>
> The true value of the 3 Year Action Plan is as a guide to inform key parts of the Annual Work Plans developed by the Department's various functional Divisions. The Divisions use these Annual Work Plans to guide their day-to-day operational priorities and establish milestones for measuring progress. The actions and recommendations in the 3 Year Action Plan come directly from the priority strategies identified in the Game Plan

Table 11-4
City of Sarasota Phase One Capital Improvements Plan

Proposed Improvement	Quantity	Unit Cost	Subtotal	Notes
Deferred maintenance, repairs, replacements			$22.6M	
Small local parks	27	Varies	$7.4M	City staff estimate
Large community parks	15	Varies	$13.7M	City staff estimate
Urban open spaces	9	Varies	$1.5M	City staff estimate
Small local parks			$20.25M	
Develop conceptual master plans for existing parks, including neighborhood engagement	±10	$25,000 average	$250,000	
Upgrade existing local parks per prototype	±10	$1M average	$10M	Walking trails, sports courts, pavilions, restrooms, playgrounds, shade trees, site furnishings, multipurpose open lawns, etc.
Acquire and develop new parks to meet ten-minute walk goal	±5	$2M average, including land acquisition	$10M	5–10 acres each

Large community parks, recreation centers, aquatics facilities			$17M	
Develop conceptual master plans for existing parks, including public engagement	10	$100,000 average	$1M	
Upgrade existing parks per prototype	5	$2M average	$10M	Walking trails, sports courts, pavilions, restrooms, playgrounds, shade trees, site furnishings, athletics fields, central gathering spaces, etc., plus new facilities required to meet residents' needs
New indoor recreation space	20,000 square feet	$300	$6M	Location, size to be determined; could be a single multipurpose center or multiple satellite facilities
Urban open spaces			$5M	
Pocket parks in Rosemary District	To be determined			Allowance for acquisition, joint use, leases, and improvements
Natural areas			$5M	
Acquisition of vacant land adjacent to existing parks	5 acres	$1M/acre average	$5M	To increase park acreage level of service
TOTAL			$69.85M	

Source: Barth Associates, LLC.

> document and are meant to clearly identify to internal staff, the public, and stakeholders, how the department will be taking more specific actions on the various phases of plan implementation. Collaboration is a key goal for this Action Plan; it identifies opportunities for internal and external collaboration to work together towards shared goals.[2]

The action plan includes recommended actions for each of the plan's five implementation strategies—adapt to the changing climate and limited resources; diversify parks and recreation services; grow the park system and recreation access; reinvest in Denver's parks and recreation resources and people; and connect to Denver's nature and culture. Each action lists the lead agency or division, the supporting divisions or divisions, external partners, three-year milestones, and supporting actions. The plan also recommends the creation of an annual report or online dashboard to report annual progress toward the milestones.

The ultimate test for an implementation strategy is whether it will result in approval and adoption of the PRSMP. Each public agency council or commission has a unique personality and culture, and the implementation strategy must respond to their individual preferences and perspectives. For example, we have had clients ask us to remove all cost estimates in order to get a plan approved; they agreed with the long-range vision and recommendations but were not willing to commit to the funding. Others have asked for full estimates for capital and operations, prioritization criteria, and year-by-year funding and phasing estimates. We have also been asked to provide estimates for only the proposed first phase of projects because of concerns of political or public perception of long-term costs. Most recently, we were asked to remove all funding projections from an implementation strategy; the city was not concerned about costs and just preferred to determine specific funding sources and phasing strategies during the normal annual budgeting process. This reinforces the importance of the one-on-one briefings, shown as step 11 in the PRSMP process (figure 11-3), to make sure that each elected official is comfortable and supportive of the proposed long-range vision and the implementation strategy.

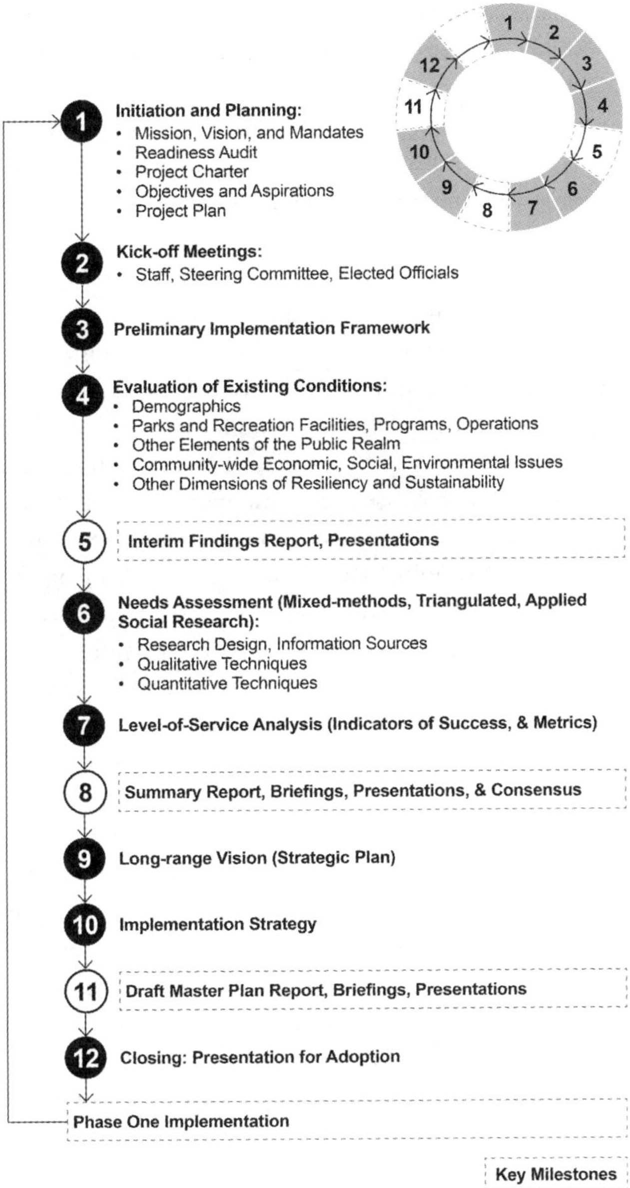

Figure 11-3: PRSMP process (Barth Associates, LLC)

One particular experience underscores the importance of understanding the perspective of the elected body and discussing implementation from the very beginning of a project. Years ago, we developed the long-range vision and implementation strategy for a PRSMP and were asked to reduce the scope of our recommendations because of the city commission's general antigovernment spending philosophy. However, our modest proposal for improvements failed to gain approval even after our one-on-one briefings. A year later, we were invited to resubmit the plan to the members of a newly elected commission, who asked why our recommendations were so modest! They requested that we update the plan to fully reflect the estimated costs of the long-range vision and provide them with maximum flexibility to implement the plan through a variety of funding sources. The revised implementation strategy stated that "project funding will be determined annually, based on Commission priorities. Potential funding sources may include, but not be limited to ad valorem taxes, county surtax, bonds, special assessments, impact fees, user fees, grants, donations, public-private partnerships and/or other sources." The revised plan was unanimously approved and adopted and is currently being implemented.

Summary

Successful approval of the implementation strategy—and subsequent approval and adoption of the entire PRSMP—is a significant accomplishment. While all of the recommendations and funding may not be approved, the authorization of even a modest first phase is cause for celebration. Then the focus turns to the planning and design of each approved improvement or program in order to generate as many community-wide benefits as possible. Once residents and elected officials see the actual benefits of the first phase of implementation, they are often eager to fund subsequent phases, and, as illustrated in figure 11-3, the PRSMP process begins all over again. Numerous communities throughout the United States have passed a series of bond or sales tax initiatives to continually fund multiple phases of parks, recreation, open space, and public realm improvements that meet residents' needs, improve the quality of their lives, and make their communities more livable, sustainable, and resilient.

CONCLUSION

The Power of Parks and Recreation System Planning

I recently had a conversation with a parks and recreation director whose agency runs a stellar youth sports program, engaging over 40 percent of the kids in the community. She had interviewed for a directorship position in a larger city and was surprised to find that she wasn't even short-listed. It turned out that the larger city was looking for someone with a broader perspective of parks and recreation to help address community issues such as social equity, economic sustainability, and resiliency to climate change. "I didn't even get to first base," she said, "but it was a great education." It opened her eyes to the reality that, in addition to sports, communities also care deeply about the role of their parks and recreation system in promoting the arts, culture, economic development, greenways, trails, water quality, habitat, and many of the other dimensions of their parks and recreation system that I've discussed in this book.

Her experience embodies the aspirations I expressed in the introduction: (1) that parks and recreation planners will gain a greater appreciation of the incredible opportunities they have to significantly influence the quality of life in their communities; (2) that parks and recreation system planning can be a platform for community leadership; and (3) that there is a need for a far more rigorous, robust, and collaborative planning process for parks and recreation systems to both increase their influence and generate greater community-wide benefits.

I hope that the opportunities to improve community quality of life, resiliency, and sustainability have become abundantly clear. Throughout this book I've discussed numerous examples of opportunities for parks and recreation systems to create jobs, increase revenues, protect natural resources, shape urban form and character, expand access, improve health and education, and strengthen families. And, in light of worsening wealth inequality, climate change, and political exhaustion, parks and recreation systems can be an oasis, bringing people together, mitigating effects of storms and severe weather, and providing an outlet for stress relief and opportunities to improve overall wellness for community members.

For those who believe that more research and analysis are necessary to "prove" the benefits generated by parks and recreation systems, I suggest that we have successfully passed the tipping point; more and more elected officials, community and business leaders, and developers are now acknowledging the irrefutable relationship between great parks and recreation systems and sustainable, resilient, and livable communities. The City Parks Alliance's excellent five-part video series, *City Parks: America's New Infrastructure*, features conversations with mayors, chief executive officers, health-care providers, and other community leaders regarding the role of parks systems in their communities. Denver's mayor, Michael Hancock, states that "study after study has shown that the more open space and the more dedication of park space that you have, the healthier your community will be. . . . One of the things that developers understand is that if I have parks, people are more likely to want to invest and live and work in an area." Similarly, Catherine Nagel, executive director of City Parks Alliance, says that "cities are looking at parks to help address pressing urban infrastructure challenges. . . . When we see the cities who have made those long term investments in urban parks and recreation systems, those cities seem to be thriving; they've put that basic infrastructure in place." Dr. Robert Zarr, founder of Park RX America and a pediatrician at UnitedHealthcare, notes that "the closer you live to green space, the more likely you are to access it, and the more likely you are to be active. For every dollar spent on creating and maintaining trails, you save three dollars in health-care expenses." Mick Cornett, former mayor of Oklahoma City, summarizes: "You can't be a great city without great parks."[1]

I've witnessed firsthand the power of parks and recreation system planning as a platform for community leadership. I've seen enlightened parks and recreation directors assigned responsibility for libraries, stormwater systems, tourism, and other elements of the public realm. I've seen other directors—who understand the far-reaching influence of the public realm—promoted to city and county management positions. And I've seen agency planners initiate transformative, visionary parks and recreation projects that have revitalized entire communities. Planners' actions and recommendations can have extremely powerful effects on the future of cities, towns, counties, and regions, says William Klein, former director of research and advisory services for the American Planning Association. Planners are "uniquely positioned" because "they are key players in . . . the five strategic points of intervention": long-range community visioning and goal setting; plan making; standards, policies, and incentives; development work; and public investments.[2] The parks and recreation system planning process provides planners with opportunities to make significant contributions in all five of these strategic points.

My hope is that planners will recognize the need for a far more rigorous, robust, and collaborative parks and recreation system planning process to both increase their influence and generate greater community-wide benefits. A common refrain throughout this book has been the need to revamp the traditional parks and recreation system planning process in order to have the greatest possible effects on our communities. It can be a huge undertaking, requiring much more time and money, but the results will be worth it.

We need to plan our parks and recreation systems as integral parts of the public realm, figuratively and physically connected to streets and bikeways, stormwater and utility facilities, and conservation lands, trails, and greenways. Only then can a parks and recreation system generate the desired community-wide impacts on resiliency and sustainability.

We also need to broaden our perspectives of a parks and recreation system, including the benefits that can be generated, to include economic development, health, social equity, crime reduction, water quality, and other dimensions of resiliency and sustainability. A broadened perspective makes it easier to recognize opportunities to generate multiple benefits.

We need to make the PRSMP process more thoughtful, robust, and rigorous by applying the best practices and principles from the disciplines of project management, strategic planning, and applied social science research. A well-organized, inclusive, and scientific process leads to a more credible and consensus-based plan—which increases the chances of successful adoption and implementation.

Finally—and perhaps most important—parks and recreation planners must be excited about the innovations and recommendations in the PRSMP and committed to their implementation. Project teams who are passionate about their projects consistently overcome the numerous obstacles and challenges that arise when implementing a bold new vision. This is particularly true for large, ambitious projects—think of the High Line or Historic Fourth Ward Park—that may take years to implement but ultimately transform entire areas and generate multiple community-wide benefits.

Regardless of your aspirations—whether you wish to transform your entire community, reposition your department or parks and recreation system as being more essential, or simply increase the quality of the services and programs you provide to your community—the new approach to parks and recreation system planning can help you meet your goals. Following the process outlined in this book will result in a PRSMP that is more relevant to the needs and issues of your community and elected officials, more collaborative, more credible, and more likely to be successfully implemented and transformative.

APPENDIX 1

PARKS AND RECREATION SYSTEM MASTER PLAN (PRSMP) CHARTER OUTLINE

1. Project title: ____

2. Sponsoring department or agency: ___________________________

3. Project manager: ____

4. Oversight team: ____

5. Estimated budget: ____

6. Project purpose and goals:

____

____

____

7. Proposed dimensions and issues to be addressed:

____

____

____

8. Other public realm subsystems to be addressed:

____

____

____

9. Expectations, outcomes, and deliverables:

____

____

____

10. Preliminary project scope of work and methodology (create separate attachment if needed):

____

____

____

11. Project team, roles, and responsibilities:

____

____

____

12. Other key stakeholders to be involved:

____

____

____

13. Consultant selection process (if needed):

____

____

____

APPENDIX 2

MASTER (TYPICAL) OUTLINE FOR A PARKS AND RECREATION SYSTEM MASTER PLAN (PRSMP)

—

Letter from mayor/elected official

Letter from parks and recreation director

Acknowledgments

Table of contents

1. Executive Summary (lively and interesting)

- Purpose of the plan
  - Catalyst
  - Specific dimensions
  - Premise, role of the public realm
  - Objectives
  - Anticipated outcomes and actions
- Summary of conditions and issues
  - Community-wide
  - Parks and recreation system—physical, organizational, programmatic, financial, policies
  - Other elements of the public realm—transportation, stormwater, utilities, schools
- Summary of needs and priorities—key findings, preliminary recommendations
- Summary of long-range vision—physical, organizational, programmatic, financial, policies
- Summary of decision-making framework—mission, vision, role, service delivery models and classifications, level-of-service (LOS) metrics, cost recovery goals, repair and replace schedule, organizational structure
- Summary of funding, phasing, and implementation strategy
- Summary action plan
  - Within 1 year
  - Within next 5 years

2. Existing Conditions and Issues

- Agency mission, vision, values, and role(s)
- Demographics
- Community-wide issues—environmental, social, economic
- Parks and recreation system
    - Physical (evaluation of aesthetics, functionality, maintenance, sustainability, resiliency, etc.)
    - Organizational
    - Programmatic
    - Financial, cost recovery
    - LOS
    - Policies
    - Partnerships
- Other elements of the public realm (overview)
    - Transportation
    - Stormwater
    - Utilities
    - Schools
- Summary of existing conditions and issues; implications for the PRSMP

3. Needs and Priorities Assessment

- Overview of purpose, process
- Social media plan
- Anecdotal techniques
    - Site observations and conversations
    - Previous and current studies
    - Local, state, and national trends research
- Qualitative techniques
    - Public outreach meetings
    - One-on-one interviews
    - Focus group meetings
    - Interactive website
    - Demographics/recreational lifestyle analysis
- Quantitative techniques
    - Statistically valid mail/telephone survey
    - Online survey
    - Benchmarking
    - LOS analysis

- Needs assessment summary
    - Key findings
    - Preliminary recommendations

4. Long-Range Vision

- Updated mission, vision, values, roles—who we are, why we exist, what we stand for, what we do
- The parks and recreation system
    - Parks and recreation facilities plan
    - Program plan
    - Maintenance and operations plans
- Integration with other elements of the public realm
- Estimated costs
- Anticipated benefits (related to original objectives)

5. Decision-Making Framework

- Service delivery models and classifications—how we deliver our parks, programs, and services
- Organizational structure, staffing plan—how we are organized to deliver our services
- Interlocal agreements and partnerships—who we partner with to deliver our services
- LOS, performance metrics—how we measure our success, needs
- Policies—what mandates direct our decision making
- Maintenance standards, repair and replacement schedule—how we maintain our system
- Operations, fees, cost recovery goals—how we operate in a fiscally responsible and sustainable manner
- Design standards—how we specify the construction of new and renovated facilities
- Business plans for enterprise facilities
- Land development regulations and codes—role and requirements for developers in contributing to the parks and recreation system
- CAPRA—how we meet or exceed the standards of the Commission for Accreditation of Parks and Recreation Agencies

6. Summary of Funding, Phasing, and Implementation Strategy

- Projected funding over next 1, 5, and 10 years
- Prioritization criteria

- Priority projects
- Phasing plan
- Plan updates
- Goals, objectives, policies
- Summary action plan
    - First 100 days
    - Within 1 year
    - Within next 5 years

APPENDIX 3

PARKS AND OPEN SPACE FUNDING WORKSHEET

—

The purpose of this worksheet is to calculate potential funding for parks and open space improvements, based on historical and projected funding. **Please fill in 1-, 5-, and 10-year funding projections for each appropriate funding source.** Note the specific sources in the Comments column.

Pay-as-You-Go	1 Year	5 Years	10 Years	Comments
City/county capital improvement program for street, park improvements				
Citywide parks improvement district				
Area parks improvement district				
Special parks assessment				
Parks conservancy, capital campaign, fund raising (bricks, naming rights, etc.)				
Tax increment financing				
Concession revenues				
Public use easements on private parcels, including rooftops, stormwater ponds, vacant lands, etc.				
Prescriptive codes, regulations				
Partnerships with schools, churches, nonprofits				
Use of other public lands (e.g., Department of Transportation underpass)				
Donations, gifts				
Interagency transfers (e.g., military)				
Impact fees: parks, transportation				
Tax-defaulted properties				

Grants: local, state, federal				
Parking fees				
Stormwater utility fees				
User fees				
Corporate sponsorships				
Land swaps				
Local sales tax				

Borrowing	1 Year	5 Years	10 Years	Comments
City/county general obligation bonds				
City/county revenue bonds				
Revolving loan fund				

Regulatory, private actions	1 Year	5 Years	10 Years	Comments
Prescriptive codes, regulations				
Zoning, land use incentives and credits				
Negotiated exactions, donations				
Legal settlements, mitigation				
Volunteers, adopt-a-park programs				
Site plan/design assistance				
Stormwater treatment design standards				
Transfer of development rights				
Water quality, conservation credits				
TOTALS				

APPENDIX 4

EXAMPLE OF A PARK EVALUATION FORM

Park Name: ______________________________

1. PROXIMITY/ACCESS/LINKAGES | Total Score: _____

Visibility from a distance

(**1** being poor visibility to the interior of the park from the surrounding neighborhood due to man-made structures or natural features that obstruct views into the park; **5** being the ability to see clearly into the park from the surrounding neighborhood)

1 2 3 4 5

Ease in walking to the park

(**1** being poor access to the park from the surrounding neighborhood due to disconnected sidewalks, lack of shade trees, unmarked pedestrian street crossings on fast, wide streets, and single-sided park frontage onto the street; **5** being ADA accessible on wide, shaded sidewalks that lead to the park, pedestrian-timed street crossings on narrow streets that lead to an interconnected park sidewalk network, multiple sides of the park facing the street)

1 2 3 4 5

Transit access

(**1** being a transit stop located within a quarter mile of the park; **5** being directional and orientational signage that directs park users to an easily accessible transit stop within a quarter mile with comfortable and sheltered seating area or [depending on the size and function of the park] a highly visible and easily accessible transit stop located on park property with bike racks, directional and orientational signage, pedestrian comfort stations, and comfortable and sheltered seating area)

1 2 3 4 5

Clarity of information/signage

(**1** being the mere presence of gateway signage and regulatory signage; **5** being a hierarchy of signage [gateway, location map, depending on the complexity of the park, identification, regulatory, directional, educational, etc.] that is clear, legible, and well maintained)

1 2 3 4 5

ADA compliance

(**1** being the park appears to be generally inaccessible due to a lack of appropriate ramps, equitable distribution of site accessibility facilities, level paving, etc., and does not appear to be easily usable by someone with special needs; **5** being the majority of the park shows evidence that its intent is to be accessible and would allow equitable use by people with all needs/abilities)

1 2 3 4 5

Lighting

(At the time of evaluation, is the park apparently lit appropriately for its typology? **1** being the park is not appropriately lit; **5** being the park is well lit and the fixtures present are energy efficient and contribute to the overall aesthetic)

1 2 3 4 5

COMMENTS:

---

2. COMFORT AND IMAGE | Total Score: _____

First impression/overall attractiveness

(**1** being a park that is perceived to be uninviting, unsafe, abandoned, dilapidated, and unmaintained; **5** being a park that is perceived to be inviting, safe, and impeccably maintained)

1 2 3 4 5

Feeling of safety
(**1** being surroundings that induce a feeling of danger due to obstruction of natural surveillance and eyes on the park, extreme pedestrian access control [high fences, single access point], lack of territorial enforcement and sense of ownership, and appearance of abandonment; **5** being surroundings that evoke a feeling of safety and security through promotion of eyes on the park, selectively placed entry and exit points, short and least sight-limiting fencing, spaces that promote proprietary concern, and well-maintained spaces)

1 2 3 4 5

Cleanliness/overall quality of maintenance (exterior site)
(**1** being unclean and damaged structures, recreational facilities, pavements, furnishings, and other hardscapes; dying, damaged, and unmaintained landscaping and the presence of litter; **5** being seamlessly maintained structures, recreational facilities, pavements, furnishings, and other hardscapes; healthy, vibrant, and well-maintained landscaping; and no litter)

1 2 3 4 5

Cleanliness/overall quality of maintenance (facilities interior)
(**1** being unclean and damaged structures, recreational facilities, pavements, furnishings, and other hardscapes; dying, damaged, and unmaintained landscaping and the presence of litter; **5** being seamlessly maintained structures, recreational facilities, pavements, furnishings, and other hardscapes; healthy, vibrant, and well-maintained landscaping; and no litter)

1 2 3 4 5

Comfort of places to sit
(**1** being uninviting, damaged, dirty, and sensorially unpleasant; **5** being inviting, neat, clean, and sensorially pleasant)

1 2 3 4 5

Protection from bad weather
(**1** being the presence of a covered structure [depending on the complexity of the park, at least one] that does not offer complete protection from the elements and is difficult to get to; **5** being covered structures [depending on the complexity of the park, several structures strategically placed] that offer complete protection from the elements and are easily accessible)

1 2 3 4 5

Evidence of management/stewardship (exterior site)
(**1** being an abandoned appearance [unmaintained landscaping, deteriorating structures, and hardscape, presence of litter]; **5** being a cared-for appearance [impeccably maintained landscaping, hardscapes, and structures and no litter])

1 2 3 4 5

Evidence of management/stewardship (facility interior)
(**1** being an abandoned appearance [unmaintained, deteriorating structures and hardscape, presence of litter]; **5** being a cared-for appearance [impeccably maintained hardscapes and structures and no litter])

1 2 3 4 5

Ability to easily supervise and manage the park or facility (interior)
(**1** being difficult to supervise [cannot easily see entrances or exits to the facility or major program areas]; **5** being easily supervised [facility is configured in a manner that allows for clear views of major amenities and all entrances and exits from a central location])

1 2 3 4 5

Condition and effectiveness of equipment and operating systems
(**1** being equipment is in poor condition and ineffective [fitness equipment is old and not well maintained, and computerized registration and facility management is not available]; **5** being equipment is in good condition and effective [all equipment is well maintained through a formal process, and fully computerized operating systems are in place and updated regularly])

1 2 3 4 5

COMMENTS:

---

3. USES, ACTIVITIES, SOCIABILITY | Total Score: _____

Mix of uses/things to do
(**1** being a single-use park that can be used only in specific weather conditions; **5** being a park that offers activities for a variety of users [children, adults, seniors] at all times during the day)

1 2 3 4 5

Level of activity
(At the time of evaluation, what is the level of activity within the site, based on appropriate level for its typology? **1** being a few people using the park at a single time period; **5** being a variety of people of different age groups using the park at all times during the day)

1 2 3 4 5

Sense of pride/ownership
(**1** being litter, vandalism, and misuse of facilities; lack of use; and lack of maintenance and upkeep; **5** being an actively used park; volunteers; "patrolling" users; signs of care, maintenance, and upkeep)

1 2 3 4 5

Programming flexibility
(**1** being inflexible, limited use due to topography, size, access, physical limitations, and single-season use; **5** being most flexible, with large range of options due to support system, shelter, and water, etc., for multiple uses; flexible topography, open space)

1 2 3 4 5

Ability of facility to effectively support current organized programming
(**1** being inability of facility to support current organized programs [space is too small or not configured properly for the programming it must support]; **5** being ability to support organized programming [facility has proper spaces that are adequate in size and makeup to allow the facility's programming to thrive])

1 2 3 4 5

Marketing or promotional efforts for the facility or activities
(**1** being poor marketing or promotional efforts for the facility or activities [no obvious efforts to promote the facility or its activities to the community it supports]; **5** being effective marketing or promotional efforts for the facility or activities [a basic marketing plan is in place that relies on a variety of promotional tools to bring users to the facility and its programs])

1 2 3 4 5

COMMENTS:

---

4. ENVIRONMENTAL SUSTAINABILITY | Total Score: _____
Stormwater management
(**1** being a drainage system that discharges water from the site without any intermediate retention or treatment, large amount of impervious surfaces; **5** being a system that successfully incorporates the reuse of stormwater where feasible and treats as much water on-site as possible through retention/detention, bioswales, wetlands, pervious paving, green roofs, and the like)

1 2 3 4 5

Multimodal capacity

(**1** being a poorly connected park that relies solely on automobile access; **5** being a park that facilitates the use of alternative modes of transportation through bicycle and adjacent mass transit facilities as well as interconnected pedestrian access routes to and within the park)

1 2 3 4 5

Facility energy efficiency

(Based on observational techniques, **1** being a clear lack of energy efficiency improvements and complete lack of facility upgrades or construction; **5** being certification of building as an energy-efficient structure or clear evidence of facility improvement or enhancement consistent with energy efficiency standards of city or other entity)

1 2 3 4 5

COMMENTS:

---

5. BUILDINGS/ARCHITECTURE | Total Score: _____

Image and aesthetics

(**1** being a building that is visually unpleasing or detracts from the surrounding park or neighborhood setting; **5** being a building that has pleasing proportions and materials and contributes to the context of the park or neighborhood setting)

1 2 3 4 5

Clarity of entry and connections to park

(**1** being a building with multiple doors that appear to be entries but are emergency exits only, or other confusing elements on the exterior; **5** being a building with a clearly defined main point of entry, pleasant lobby space and sense of arrival, and clear access to outdoor recreation)

1 2 3 4 5

Interior layout
(**1** being an interior layout that is confusing or inefficient; **5** being a well-organized interior layout)

1 2 3 4 5

Interior finishes, furniture, and equipment
(**1** being interior finishes, furniture, and equipment that are worn, damaged, or outdated; **5** being finishes, furniture, and equipment that are undamaged, well maintained, and aesthetically pleasing)

1 2 3 4 5

Functioning dimensions of spaces
(**1** being spaces that are incorrectly sized or otherwise ill-fitted for their current function [e.g., spaces too small or ceilings too low for a competition court]; **5** being spaces of ample size and volume for their function, based on current guidelines)

1 2 3 4 5

Structural integrity
(**1** being dangerous structural conditions as determined by visual observation; **5** being no visible evidence of loss of integrity of any structural members)

1 2 3 4 5

Building enclosure
(**1** being visibly obvious openings or breaches in exterior roof or walls; **5** being no evidence of need for repair of components of the building enclosure, and all materials maintained with weatherproof finishes)

1 2 3 4 5

Building systems
(**1** being building's mechanical, electrical, or plumbing systems in obvious visual need of repair; **5** being all mechanical, electrical, and plumbing systems observed to be in operating order and well maintained)

1 2 3 4 5

Energy and sustainability
(**1** being that the building has deficiencies in insulation, energy-efficient mechanical systems, or use of sustainable materials; **5** being visual evidence that building components appear to be energy efficient and have appropriate use of sustainable materials or systems)

1 2 3 4 5

COMMENTS:

---

6. OPPORTUNITIES TO CREATE HIGH-PERFORMANCE PUBLIC SPACES TO IMPROVE RESILIENCY AND SUSTAINABILITY

	Existing (1–5)	Opportunities (1–5) (state specifics)
Economic Criteria		
• The space creates and facilitates revenue-generating opportunities for the public sector and/or the private sector.		
• The space creates meaningful and desirable employment.		
• The space indirectly creates or sustains good, living-wage jobs.		
• The space sustains or increases property values.		
• The space catalyzes infill development and/or the reuse of obsolete or underused buildings or spaces.		
• The space attracts new residents.		
• The space attracts new businesses.		
• The space generates increased business and tax revenues.		
• The space optimizes operations and maintenance costs (compared with other similar spaces).		

Environmental Criteria		
• The space uses energy, water, and material resources efficiently.		
• The space improves quality of both surface water and groundwater.		
• The space serves as a net carbon sink.		
• The space enhances, preserves, promotes, or contributes to biological diversity.		
• Hardscape materials were selected on the basis of longevity of service; social, cultural, and historical sustainability; regional availability; low carbon footprint; and/or other related criteria.		
• The space provides opportunities to enhance environmental awareness and knowledge.		
• The space serves as an interconnected node within larger-scale ecological corridors and natural habitat.		
Social Criteria		
• The space improves the neighborhood.		
• The space improves social and physical mobility through multimodal connectivity—automobile, transit, bike, pedestrian.		
• The space encourages the health and fitness of residents and visitors.		
• The space provides relief from urban congestion and stressors such as social confrontation, noise pollution, and air pollution.		
• The space provides places for formal and informal social gatherings, art, performances, and community or civic events.		

APPENDIX 5

EXAMPLE OF A STATISTICALLY REPRESENTATIVE SURVEY

Let your voice be heard today! The City of Sarasota would like your input to help determine parks and recreation priorities for our community. Parks and recreation facilities contribute significantly to your quality of life, and your opinions are very important to us. This survey will take 15–20 minutes to complete. We greatly appreciate your time. If you prefer to complete the survey online, please go to [insert link].

1. **Parks, recreation, and open spaces provide a multitude of benefits. From the following list, please select the top FIVE benefits that are MOST IMPORTANT to you and your household.**

____(01) Community character (quality of the built environment, neighborhoods, streetscapes, etc.)
____(02) Community safety
____(03) Conservation of natural areas
____(04) Economic development (helping the city to be more vibrant, increasing property values, and attracting/retaining business)
____(05) Education (arts, culture, science, etc.)
____(06) Food production education/community gardens
____(07) Neighborhood/community open space for social interactions and play (creating a sense of community/bringing people together)
____(08) Recreation and athletics
____(09) Sustainability (ecological, fiscal, and social equity)
____(10) Transportation/connectivity (e.g., bike lanes, greenways)
____(11) Preservation of the heritage of the City of Sarasota
____(12) Promotion of holistic health (physical, social engagement, psychological), wellness, and fitness
____(13) Youth development
____(14) Other (please specify) ____________________

2. Please check ALL the City of Sarasota parks that you or members of your household have visited during the past 12 months.

____(01) A.B. Smith Park
____(02) Arlington Park
____(03) Avion Park
____(04) Bay Walk Park
____(05) Bayfront Community Center
____(06) Bayfront Park and Marina/Island Park
____(07) Beneva Road Park
____(08) Bird Key Park
____(09) Bobby Jones Golf Course
____(10) Bonita Park
____(11) Boulevard Arts Parks
____(12) Centennial Park
____(13) Charles Ringling Park
____(14) MLK Park
____(15) Eastwood Park
____(16) Eloise Werlin Park
____(17) Firehouse Park
____(18) Fredd Atkins Park
____(19) Fruitville Road Park
____(20) Galvin Park
____(21) Gillespie Park
____(22) Hart's Landing
____(23) Indian Beach Park
____(24) J.D. Hamel Park
____(25) John Ringling Causeway Park
____(26) Ken Thompson Park
____(27) Laurel Park
____(28) Lemon Avenue Mall
____(29) Lido Beach and Pool
____(30) Links Plaza Park
____(31) Little Five Points
____(32) Lukewood Park (North)
____(33) Lukewood Park (South)
____(34) Mary Dean Park
____(35) McClellan Parkway Park
____(36) Municipal Auditorium
____(37) New Pass Fishing Pier
____(38) Nora Patterson Bay Island Park (North)

____(39) North Lido Beach Park
____(40) North Water Tower Park
____(41) Orange Avenue Park
____(42) Otter Key Park
____(43) Payne Park
____(44) Payne Park Tennis Center
____(45) Paul Thorpe Park
____(46) Pioneer Park
____(47) Ringling Boulevard Park
____(48) Robarts Memorial Park
____(49) Robert L. Taylor Community Complex/David Cohen Park
____(50) San Remo Park
____(51) Sarasota Fairgrounds
____(52) Sarasota Lawn Bowling
____(53) School Avenue Greenway
____(54) Selby Five Points Park
____(55) Seminole Linear Park
____(56) Shenandoah Park
____(57) St. Armands Circle Park
____(58) Tony Saprito Pier
____(59) Tuttle Walkway Park
____(60) Waterfront Park
____(61) Whitaker Gateway Park

3. Please check ALL the reasons that prevent you or other members of your household from using parks, greenway trails, and recreation facilities of the City of Sarasota more often.

____(01) Facilities are not well maintained
____(02) I do not feel safe at parks/facilities
____(03) I do not know where parks are located
____(04) I use facilities offered by surrounding communities
____(05) I use private facilities
____(06) Lack of parking
____(07) Lack of transportation
____(08) Parks are not easily accessible by walking, biking, or driving
____(09) Parks are not easily accessible to the disabled
____(10) Parks do not contain facilities or amenities that are appropriate for my family and me
____(11) Parks/facilities are too far from my home
____(12) Park operating hours are not convenient

____(13) Other communities offer recreation facilities that are closer to my home or are of higher quality

____(14) Other (please specify) ________________

4. Please indicate if you or any member of your household has a need for each of the parks and recreation amenities listed below by circling Yes or No.

If Yes, please rate all of the following parks and recreation amenities of this type on a scale of 5 to 1, where 5 means the needs of your household are 100% met and 1 means 0% met.

	Type of Amenity	Do You Have a Need for This Amenity?		If Yes, How Well Are Your Needs Being Met?				
				100% Met	75% Met	50% Met	25% Met	0% Met
01	Baseball/softball fields	Yes	No	5	4	3	2	1
02	Boating access—motorized	Yes	No	5	4	3	2	1
03	Boating access—nonmotorized (e.g., canoe, kayak)	Yes	No	5	4	3	2	1
04	Community/recreation/teen centers	Yes	No	5	4	3	2	1
05	Community gardens	Yes	No	5	4	3	2	1
06	Disc golf course	Yes	No	5	4	3	2	1
07	Fishing pier							
08	Dog park	Yes	No	5	4	3	2	1
09	Game tables (e.g., chess, checkers, dominoes)	Yes	No	5	4	3	2	1
10	Golf course	Yes	No	5	4	3	2	1
11	Indoor fitness centers	Yes	No	5	4	3	2	1
12	Indoor gymnasiums (basketball, volleyball)	Yes	No	5	4	3	2	1
13	Indoor gymnastics area	Yes	No	5	4	3	2	1
14	Indoor nature center	Yes	No	5	4	3	2	1
15	Indoor swimming pool	Yes	No	5	4	3	2	1
16	Large community parks	Yes	No	5	4	3	2	1

17	Multipurpose fields	Yes	No	5	4	3	2	1
18	Natural areas/nature parks	Yes	No	5	4	3	2	1
19	Neighborhood parks	Yes	No	5	4	3	2	1
20	Outdoor basketball courts	Yes	No	5	4	3	2	1
21	Outdoor fitness equipment	Yes	No	5	4	3	2	1
22	Outdoor football/soccer/lacrosse fields	Yes	No	5	4	3	2	1
23	Outdoor swimming pool	Yes	No	5	4	3	2	1
24	Park shelters and picnic areas	Yes	No	5	4	3	2	1
25	Paved multipurpose trails	Yes	No	5	4	3	2	1
26	Performing arts center	Yes	No	5	4	3	2	1
27	Pickleball courts	Yes	No	5	4	3	2	1
28	Playgrounds	Yes	No	5	4	3	2	1
29	Restrooms at existing parks	Yes	No	5	4	3	2	1
30	Sand volleyball	Yes	No	5	4	3	2	1
31	Senior centers	Yes	No	5	4	3	2	1
32	Sidewalks	Yes	No	5	4	3	2	1
33	Skate park	Yes	No	5	4	3	2	1
34	Spraygrounds/splash pads	Yes	No	5	4	3	2	1
35	Tennis courts	Yes	No	5	4	3	2	1
36	Unpaved walking and hiking trails	Yes	No	5	4	3	2	1
37	Food concessions	Yes	No	5	4	3	2	1
38	Park benches/seating	Yes	No	5	4	3	2	1
39	Other (please specify) ____________________	Yes	No	5	4	3	2	1

5. **Which FOUR amenities from the list in question 4 are MOST IMPORTANT to your household?** *(Write in your answers below using the numbers from the list in question 4, or circle NONE.)*

1st: ____ 2nd: ____ 3rd: ____ 4th: ____ NONE

6. Please indicate if you or any member of your household has a need for each of the parks and recreation activities/programs listed below by circling Yes or No.

If Yes, please rate all of the following parks and recreation activities/ programs of this type on a scale of 5 to 1, where 5 means the needs of your household are 100% met and 1 means 0% met.

	Type of Activity/Program	Do You Have a Need for This Activity/ Program?		If Yes, How Well Are Your Needs Being Met?				
				100% Met	75% Met	50% Met	25% Met	0% Met
01	Adult athletic leagues	Yes	No	5	4	3	2	1
02	Adult education (e.g., GED, degree, trade)	Yes	No	5	4	3	2	1
03	Adult fitness/wellness	Yes	No	5	4	3	2	1
04	Adult learn to swim	Yes	No	5	4	3	2	1
05	Adult performing arts/dance	Yes	No	5	4	3	2	1
06	Athletic special events (e.g., 5K, marathons)	Yes	No	5	4	3	2	1
07	Before- and after-school programs	Yes	No	5	4	3	2	1
08	Camps (e.g., summer/school break)	Yes	No	5	4	3	2	1
09	Child day care	Yes	No	5	4	3	2	1
10	Community meetings	Yes	No	5	4	3	2	1
11	Community special events (e.g., concerts, green markets, festivals)	Yes	No	5	4	3	2	1
12	Cooking classes	Yes	No	5	4	3	2	1
13	Date night/parents' night out child care	Yes	No	5	4	3	2	1
14	Digital media, photography programs	Yes	No	5	4	3	2	1
15	Education lecture series	Yes	No	5	4	3	2	1
16	Footgolf	Yes	No	5	4	3	2	1
17	Galas, formal events	Yes	No	5	4	3	2	1
18	Gymnastics	Yes	No	5	4	3	2	1
19	Language classes	Yes	No	5	4	3	2	1
20	Movies in the park	Yes	No	5	4	3	2	1

21	Music programs	Yes	No	5	4	3	2	1
22	Nature programs/environmental education	Yes	No	5	4	3	2	1
23	Outdoor dining	Yes	No	5	4	3	2	1
24	Preschool programs	Yes	No	5	4	3	2	1
25	Programs for people with disabilities	Yes	No	5	4	3	2	1
26	Senior education (e.g., computer, special interest classes)	Yes	No	5	4	3	2	1
27	Senior leisure programs	Yes	No	5	4	3	2	1
28	Teen programs	Yes	No	5	4	3	2	1
29	Temporary art exhibits	Yes	No	5	4	3	2	1
30	Video games/virtual gaming	Yes	No	5	4	3	2	1
31	Water fitness	Yes	No	5	4	3	2	1
32	Youth arts/painting/crafts/drawing classes	Yes	No	5	4	3	2	1
33	Youth athletic leagues	Yes	No	5	4	3	2	1
34	Youth education (e.g., computer, programming, special interest classes)	Yes	No	5	4	3	2	1
35	Youth fitness/wellness	Yes	No	5	4	3	2	1
36	Youth learn to swim	Yes	No	5	4	3	2	1
37	Youth performing arts/dance	Yes	No	5	4	3	2	1
38	Other (please specify) ____________ ________________________	Yes	No	5	4	3	2	1

7. **Which FOUR activities/programs listed in question 6 are MOST IMPORTANT to your household?** *(Write in your answers below using the numbers from the list in question 6, or circle NONE.)*

1st: ____ 2nd: ____ 3rd: ____ 4th: ____ NONE

8. Please indicate how supportive you would be of each of the following actions that the City of Sarasota could take to improve the parks and recreation system.

	Action	Very Supportive	Somewhat Supportive	Not Sure	Not Supportive
01	Acquire land for developing parks and recreation facilities	4	3	2	1
02	Acquire land for developing sports/ athletics fields and courts	4	3	2	1
03	Acquire land for developing sports complexes for travel leagues' regional/ national competitions that attract tourism	4	3	2	1
04	Acquire land to preserve greenspace and tree canopy and provide access to natural areas	4	3	2	1
05	Acquire land to develop more greenways and trails	4	3	2	1
06	Completely redesign and renovate existing parks to meet residents' needs and priorities	4	3	2	1
07	Develop a teen center	4	3	2	1
08	Develop an indoor pool/aquatics center	4	3	2	1
09	Develop new athletics fields and courts	4	3	2	1
10	Develop new greenways, trails, high-quality bicycle facilities, and shaded sidewalks that enhance connectivity	4	3	2	1
11	Develop new parks and recreation facilities to meet residents' needs and priorities	4	3	2	1
12	Expand park resources to improve facility maintenance	4	3	2	1
13	Expand recreation and staff resources to offer more programs	4	3	2	1
14	Increase funding for improving, renovating, and expanding existing parks and recreation facilities	4	3	2	1

15	Offer more programs and special events that bring families together	4	3	2	1
16	Renovate and make improvements to existing parks and recreation facilities to meet residents' needs and priorities	4	3	2	1
17	Provide additional parking in parks	4	3	2	1
18	Do nothing—leave parks the way they are	4	3	2	1
19	Other (please specify) ____________ ____________	4	3	2	1

9. Which FOUR items listed in question 8 are MOST IMPORTANT to your household? *(Write in your answers below using the numbers from the list in question 8, or circle NONE.)*

1st: ____ 2nd: ____ 3rd: ____ 4th: ____ NONE

10. Parks and recreation systems have the potential to help address some of the complex social, economic, and environmental challenges facing communities. From the following list, please select the top FIVE challenges that are MOST IMPORTANT to your household.

____(01) Community safety
____(02) Flooding
____(03) Homelessness
____(04) Lack of workforce housing
____(05) Limited access to healthy foods such as fresh fruits and vegetables and whole foods
____(06) Limited access to multimodal transportation options (e.g., sidewalks, bikeways, trails, transit)
____(07) Limited adult education
____(08) Poor health
____(09) Poverty
____(10) Preservation of natural areas
____(11) Retaining/attracting youth and young families
____(12) Sea-level rise
____(13) Substandard childhood education
____(14) Traffic congestion
____(15) Water quality
____(16) Other (please specify) ____________

The following demographic information is requested to validate the survey; all responses will remain confidential.

11. Counting yourself, how many people in your household are:

Under age 5: ____
Ages 5–9: ____
Ages 10–14: ____
Ages 15–19: ____
Ages 20–24: ____
Ages 25–34: ____
Ages 35–44: ____
Ages 45–54: ____
Ages 55–64: ____
Ages 65–74: ____
Ages 75+: ____

12. What is your age? ____ years

13. Your gender: ____(1) Male ____(2) Female

14. Which of the following best describes your race? *(Check all that apply.)*

____(1) White/Caucasian
____(2) African American/Black
____(3) American Indian/Alaska Native
____(4) Asian/Pacific Islander
____(5) Other: ____________________

15. Are you or other members of your household of Hispanic, Latino, or Spanish ancestry?
____(1) Yes ____(2) No

16. What is your household income?

____(1) Under $25,000
____(2) $25,000–$49,999
____(3) $50,000–$74,999
____(4) $75,000–$124,999
____(5) Over $125,000

17. Do you have any other thoughts or ideas that you would like to share regarding the City of Sarasota's parks and recreation system?

This concludes the survey—Thank you for your time!

Please return your survey in the enclosed postage-paid envelope addressed to:

ETC Institute, 725 West Frontier Circle, Olathe, KS 66061

APPENDIX 6

STAKEHOLDER INTERVIEW TALKING POINTS

1. **Review of scope and methodology:** Do you have any questions about the project scope or methodology? Are there any additional meetings, workshops, presentations, or other outreach efforts that we should consider?
2. **Needs:** Based on what you know, see, and hear about your community, what do you believe are the top-priority parks and recreation needs (i.e., facilities or programs that are important but are not being provided adequately)?
3. **Broader city needs:** Thinking more broadly about your community and its constituents, what do you believe are the top-priority social, economic, and environmental needs of the community?
4. **Priorities:** Of the needs listed above, what are your top three priorities?
5. **Benchmark communities:** As we analyze and plan the community's parks and recreation system, are there any communities we should try to emulate?
6. **Funding and implementation:** Assuming that the parks and recreation master plan will identify hundreds of millions of dollars in desired and needed improvements, what funding source or sources would you support?

   Pay-as-You-Go:
   - General fund or capital improvement program
   - Sales tax
   - Park impact fees
   - Grants
   - User fees
   - Special assessments
   - Other (please specify)

   Borrowing:
   - General obligation bonds
   - Revenue bonds
   - Other (please specify)
7. **Other:** Is there anything else you would like to discuss?

NOTES

Introduction: A Framework for Community Sustainability and Resiliency

1. Peter Harnik, *Inside City Parks* (Washington, DC: Urban Land Institute, 2000), 3.
2. Alexander Garvin, *The American City: What Works, What Doesn't* (New York: McGraw-Hill, 2002), 32.
3. Harnik, *Inside City Parks*, xiii.
4. James D. Mertes and James R. Hall, *Park, Recreation, Open Space, and Greenway Guidelines* (Arlington, VA: National Recreation and Park Association, 1996), 37.
5. American Planning Association, *Planning and Urban Design Standards* (Hoboken, NJ: John Wiley & Sons, 2006), 39.
6. Peter Harnik, *Urban Green: Innovative Parks for Resurgent Cities* (Washington, DC: Island Press, 2010), 5.
7. Mertes and Hall, *Park, Recreation*, 59.
8. Megan Lewis, ed., *From Recreation to Re-creation: New Directions in Parks and Open Space System Planning* (Washington, DC: American Planning Association, Planning Advisory Service, 2008), vi.
9. Galen Cranz and Michael Boland, "Defining the Sustainable Park: A Fifth Model for Urban Parks," *Landscape Journal* 23, no. 2 (January 2004): 103, http://www.doi.org/10.3368/lj.23.2.102.
10. City of Bellevue, Washington, "Comprehensive Plan," https://bellevuewa.gov/city-government/departments/community-development/planning-initiatives/comprehensive-plan.

Chapter 1: Parks and the Public Realm

1. Alexander Garvin, *The Planning Game: Lessons from Great Cities* (New York: W. W. Norton, 2013), 14.
2. Spiro Kostof, *The City Shaped: Urban Patterns and Meanings through History* (Boston: Bulfinch Press, 1991), 217.
3. Jon A. Peterson, *The Birth of City Planning in the United States, 1840–1917* (Baltimore: Johns Hopkins University Press, 2003), 32.

4. Peterson, *Birth of City Planning*, 33.
5. Peterson, *Birth of City Planning*.
6. Mel Scott, *American City Planning since 1890* (Washington, DC: American Planning Association, 1995), 11.
7. National Recreation and Park Association, "Synopsis of 2010 Research Papers: The Key Benefits," p. 8, https://www.nrpa.org /uploadedFiles/nrpa.org/Publications_and_Research/Research /Papers/Synopsis-of-Research-Papers.pdf.
8. Alexander Garvin, *The American City: What Works, What Doesn't* (New York: McGraw-Hill, 2002), 32.
9. Allan B. Jacobs, *Great Streets* (Cambridge, MA: MIT Press, 1993), 6.
10. Art Lerner-Lam, "Hurricane Sandy: A Climate Change Wakeup Call," Lamont-Doherty Earth Observatory, November 7, 2012, https://www.ldeo.columbia.edu/news-events/a-climate -change-wakeup-call.
11. David Rouse, "Parks and Resilience: A Whole Community View" (PowerPoint presentation to the National Recreation and Park Association, Rockefeller Foundation, 2017).
12. Rockefeller Foundation and ARUP, *City Resilience Index Understanding and Measuring City Resilience*, 2017, https://assets .rockefellerfoundation.org/app/uploads/20171206110244/170223 _CRI-Brochure.pdf.
13. "Historic Fourth Ward Park," Atlanta BeltLine, https://beltline .org/parks/historic-fourth-ward-park/.
14. Tyler Falk, "High Line Park Attracts $2 Billion in New Developments, Other Cities Follow," ZDNet, August 3, 2011 (originally published on Smartplanet.com), https://www.zdnet.com /article/high-line-park-attracts-2-billion-in-new-development s-other-cities-follow/.
15. "Plexus (n.)," *Merriam-Webster.com Dictionary*, http://www .merriam-webster.com/dictionary/plexus.
16. Megan Lewis, ed., *From Recreation to Re-creation: New Directions in Parks and Open Space System Planning* (Washington, DC: American Planning Association, Planning Advisory Service, 2008), v.
17. City of Portland, Oregon, "2035 Comprehensive Plan," December 2018, I-34, https://beta.portland.gov/sites/default/files/2019 -08/comp_plan_intro.pdf.
18. City of Portland, Oregon, "2035 Comprehensive Plan."

19. City of Portland, Oregon, "Citywide Systems Plan," July 2014, https://www.portlandoregon.gov/bps/article/497435.
20. Karyl Ramsey, "A Systems Perspective on Public Agency Collaboration for the Emergence of Sustainable Solutions to Social Problems" (PhD diss., Saybrook University, June 2010).
21. City of Denver, Colorado, "Small Area Plans," https://www.denvergov.org/content/denvergov/en/community-planning-and-development/planning-and-design/how-we-plan/small-area-plans.html.

Chapter 2: Multiple Dimensions of Parks and Recreation Systems

1. Richard J. Dolesh, "Top Trends in Parks and Recreation for 2019," *Parks & Recreation Magazine*, January 7, 2019, https://www.nrpa.org/parks-recreation-magazine/2019/january/top-trends-in-parks-and-recreation-for-2019/.
2. John L. Crompton, *Community Benefits and Repositioning: The Keys to Park and Recreation's Future Viability* (Ashburn, VA: National Recreation and Park Association, 2007), 75.
3. Crompton, *Community Benefits*, 62.
4. National Recreation and Park Association, "Benefits of CAPRA Agency Accreditation," https://www.nrpa.org/certification/accreditation/CAPRA/benefits-of-capra-agency-accreditation/.
5. "PATH Foundation," https://pathfoundation.org/.
6. Atlanta BeltLine, "Wherever You Want to Go, Atlanta BeltLine Takes You There," https://beltline.org/the-project/project-goals/.
7. Timothy Beatley, *Biophilic Cities: Integrating Nature into Urban Design and Planning* (Washington, DC: Island Press, 2011), 46, 45.
8. City of Atlanta, Georgia, "Urban Ecology Framework," https://www.atlantaga.gov/government/departments/city-planning/urban-ecology-framework.
9. Philly Watersheds, "Green City, Clean Waters," http://archive.phillywatersheds.org/what_were_doing/documents_and_data/cso_long_term_control_plan.
10. American Planning Association, "Healthy Communities Policy Guide," 2017, 3, https://www.planning.org/policy/guides/adopted/healthycommunities/.
11. Robert Wood Johnson Foundation and University of Wisconsin Population Health Institute, County Health Rankings & Roadmaps, "Policies & Programs: Policies and Programs That Can

Improve Health," 2018, filtered by "Scientifically Supported," http://www.countyhealthrankings.org/take-action-to-improve-health/what-works-for-healthpolicies?f%5B0%5D=field_program_evidence_rating%3A1.

12. Atlanta Regional Commission, "Atlanta Region Plan 2040: What Is Planning for Social Equity?," http://documents.atlantaregional.com/plan2040/quickguides/tp_PLAN_2040_FS_Social_Equity.pdf.
13. University of Minnesota, Institute on Community Integration, "Check & Connect," http://checkandconnect.umn.edu/.
14. Blair Kamin, "Millennium Park: 10 Years Old and a Boon for Art, Commerce and the Cityscape," *Chicago Tribune*, July 12, 2014, http://www.chicagotribune.com/news/columnists/ct-millennium-park-at-10-kamin-0713-met-20140712-column.html.

Chapter 3: High-Performance Public Spaces

1. Diane Steinle, "Officials' Creative Vision Led to Thriving Clearwater Beach," Tampa Bay Times, July 3, 2014, http://www.tampabay.com/opinion/columns/steinle-officials-creative-vision-led-to-thriving-clearwater-beach/2187036.
2. Florence Snyder, "7 Things You Should Do in Tallahassee's Gaines Street," n.d., Visit Florida, https://www.visitflorida.com/en-us/cities/tallahassee/7-things-you-should-do-in-tallahassees-gaines-street.html.

Chapter 4: A New Approach to Parks and Recreation System Planning

1. Landscape Architecture Foundation, "Case Study Briefs," Landscape Performance series, https://www.landscapeperformance.org/case-study-briefs.
2. United Nations Educational, Scientific and Cultural Organization (UNESCO), International Institute for Educational Planning (IIEP), "Strategic Planning: Concept and Rationale," Working Paper 1, 2010, http://unesdoc.unesco.org/images/0018/001897/189757e.pdf.
3. John M. Bryson, *Strategic Planning for Public and Nonprofit Organizations: A Guide to Strengthening and Sustaining Organizational Achievement* (San Francisco: Jossey-Bass, 1995), 8.

4. Rebecca Reviere et al., eds., *Needs Assessment: A Creative and Practical Guide for Social Scientists* (New York: Routledge, 1996), 15.
5. David Epstein, "Chances Are, You're Not as Open-Minded as You Think," *Washington Post*, July 20, 2019, https://www.washingtonpost.com/opinions/chances-are-youre-not-as-open-minded-as-you-think/2019/07/20/0319d308-aa4f-11e9-9214-246e594de5d5_story.html.

Chapter 5: Initiating and Planning the PRSMP Process

1. Terry A. Clark, *Project Management for Planners: A Practical Guide* (Chicago: Planners Press, 2002).
2. Victor Bekkers, Jurian Edelenbos, and Bram Steijn, "Linking Innovation to the Public Sector: Contexts, Concepts and Challenges," in *Innovation in the Public Sector: Linking Capacity and Leadership*, ed. Victor Bekkers, Jurian Edelenbos, and Bram Steijn (London: Palgrave Macmillan, 2011), 27.
3. Everett M. Rogers, *Diffusion of Innovations*, 5th ed. (New York: Free Press, 2003), 414.
4. Bilge Erdogan et al., "Collaboration Environments for Construction: Management of Organizational Changes," *Journal of Management in Engineering* 30, no. 3 (May 2014): 1–14, http://dx.doi.org/10.1061/(ASCE)ME.1943-5479.0000231.
5. Clark, *Project Management*, 35.

Chapter 6: The Preliminary Implementation Framework

1. David Rouse, "Sustaining Places: The Role of the Comprehensive Plan" (PowerPoint presentation to the American Planning Association, 2012).
2. Rouse, "Sustaining Places."

Chapter 7: Existing Conditions Analysis

1. Betty Van der Smissen, Merry Moiseichik, and Vern J. Hartenburg, eds., *Management of Park and Recreation Agencies* (Ashburn, VA: National Recreation and Park Association, 2005), 128, 129.
2. City of Seattle, Washington, Seattle Parks and Recreation, *2017 Parks and Open Space Plan*, August 7, 2017, 7, https://www.seattle

.gov/Documents/Departments/ParksAndRecreation/Policies Planning/2017Plan/2017ParksandOpenSpacePlanFinal.pdf.

Chapter 8: The Needs Assessment

1. Los Angeles County Department of Parks and Recreation, "Executive Summary of the Los Angeles Countywide Comprehensive Parks & Recreation Needs Assessment," May 3, 2016, https://lacountyparkneeds.org/wp-content/uploads/2016/05/Executive-Summary.pdf.
2. Floyd J. Fowler Jr., *Survey Research Methods*, 4th ed., Applied Social Research Methods Series, No. 1 (Thousand Oaks, CA: SAGE, 2009).
3. Alan Bryman, *Social Research Methods*, 4th ed. (Oxford: Oxford University Press, 2012), 24.
4. Bryman, *Social Research Methods*, 171.
5. Bryman, *Social Research Methods*, 185.
6. Jacob Bogage, "Youth Sports Study: Declining Participation, Rising Costs, and Unqualified Coaches," *Washington Post*, September 6, 2017, https://www.washingtonpost.com/news/recruiting-insider/wp/2017/09/06/youth-sports-study-declining-participation-rising-costs-and-unqualified-coaches/?noredirect=on&utm_term=.d12db027820a.
7. Florida Department of Environmental Protection, "SCORP: Outdoor Recreation in Florida," 2013, https://floridadep.gov/parks/florida-scorp-outdoor-recreation-florida.
8. Athletic Business, "Infographic: The Benefits of Youth Sports," July 2017, https://www.athleticbusiness.com/recreation/infographic-the-benefits-of-youth-sports.html.
9. James D. Mertes and James R. Hall, *Park, Recreation, Open Space, and Greenway Guidelines* (Arlington, VA: National Recreation and Park Association, 1996), 58.
10. Esri, "Tapestry Segmentation," https://www.esri.com/en-us/arcgis/products/tapestry-segmentation/overview.

Chapter 9: Level-of-Service Alternatives

1. James D. Mertes and James R. Hall, *Park, Recreation, Open Space, and Greenway Guidelines* (Arlington, VA: National Recreation and Park Association, 1996), 58–59.

2. Dan Buettner, "Power 9: Reverse Engineering Longevity," Blue Zones, https://www.bluezones.com/2016/11/power-9/.
3. Mertes and Hall, *Park, Recreation*, 6.
4. Greg Hise and William Deverell, *Eden by Design: The 1930 Olmsted-Bartholomew Plan for the Los Angeles Region* (Berkeley: University of California Press, 2000).
5. Denver Parks & Recreation, "Denver Parks and Recreation 2017 Game Plan Update: Existing Conditions Report," March 2017, 54, https://www.denvergov.org/content/dam/denvergov/Portals/Denveright/documents/Game%20Plan/DPR-Game-Plan_existing-conditions-report_03022017.pdf.
6. Denver Parks & Recreation, "2017 Game Plan Update," 121.

Chapter 10: Developing a Long-Range Vision

1. John M. Bryson, *Strategic Planning for Public and Nonprofit Organizations: A Guide to Strengthening and Sustaining Organizational Achievement* (San Francisco: Jossey-Bass, 1995), 27.
2. Bryson, *Strategic Planning*, 69.
3. Peter Harnik, "The Excellent City Park System: What Makes It Great and How to Get There," Trust for Public Land, 2003, http://cloud.tpl.org/pubs/ccpe_excellentcityparks_2006.pdf.
4. "What Is Placemaking?," Project for Public Spaces, 2007, https://www.pps.org/article/what-is-placemaking.
5. "The Power of 10+," Project for Public Spaces, https://www.pps.org/article/the-power-of-10.
6. Hazards Planning Center, "Naturally Resilient Communities," American Planning Association, https://www.planning.org/nationalcenters/hazards/naturallyresilient/.
7. James D. Mertes and James R. Hall, *Park, Recreation, Open Space, and Greenway Guidelines* (Arlington, VA: National Recreation and Park Association, 1996).
8. "Oklahoma City Parks Master Plan," August 2013, prepared for the City of Oklahoma City and the Oklahoma City Community Foundation by Wallace Roberts & Todd, LLC, https://www.okc.gov/home/showdocument?id=1526.

Chapter 11: Implementation Strategy

1. Baker Galloway, "Pros/Cons of Design-Bid-Build vs. Construction Manager at Risk vs. Design/Build—What's the Difference?" *News Blog*, Jackson Galloway, April 5, 2016, http://www.jacksongalloway.com/news/2016/4/12/comparing-three-popular-construction-contracting-methods-designbuild-design-bid-build-and-construction-manager-at-risk.
2. Denver Parks & Recreation, "Denveright: Game Plan for a Healthy City," May 2019, 228, https://www.denvergov.org/content/dam/denvergov/Portals/Denveright/documents/Game%20Plan/GamePlan_FinalReport.pdf.

Conclusion: The Power of Parks and Recreation System Planning

1. City Parks Alliance, "City Parks: America's New Infrastructure—Overview," YouTube video, September 18, 2017, https://www.youtube.comwatch?v=AEFXFeSC75U.
2. Samuel Staley, "When Planning Matters," blog post, *Planetizen*, March 12, 2008, https://www.planetizen.com/node/30091.

INDEX

Page numbers followed by "b", "f" and "t" indicate boxes, figures and tables.